"*Mourning Companion Animals* is an empathetic, essential guide for navigating the difficult terrain of pet loss. Integrating her deep understanding of clinical social work with trauma-informed strategies, Stone delivers a powerful and comforting blueprint for grief management. This book is not just an invaluable resource; it is a heartfelt legacy to the animals we've loved and lost, destined to resonate deeply with anyone who has experienced the unique sorrow of losing a beloved pet."

Dr. Katherine Compitus, *expert applied anthrozoologist and professor of clinical social work, New York University*

"Over the years, my grief response to the inevitable passing of my animal companions impacts me just as much as – and admittedly maybe even more – as the grief response to the passing of any other beloved family member or friend. Susan Stone's wonderful, thorough, and thought-provoking book teaches us how to deal with that grief and helps us understand that our animals never really die if they live on in our hearts and in our memories."

David Frei, *longtime host of NBC's National Dog Show and Westminster Kennel Club*

"I first met Dickens and his person, Susan Stone, during my early years as a veterinarian at The Oradell Animal Hospital when a friendship emerged based on our united dedication to the human-animal bond and the grief that can follow loss. This insightful book touches on all areas of animal-companion loss. It is a must read not only for mental health professionals, but for those who treat, care for, and support animal companions and those who love them."

Dr. John G. DeVries, *DVM, diplomate of the American Board of Veterinary Practitioners*

Mourning Companion Animals: Guiding Clients from Loss to Legacy

Mourning Companion Animals is a guidebook for mental health clinicians searching for effective, compassionate resources to guide their clients through the often-devastating experience of animal companion loss.

Chapters offer powerful and comprehensive strategies to heal animal companion loss based in sound, evidenced-based, theoretical perspectives. The included author-generated inventory, the animal companion bereavement questionnaire, provides further assistance in clinician exploration of each client's unique bond with their lost companion.

The book's content is the result of more than 25 years of extensive work within the human-animal bond, clinical training in the referenced therapies, and application of major psychodynamic theories.

Susan Dowd Stone MSW, LCSW, is an adjunct associate professor at New York University's Silver School of Social Work and an award-winning advocate, speaker, author, and clinician whose lengthy career has focused on the human-animal bond.

Mourning Companion Animals

Guiding Clients from Loss to Legacy

Susan Dowd Stone

Routledge
Taylor & Francis Group

NEW YORK AND LONDON

Designed cover image: Shekularaz © Getty Images

First published 2024
by Routledge
605 Third Avenue, New York, NY 10158

and by Routledge
4 Park Square, Milton Park, Abingdon, Oxon, OX14 4RN

Routledge is an imprint of the Taylor & Francis Group, an informa business

© 2024 Susan Dowd Stone

Library of Congress Cataloging-in-Publication Data
Names: Stone, Susan Dowd, author.
Title: Mourning companion animals : guiding clients from loss to
   legacy / Susan Dowd Stone.
Description: New York, NY : Routledge, 2024. | Includes
   bibliographical references and index.
Identifiers: LCCN 2023048155 (print) | LCCN 2023048156 (ebook) |
   ISBN 9780367694234 (pbk) | ISBN 9780367694302 (hbk) |
   ISBN 9781003145929 (ebk)
Subjects: LCSH: Pet owners—Psychology. | Pet loss. | Pets—Death. |
   Bereavement—Psychological aspects.
Classification: LCC SF411.47 .S77 2024 (print) | LCC SF411.47
   (ebook) | DDC 155.9/3—dc23/eng/20240102
LC record available at https://lccn.loc.gov/2023048155
LC ebook record available at https://lccn.loc.gov/2023048156

ISBN: 978-0-367-69430-2 (hbk)
ISBN: 978-0-367-69423-4 (pbk)
ISBN: 978-1-003-14592-9 (ebk)

DOI: 10.4324/9781003145929

Typeset in Palatino
by Apex CoVantage, LLC

This book is lovingly dedicated to
Jack Holden Raife
taken too soon and of comfort to every animal he met
and
Dickens, aka Blue Skye Christmas Triumph
also taken too soon and of comfort to every human he met.

Contents

Acknowledgments. x

Introduction 1

1 The experience of animal companion loss. 5

2 The impact of trauma on animal companion loss 26

3 Considerations of attachment theory in animal
  companion loss 45

4 Assessment strategies for animal companion loss. 68

5 Psychodynamic approaches to healing animal
  companion loss 90

6 Cognitive behavioral approaches to healing animal
  companion loss 114

7 Trauma approaches to healing animal companion loss . . .137

8 Anticipatory mourning in animal companion loss 157

9 Legacy creation following animal companion loss 174

Bibliography 192
Index 217

Acknowledgments

Writing this book began as a personal and impassioned project. But over the years – as I read the wise words of those who study the human-animal bond, worked with those whose lives included a fascination and collaboration with animals, and entered the profession of clinical social work – it became a much larger endeavor.

In the world of Animal-assisted therapy, my experience as a certified Pet Partners team trainer and evaluator was guided by Anne R. Howie, CCA, CGFT, LICSW, ACSW; Maureen Frederickson, LCSW; Stephanie LaFarge, PhD; and Greer Griffith, MFT. Their devotion and enthusiasm for celebrating canines have never wavered.

I am grateful for the leadership, support, and friendship of David Frei, author and promoter of animal-assisted therapy programs through his founding of Angel on a Leash and his association with Pet Partners (formerly known as Delta Society). He has been the cohost of NBC's *National Dog Show* since its inception in 2002 and was "the voice" of the Westminster Kennel Club dog show for 27 years. David has been described by *New York* magazine as "probably the most well-known human in the world of canines." His life has been devoted to the support and acknowledgment of the human-animal bond.

Several hospitals and institutions worked with me to sponsor groundbreaking AAI programs in their psychiatric units, and their trust has benefited thousands of hospitalized people. I am indebted to Oradell Animal Hospital, in Paramus, New Jersey, which supported the formation of the pet bereavement group I facilitated for 14 years. In particular, I want to thank the most expert and compassionate veterinarian of my pack, John G. DeVries, DVM and Diplomate of the American Board of Veterinary Practitioners (DABVP), for his guidance of the group's formation. Nancy Miles, RRT, found ever-larger spaces to house the growing program, which also benefited from her unfailing support. I am grateful to colleague and friend Nancy Osgoodby, LCSW, for her willingness to continue the group in a virtual environment, allowing more participants. I credit Heather Troyer, DVM, a most knowledgeable and caring professional, for her inclusion of mental health services while developing the hospice program at Oradell Animal Hospital. Among the nation's most expert and empathic vet techs is Jennifer Grady Holmes, CVT, VTS, (ECC) – affiliated with Cornell University Veterinary Specialists and Oradell Animal Hospital – who has my sincere thanks for her willingness to fact-check my animal health-related content.

I am indebted to my colleagues at New York University's Silver School of Social Work. In particular, I want to thank the most talented and dedicated Dr. Katherine Compitus, DSW, LCSW-R, MSEd, MA, C-AAIP – a renowned educator, practitioner, and author in the field of the human-animal bond – for her commitment to the development of a curriculum focusing on the importance of educating clinical professionals. I also want to acknowledge the visionary Ben Sher, MA, LMSW, Director of the Office of Global and Lifelong Learning, for his encouragement of veterinary social work content in the post-master's and continuing education programming. Ernest Gonzales, PhD, MSSW, has my warmest thanks for his support of veterinary social work content in the MSW program. I'm grateful to NYU for its sponsorship of an animal-assisted therapy club, of which I am the faculty advisor, and for its acknowledgment of the importance of this community service.

I have such admiration for Julia Prem, a friend who has devoted her life to the care of Earth's animal inhabitants. She continues to rescue, rehab, and rehome all manner of creatures. Her selflessness in this effort is extraordinary.

In creating this book, I was fortunate in assistance from enthusiastic collaborators. Once the book's goals were clear, the open-hearted and open-minded Anna Moore at Routledge encouraged the proposal and tracked it toward completion. Thanks also to Ellie Broadhurst, Editorial Assistant, who kept me informed of each step of the process. Equal appreciation is extended to the copy editor (vaishnavi madhavan) for the meticulous editing of the manuscript.

My editor, Samantha Shubert, balanced masterful storytelling with editorial excellence. Samantha's guidance was expert, creative, respectful – and always diplomatic! I thankfully recall her reassuring availability during "pivotal" editorial moments with gratitude. My dear friend, Ellen B. Unger J.D., offered consistent encouragement throughout this project and generously volunteered meticulous citation review to ensure timely adherence to production deadlines.

My family and friends lent support throughout this project, often sharing stories of their own animal bonds. I would like to thank my daughter Julia and Mr. Hyde, Freddy and Harmony, Perrie and Patches, Stephen and Seanny, Nancy and Alex, Rebecca and Ash, David and Ellway, Ray and Cobra Knight, Pat and Mags, Oliver and Petunia, Michael and Max, Ken and Harlow, Nancy and Cherokee, Sylvia and Sonny, and Ellen and Bear.

Special thanks to the loved ones who patiently tolerated absences, especially my 7-year-old grandson, Freddy Wardell, who constantly inquired about the book's progress, sought assurance that turtles would be included, and never tired of hearing the animal case studies. Walks and gardening with Freddy offered respite from writing conundrums, while revealing his own respectful view of animal life.

Departed loved ones, whose voices and legacies are with me still, include my sister Nancy Raife and her ever-increasing pack of canines; Frederick Rish, who always paused to greet sentient creatures; and Finvola Drury, AIDS researcher and poet, who gave her life working with dying men and offering comfort by arranging visits with furry creatures. There is a special place in my heart for the person to whom this book is dedicated: Jack Holden Raife, who died far too young, but whose life was lived with an abiding love of animals.

Profound thanks to the clients who trusted me with their grief, bringing constant perspective and new dimensions in their revelations of what was shared and experienced with their animal companions.

I would like to thank the readers of this book, with the hope that you will find a way to integrate animal family members more fully into your professional lives and clinical work.

My humblest appreciation is extended to animals themselves for sharing their life-changing gifts with humans as we fumble our way to recognition of all they are and all they give to enhance our lives.

Finally, I would like to acknowledge one who profoundly enhanced the existence of this human steward and who was the force behind this book's creation: my mighty mentor, a dog named Dickens.

Introduction

Our wood-sided Ford station wagon pulled into the yard of the old family homestead. What had once been the working farm of my immigrant Irish forebears was now a gathering place for their descendants. The barn had become a guesthouse, and the meadows had all gone to tall grass and spindly trees. The gate that separated the grounds from the pastures hadn't seen the passage of farm animals for many years.

The only presence in the yard on that warm, early-summer day in 1959 was Friskie, a black Labrador retriever with a graying face, thickened body, and arthritic legs that somehow supported him as he dutifully acknowledged our arrival.

Friskie belonged to everyone in our extended clan. He anchored our Thanksgivings and Christmases, our summers and autumns, our feasts that extended outside and into the evenings. Hobbling his way from music room to living room, hopefully following the latest tray of food wherever it led, giving and receiving affection to all who approached, he was a polite and social creature, tender with the babes and rambunctious with the ball players. He was always on duty, ready to listen or mediate a family crisis with stoic wisdom.

One morning in his sixteenth year, he failed to rise from his bed in the corner of the kitchen. When Friskie was buried in the back field under an apple tree, most family members were present, united in grief. No one found the whispered anguish or plentiful tears to be strange or excessive. In the springtime that followed, everyone agreed, that apple tree bore more fruit than ever before. Songbirds lingered and nested in its branches.

DOI: 10.4324/9781003145929-1

This is not an unusual story. Many of us – perhaps most of us – have, at some point, lived with creatures we loved. Animal stewards cross all social and cultural lines, and soaring adoption rates suggest that such relationships can provide visceral and existential comfort. Whether this is due to pure enjoyment of life with animals, increased social alienation, increased mental illness – -202 22.8 percent among adult Americans (NIMH 2021) and probably even higher – or other reasons, we will never know.

But one thing is clear: The important roles that animals serve – from distracting amusers to transformative healers – mean that their deaths can provoke profound loneliness and exacerbate affective disturbances in their human stewards.

There are resources, books, and websites that help mourners cope with the initial shock of the loss of their animals. But the clinical community may sometimes underestimate the impact of their deaths in triggering mental health crises in both vulnerable or the most well-adjusted clients.

This perception is not lost on most human stewards. They may hesitate to share the intensity of their feelings, lest they be viewed as somehow shameful. Their grief, which might have been moderated by the interventions that are reliably applied after human losses, therefore continues, unacknowledged and untreated.

Most Americans describe animal companions as family members. It is no surprise, then, that animal companion deaths may cause as much anguish as the loss of any other deeply valued relationship.

The problem is that this grief is not always accorded the same significance. Time off for animals' illnesses and deaths is not included in family leave policies. Among some clinicians, mourning a companion animal beyond a week or two may be viewed as pathological; surely, intense grief over a dog might suggest a deeper issue or previous trauma. Lastly, there are no widely accessible societal rituals that might validate a mourner's pain and lead to comfort and resolution.

It's ironic that these attitudes persist at the same time that American society increasingly seeks to elevate the status of animals. More than 90 law schools host programs in animal law (Rollins, 2008), and animal cruelty may be prosecuted as felonies in all 50 states (Henderson et al., 2022). The Supreme Court recently upheld a California law requiring humane confinement of pigs destined for consumer purchase. In confronting the ethics of how we treat these sentient beings, we are faced with the paradox of advocating for creatures that provide us with emotional, familial, and biological sustenance. In promoting social justice and mental health, the lives of animals and humans, including marginalized populations, are intrinsically linked. "By recognizing the ways human social factors negatively affect people and wildlife, we can change our behavior for the benefit of society" (Schmidt & Garroway, 2022).

Having been immersed in the study of the human-animal bond for nearly 30 years, I've learned that there is an enormous unmet need for mental health services for those intensely grieving companion animals – as well as the wilder creatures whose losses echo our own viability.

My education and experiences have led me to offer my fellow clinicians this text to guide the treatment of clients experiencing animal companion loss. In presenting the respected research of those who have made animals' high sentience their lives' study or profession – animal behaviorists, ethicists, philosophers, scientists, neurologists, and veterinary caregivers – along with the findings of those who apply psychological theory and interventive strategies for people struggling to manage significant loss – my goal is both to further understanding within our clinical communities of the deep connection that causes such grief and also to suggest evidence-based strategies to heal it. The intersection of these worlds may be found in attachment theory, with the introduced hypothesis that human-animal dyads form their own attachment styles based on the attachment capacities of both human and animal.

Because trauma is so often a complicating factor in animal companion death, it has been addressed in its own chapter, as is assessment, including the introduction of the Animal Companion Bereavement Questionnaire, meant to provide further clinical guidance during assessment. The goal of the questionnaire is to lead to a more complete understanding of each human-animal relationship.

I then consider the application of specific evidence-based strategies to those experiencing various reactions to animal companion loss.

Although advances in veterinary technology now offer life-extending treatments, these options often lack the mental health support found in hospice programs for humans. For this reason, I apply the sound theories and strategies of work in anticipatory mourning to animal companion loss – a stage of grief that would greatly benefit from the expertise of my fellow clinicians.

Finally, I propose the idea of legacy creation as an essential element in healing from animal companion loss, reflective of David Kessler's sixth stage of grief: finding meaning (2019).

I firmly believe that our community of talented mental health professionals are prepared to guide and treat the considerable pain their clients may experience following animal companion death. I hope this work will alert my colleagues to the severity of the problem, encourage them to include animal family members in initial assessments, and align themselves with their clients' views that animals are full-fledged family members whose adoptions and deaths may represent pivotal life events. In doing so, we will ensure that all beloved relationships receive equal clinical focus.

Historically, clinical practitioners have vigorously responded to social and mental health crises with education, advocacy, and intervention. By drawing attention to the invalidation or undertreatment of those mourning companion animals, I hope that we can likewise begin to reverse this often-overlooked but deeply impactful experience. This book will also stress the power of humans to heal and protect animals.

By simply considering the proposed options in this text, your much-needed advocacy begins.

Susan Dowd Stone
Rensselaerville, New York, August 2023

1

The experience of animal companion loss

The email had arrived at 2:47 a.m.

"Can you please help us? We had to put our Matty down today. We don't know where to turn. We are devastated. The pain is terrible. Please respond. Thank you."

Messages like this have arrived regularly, sometimes daily, via a simple website – www.petlosshelp.org – created in 2008.

As always, I try to imagine the suffering, the desperation, the isolation that would lead someone to send a stranger a panicked cry for help in the middle of the night. The minimal expectation of any response is moving. Even those of us who understand the profound impact of companion animals on their human stewards can be surprised by the intensity of their need.

Such messages may be just the beginning of an often-futile quest for help. Before the website existed, very few resources – online or community-based – helped people in such distress.

It was intended to serve as a "first responder" option, whose mission was to answer common questions like, "Is there something wrong with me for feeling this degree of pain over the loss of my cat?" and "How will I manage and recover from this pain?" Compassionate assurance is offered that such reactions to loss

DOI: 10.4324/9781003145929-2

are entirely normal and that there are indeed paths to healing, even if that seems hard to believe in the immediate anguish of animal companion death.

As we mourn in proportion to what we have lost, losing these creatures may include losing aspects of ourselves. If the mourning process is normative, those aspects will return in time, all the richer for our having shared our lives and loving connections with animals. If it is unsupported or triggers excessive guilt or symptoms of trauma, it may persist.

Over time, it became apparent that there is no creature – domesticated or feral – incapable of inspiring humans and being mourned. My responses encouraged mourners to share the story of their animals' lives. Eventually the site hosted proud tributes to every imaginable species, including hamsters, goldfish, ferrets, lizards, piglets, and birds, in addition to canines and felines, attesting to the importance, sometimes transformative, of these creatures in the lives of the humans who cared for and about them.

Their stories and photographs are quickly posted with the further assurance that they will not expire. The gratitude received for maintaining this modest website is both humbling and troubling. It seems so little in response to the enormity of their suffering.

I have spent 30 years of professional and personal experience observing, studying, counseling, volunteering, and immersing myself in the wonders of animal life on our planet. For 14 of those years, I facilitated an animal companion bereavement support group embedded in a large veterinary practice, where hundreds of compelling stories of how and why humans intensely grieve companion animals expanded this understanding. Concurrently, I counseled veterinary staff members, presented at conferences, guided practices to develop response plans for bereaved clients and beleaguered staff members, and observed the ways animals can help humans heal. Through these activities, it became obvious that the stresses on veterinary caretakers are considerable and that they are still without sufficient support, even as the moral and ethical components of their work increase along with the numbers of clients.

I have learned so much – along with those who have made the study of animals their life's work – about the majesty and transformative power of the human-animal bond. My belief is that this bond is indeed fueled and maintained by interactive social and emotional reciprocity, not at all solely the projected assumptions of anthropomorphism. Scientific works like the Cambridge Declaration of Consciousness (Low et al., 2012) conclude that animals possess the necessary neurological components (even without a neocortex) for emotions and undoubtedly experience them. Mark Bekoff (2007, p. 15) reminds us that, "lacking a shared language, emotions are perhaps our most effective means of cross-species communication." Jack Panksepp (1998, pp. 246–260) notes how similar chemistries prepare human and nonhuman mammals for creating the bond of motherhood. Such research encourages the application of time-honored theories of attachment as applicable to both members of the human-animal dyad. This led to my conjecture that animals have capacities for attachment that can support or thwart interactions with their human stewards.

Finally, observing the healing power of animals throughout the decades in animal-assisted therapy (AAT) programs showed me that animals have the capacity for empathy and the urges to comfort, sometimes in ways that appear miraculous.

Incidence of animal companion stewardship

The adoption of animals has been increasing across socioeconomic, racial, and ethnic strata. Throughout the last decade, the number of households with animals has increased; it is now estimated that 70 percent of American households steward a pet (American Pet Products Association, 2021). The American Veterinary Medical Association broke down ownership by species in a 2022 survey: Of households with pets, 45 percent have dogs; 26 percent have cats; 2.7 percent have fish; and 2.5 percent have birds. Households with "exotic" pets – ferrets, rabbits, and reptiles – have also increased, as have those with pet livestock and poultry (especially chickens) and other animals like hamsters, guinea pigs, and gerbils (American Veterinary Medical Association, 2022).

Adopted animals may serve different purposes in the lives of their stewards, ranging from emotional reliance to practical assistance. Regardless of statistics and popularity, their deaths may be acutely felt. While one might wonder if a chicken qualifies as a companion animal, one need only meet a client who patiently bathed a lice-infested hen in her kitchen sink for two weeks; so attached was she to this proud creature. Some hospitalized clients from rural areas have requested visits from their farm animals, including a famous Rhode Island Red therapy rooster who was affectionately known as "chicken in a basket." Human stewards are the ones who decide which creatures are significant to their lives.

Although animal companion bereavement is usually associated with cats and dogs, many clients do not live with, or even regularly interact with, a particular animal but nonetheless respond deeply to their presence and mourn their absence. For example, a Wyoming woman whose ranch crossed three state borders would search each spring for the hilltop silhouette of Guapo ("handsome" in Spanish), the bull who fathered many of her calves. When two years went by without a sighting, she mourned the loss of this magnificent but distant creature who represented the generativity and continuance of her lands.

Animals in the wild can be said to be of emotional support as well. Many humans rely on their presence when seeking comfort, a sense of innocence, or spiritual affirmation. Their migratory paths and patterns can anchor the seasons of our lives. The impact of animals, seen and unseen, may be an increasingly important area of clinical exploration, especially amid heightened awareness of the fragility of our natural world.

Given the increase of animal presence in human lives, combined with their generally shorter life spans, we may conclude that most human stewards will outlive their companion animals. Depending on the qualities inherent in each relationship, such stewards may find themselves in the predicament of the visitor to www.petlosshelp.org: awake in the middle of the night, in the midst of emotional suffering they did not anticipate. With little support or guidance toward a way forward, their mourning may become prolonged, resulting in a persistent compromise to quality of life and mental health stability.

The pivotal roles of animals in human lives

The relationship between humans and animals has been studied since ancient times. Cave art indicates animals' importance to man's earliest days, and canine companionship is evident in 8,000-year-old drawings from the Arabian Peninsula (Compitus, 2021). Modern-day questions delve into understanding animals' emotional lives as reflected in their bond with humans. There is no doubt of their continuing impact on human lives across biopsychosocial realms.

While the loss of domestic animal companions is the primary focus of this book, it is also intended to address other expressions of bereavement related to anticipated and actual threats to animal survival. We can be greatly saddened and concerned about their potential extinction and endangerment of habitats, the millions lost to forest fires, the thousands of sea creatures washed up on our shores.

Our own sense of powerlessness is revealed in the disappointment we feel when migratory birds do not appear, when our sightings of majestic whales decrease as our seas warm, when turtles that leave the ocean's protection to nest are destroyed. We may link these external environmental threats with a sense of our own vulnerability. With our social worker person-in-environment beliefs about impacts on human emotional life, we cannot dismiss the impact of the fragility of animal life on basic human perceptions of safety.

While donations to animal-related (and environmental) causes make up only 3 percent of all donations, according to Faunalytics (2018), the constancy of these donors illustrates a capacity for being deeply moved by the plight of animals they may have never even encountered. Media stories that plead for help in animal rescue elicit extraordinary response. From baby seals to dolphins caught in nets, from GoFundMe requests for Rover's hip replacement to reuniting animal and human war buddies, from fundraisers for no-kill shelters to adoption programs, from advocacy for gorillas in distant countries to protests of inhumane conditions of animals raised for food, donors are moved to action.

Related areas of interest are in funding organizations that support animal shelters in order to reduce the incidence of euthanasia; causes that try to safeguard animal habitats, prevent extinction, and respond to animal abuse; and advocacy to legally recognize the status of domestic animals as family members (NP Source, 2023; National Philanthropic Trust, 2021).

On a societal level, we acknowledge that animals exert physical and emotional curative powers that enhance our lives and even heal us (Brunke, 2008; Horowitz, 2019; Cherniack & Cherniack, 2014; Katcher & Beck, 2010). We erect statues, honor them, make them central to stories of love and loyalty. We publicly exhibit our love for these faithful companions and their wild counterparts in print, documentaries, and internet accounts. We rejoice in stories that tell of unlikely sustaining relationships between humans and animals. *My Octopus Teacher*, a well-regarded documentary film that explored the close bond between a man and a magnificent sea creature, was just the latest account about the possibility of deep connections between species, and the belief that one can be transformed by such relationships.

A rising body of research documents the healing value and contributions of animals in our society (Rehn et al., 2023, Horton et al., 2023, Compitus, 2021, Frei, 2011, Fine, 2010). Stories of animals' enhancement of human life and mental health are far from anecdotal. Study after study yields consistently remarkable results of animal contributions to psychological stability and improved self-esteem when incorporated into programs addressing a wide range of health and mental health issues (van der Kolk, 2014, p. 251). Indeed, 86 percent of animal stewards say their animals have a positive impact on their mental health (American Psychiatric Association, 2023). Sixty percent of hospice programs use complementary pet therapists, and 60 percent of U.S. colleges have pet therapy programs.

The U.S. has more than 500,000 service animals to ease physical and mental ailments, and the country boasts more than 50,000 trained therapy dogs (The Zebra, 2023b). Wellness and visiting programs are well established at hospitals, nursing homes, and assisted living facilities.

Animals' abilities to help heal trauma, increase self-esteem, and encourage safe emotional experiencing has resulted in numerous programs. The Brewster, New York–based Green Chimneys (Morris et al., 2019; Ross, 2011, Kaufmann et al., 2015) helps children with behavioral or autistic spectrum disorders acquire positive self-regard through caring for animals. Equine-based mental health programs encourage mental and physical rehabilitation (White-Lewis, 2019). Matching incarcerated individuals with animals for whose care they are responsible can foster competency and compassion (Larkin, 2017; Doyon-Martin & Gonzalez, 2022; Karkdijk et al., 2022; Hediger et al., 2022). Ponies working in rehabilitative programs for children can inspire them to walk further distances. Animals in addiction recovery programs can inspire clients to sustain progress and combat urges (Broadfield, 2020).

We see yet another side to animals as symbols of motivation and hope in the protection of human life provided by dogs working in law enforcement, service dogs patiently accompanying disabled humans, and search-and-rescue animals locating survivors of disasters or kidnapping (Quinn, 2017). These almost-mystical abilities have been documented since human beings first attempted to live closely with other sentient beings (Fujisawa et al., 2016).

But all these acknowledgments of animal contributions have not yet led to an equal understanding of the significant mental health impact animal companion loss may have on individuals and communities. As mental health professionals, we can begin responding to this problem by simply inquiring about animal family members at initial assessment, asking about their importance and roles in our clients' lives.

Aspects of animal companion loss

Intellectually, we may be aware that we will enjoy a decade or two at most with our animal companions, depending on the species. But we may also feel that they will live forever, their innocence somehow protecting them from death. The shock experienced when they die pierces such magical thinking. We are never quite prepared for these losses, regardless of our acknowledgment of their natural life spans or physical compromises.

Many factors influence the intensity and length of active grieving, and there is a wide range of responses to animal companion death. Some people are only minimally affected by their loss and quickly move on, perhaps relieved that responsibility from their care has ended. Sometimes the closeness of a working human-animal partnership or the length of the association with a beloved, long-lived cat is the deciding factor. But a puppy that survived only four months can elicit escalating grief depending on the circumstances of its acquisition or the investment in saving its life. Each experience of such losses will reflect the qualities of the human-animal dyad and the reliance placed on those qualities to imbue daily life with companionship and joy.

Trauma often accompanies these losses, further complicating healing. For example, animal stewards are often shocked to learn of severe or terminal illness, because the stoicism of their animals disguises their suffering. The suddenness of accidents, abuse, kidnapping, or missing animals can add to the already-difficult experience of loss.

Expressions of grief following the loss of companion animals range from mild and transient sorrow to severe disruptions in self-perception, attachment to life, and long-ranging grief equal to – or worse than – what follows human death (Wilson et al., 2021; Uccheddu et al., 2019).

In general, grief responses to animal companion loss can be divided into emotional, behavioral, psychological, and spiritual responses:

Emotional responses include denial, intrusive thoughts, inability to accept the loss, intense tearfulness, disorientation, disbelief, shock, somatic complaints, anger or rage, guilt, isolation, depression, ruminating about the final days/hours, and feeling out of control or that the pain is unbearable. Cognitive distortions, second-guessing decisions around end-of-life choices, or feeling the animal is angry at the steward are also common in the aftermath of death.

Behavioral responses are widely varied and may include wanting to sleep with the departed companion's toys or blankets, avoiding sleeping in the bed shared with the animal, insomnia, loss of appetite, inability to give away the animal's possessions, continuing a routine as if the animal were still alive, withdrawing from those who do not support their grief (or even those who do), and feeling critical and angry toward those involved at the time of death. Mourners may not tolerate being around other animals; conversely, they may impulsively acquire other animals of the same or different species in attempts to distract from their pain. Some individuals will have ashes made into jewelry, plan funerals, or create memorials that include planting trees, posting stories online, and arranging home altars with pictures and mementos.

Psychological responses include symptoms of depression, anxiety, or PTSD that may exacerbate underlying or ongoing mood disorders, confounding their treatment if not specifically addressed. Such symptoms may challenge important relationships when the degree of suffering is differently experienced or not shared, creates feelings of disorientation, alienation, pervasive guilt, and results in an overall loss of hope.

Clients mourning companion animals often feel their pain is unbearable and wonder how they will survive the loss of their perceived soulmate, a connection to the universe found in no other association. They may verbalize a wish to join the departed animal or end their own lives, especially if they are concurrently experiencing a mental health issue or have no other social interaction or emotional support. Persistent considerations of suicide could signal a severe depression that is developing or has worsened; of course, this must be carefully monitored, with appropriate action taken to ensure physical safety or alert family members.

The death of a companion animal can pull the rug out from under a fragile family whose anchor was the animal's steady support. When an animal is the sole conduit or facilitator of participation in "normal life" – for example, a service animal who assists a human with disabilities, the sole companion in an otherwise isolated life, or the stabilizing force for a child's emotion regulation issues – the reactions to its loss can be devastating and go well beyond the immediate impact of its death if not supported, treated, and remediated.

Clients in recovery, who may have depended on that connection to bring distraction, stability, and soothing during escalation of urges or depressive moments, may find their adherence greatly challenged when that steady support is lost. Additionally, the lack of preparedness for the emotional magnitude of loss can further challenge recovery through the emotional dysregulation that can be triggered by loss.

Spiritual responses include feeling that aspects of one's soul have been lost, or that one's essence has now departed along with the animal; a renewed or first-time emergence of thoughts of an afterlife; anger at God or another universal being; rage at the suffering of the lost innocent; and a need to connect to nature as a conduit or portal to the lost animal. Sometimes bereaved animal companion owners reach out to animal communicators hoping for assurance that the animal has passed into animal heaven or is not angry about the circumstances of its death. Mourners sometimes hesitate to reveal instances in which they feel the presence of their departed companions. They may report seeing a fleeting shadow, hearing a soft whinny from the barn, feeling a strong presence in the room, or even sensing little paws walking on the bed at night. They may dream vividly and awaken with the sense of their pet's smell and warmth in the room, certain they were briefly reunited. They worry about sharing such experiences for fear that others will believe they've lost their minds.

Much is made of the fact that animals seem to love us uncondi-tionally, and that can be a compelling factor in decisions to adopt. But it is equally significant that these sentient beings allow us our own expression of unconditional love for them – the oppor-tunity to love without restraint, worry of rejection, or emotional manipulation that may not be trusted in human relationships. Although your dog is well aware that sweetly tilting his head will entice you to take him for a walk, he will never ask for a divorce. Your cat will not refuse to do her homework, your canary will not care if you do not have the voice of Pavarotti. Animals will not gossip about our failings, judge us for poor financial planning, or abandon us for another steward because we have grown older or less attractive. These creatures are safe holders of the kind of undying love we hope to experience – but which can be frustratingly elusive in human relationships. Our need to *give* unconditional love is safe with them, an emotional transaction greatly disrupted by their deaths.

Indeed, prolonged mourning for companion animals that has not been explored or understood may sometimes be viewed as evidence of pathological maladjustment, an inability to suf-ficiently attach to human relationships that could mitigate the effect of these losses. But that may be a mistaken impression. Some people cautiously report that they are mourning an animal companion more than close relatives. Family members or part-ners may also differ in their reaction to the loss of a specific animal, or mourn differently for different animals, but this var-iety in grieving reflects a completely normative human experi-ence of loss, disenfranchised only by society's unwillingness to accord it the attention it deserves.

Among the most grief-protracting and damaging elements following the death of an animal companion is the mourner's self-invalidation of the experience, a conclusion of defectiveness. The pervasive expectation that one should quickly adapt and move on from the loss of a mere animal – despite an awareness that this creature provided the only socialization in someone's world or sustained its steward through other losses – may prompt a sense of shame. How could one shed endless tears over a ferret, pig, turtle, bird, or pony?

Stewards mourning animals may, therefore, feel the need to repress their emotions or be cautious in expressing profound grief, lest family members and friends question their mourning as excessive. Mourners may be fearful that the intensity of their sorrow will be patronized or viewed pathologically even when shared within a therapy context. They may feel shame upon acknowledging that this grief feels greater than that they have ever experienced. Marinated in a perspective that such mourning is unwarranted, they may doubt themselves and feel even greater shame, furthering an already-isolative experience.

Differences in societal response to animal and human mourning

While research on and clinical assistance for grief following human loss (Zisook & Shear, 2009) is plentiful, stewards grieving companion animals may have a different experience. Because society is less validating of severe grief following animal companion loss, many of the supports and rituals that help humans cope and recover from the loss of loved ones are not available to them.

The death of a human loved one is validated as a catastrophic life event. Family members and friends appear from great distances to support one another. If the death took place in a hospital, bereaved family members receive opportunities for practical and emotional support. Funeral services are arranged to allow an entire community of friends and relatives to grieve with the mourners. Each anniversary and holiday in the first year following a death is understood as a time of great emotional suffering for those left behind.

Support groups are available to the mourner long after that first year is endured, while friends patiently and empathically listen to stories of the deceased person's life for months and years. Casseroles from anonymous neighbors are left at the door, and donations flood into causes of choice. Obituaries document a life well lived, detailing accounts of relationships and associations. Cemeteries maintain graves "eternally" so that mourners may visit and spend time communing with their lost loved ones. We surround human mourners with validation, cry with them, touch shoulders, give hugs, take them to dinner, murmur comforting words during the initial period of mourning and for many months and years thereafter.

Mental health studies consistently demonstrate the centrality of these societally accepted, built-in processes and rituals that help mourners heal (Mathew, 2021; Daniel, 2021); there is never the suggestion that one forget the relationship or replace it with another. Any expectation of resolution following human loss is patient and compassionate; there is never the suggestion that mourning beyond a month or two indicates a pathological attachment to the deceased. It's understood that such a loss may redefine the life of the mourner.

Yet such empathy, ritual validation, and social support are rarely available for stewards suffering animal companion loss. Their search for support and ways of honoring the animal's life are few and generally relegated to the periphery of the grief and loss industry.

Helping clients recover from animal companion loss may include attempting to integrate similar rituals and resources for the mourner within a more private, individualized context. While animal funeral services are increasingly available, the hit-or-miss search for them may haunt a steward for years if they find no option for appropriately memorializing or celebrating an animal's life after a sudden and shocking loss, which gives no time for such considerations. Without the opportunity to create satisfying rituals and legacy, this unmet need discourages peaceful closure, leaving their grief still primarily focused on the physical loss of the animal. Mourning may remain suspended, while denial continues.

While the experience of mourning companion animals shares some similarities to mourning following human death – such as working through stages of denial, anger, bargaining, depression, and acceptance (Kübler-Ross, 1970) – the recovery tasks and qualities of emotional pain within each stage may be experienced very differently. Denial may be prolonged when the animal's body is not seen after running away or being kidnapped; anger may be directed at healthcare providers who encouraged the decision to euthanize; bargaining may be complicated when a diagnosis of illness is sudden; and depression may greatly delay the move to acceptance. David Kessler (2019) adds a sixth stage to Elisabeth Kübler-Ross's: finding meaning. Creating a legacy of the animal's life – something humans eventually embrace as they recover – is equally important to the resolution of animal companion grief.

Most animal companion stewards perceive animals as true family members and regard them as their children (Bouma et al., 2021), even within families that include human children. But among outsiders, holiday cards giving animals equal status may be viewed as simply "cute," but not taken seriously. Holidays and anniversary dates may pose special challenges for those mourning companion animals (Stone, 2006).

Validating the status of companion animals as equal family members is essential in creating the appropriate time and space for grieving, yet among friends and clinicians who do not understand this perception, reactions of loss may be viewed as an indulgent projection or not given appropriate weight as the triggering event for persistent depression following such loss.

The experience of traveling for miles to find a support group, calling multiple hotlines only to find many disconnected, or writing to strangers on the internet in a desperate search for support seems to signal that animal companion deaths should remain a private struggle.

Those who wrote to www.petlosshelp.org would initially receive the suggestion to attend a local animal companion bereavement group – and were fortunate if they found such an option in their area. Such greatly needed meetings are still too rare and, due to their paucity, may be located inconveniently. Their virtual counterparts, while well intended, lack the visceral connection of presence that was a major component of the human-animal bond.

The bereavement group I facilitated hosted participants from all walks of life and economic strata: artists who were suddenly more isolated when a senior cat passed away; retired physicians who found release and connection with a mimicking parrot;

policemen who had formed the deepest bond of their lives with K-9 partners; hunters who had lost their nature-loving buddies, couples struggling with childlessness who had found their family in a litter of adopted bunnies; empty nesters who had lost their last connection to their grown children.

They would enter, sometimes solemn and sobbing, clutching pictures they had been encouraged to bring, showing one another remnants of these transformative beings: hair clipped from a tail, clay imprints of paws, a favorite squeaky toy.

All found some relief in simply sitting for 90 minutes among others who understood their pain and heard their stories. Physically and emotionally sharing their grief added to the feelings of comfort. They needed to connect, to share stories, to hear reassurance that they were not crazy for grieving the loss so acutely. They found themselves in good company among other stewards who never expected that cherishing an animal could devastate their lives.

Simply telling their stories to a roomful of receptive mourners often brought the first comfort they had felt. Despite the sad reason for these gatherings, there was much humor and warmth generated in descriptions of their pets' antics, their manipulations of their human stewards, and their often-hilarious responses to attempts to control, discipline, or manage their behavior. Participants were released from their self-imposed repression, free to mourn without fear that their grief reflected some psychological defect.

When these groups would conclude, many participants verbalized deep gratitude that they existed at all. They valued sharing this time of simply being among others walking the same journey, and observing how other "normal" people were experiencing the same kind of grief.

This was not a psychotherapy group – it hardly mattered what the facilitator said. Instead, mourners left with encouragement that they would survive those first weeks, that their grief was warranted, that the pain would lessen over time, that there was a path forward, all important messages of hope to which participants clung.

The group continued to grow, and the number of people wishing to attend quickly eclipsed the facility's capacity. First it outgrew its assigned room and eventually a larger lecture hall.

A list of professionals who dealt with animal companion loss was kept at the desk, but these clinicians were sometimes perceived as the weirdos of psychotherapists, who probably had their own questionable fixation on animals. If the grief of those mourning companion animals was pathologically unwarranted, then it surely followed that those willing to devote professional expertise to their support could also be suspect.

While most clinicians would readily support a current client mourning a lengthy relationship with a dog, the grief of someone unable to right their emotional equilibrium weeks after the death may be viewed as alarmingly excessive. Acute grief over the loss of an animal may be considered a mere trigger to returned depression, unremitting anxiety, or emergence of psychotic symptoms rather than the cause – especially if the clinician was unaware of the animal's significance in the client's life or even that the loss of a beloved animal could be the exacerbating cause to prolonged mental health issues. The mourner, sensing this question further invalidates their own grief, may withdraw from the discussion, thwarting their potential for healing.

Such disconnects can create a therapeutic impasse, alienating clients who again wonder if indeed their reaction is "normal." If it were, wouldn't there be as many programs and services for mourners of animal companions as there are for humans?

In the past, there did indeed exist a tendency to assume that mourning a companion animal beyond a week or two was potentially reflective of a pathologically maladjusted person unable to find solace or perhaps equivalent companionship among humans (Spain et al., 2019). Instead of recognizing, validating, and honoring a person's ability to deeply connect with another species, it might instead be skeptically viewed as an inability to appropriately bond with human counterparts.

We have all heard of individuals who lived alone, save for a fish or a canary. The "cat lady" with eight felines roaming around her Victorian house with no other visitors is the stuff of horror stories. She is seen as potentially dangerous, witchlike, somehow defective or incapable of sustaining human familial relationships, rather than someone who has enriched her life with sentient beings.

Yet, despite society's judgment of what is "worth" mourning, humans grieve based on what each has experienced during their time with any living being. Profound experiences with animals are not footnotes but major, sometimes life-changing, relationships in which much was learned, held, revealed, felt, shared, and lived.

The ability to share love transcends attempts to diminish some experiences. The impact of giving and receiving love cannot be invalidated simply because that love was inspired by a dog's steady gaze. Indeed, there is an enormous disconnect between what we have researched and publicly accepted about the contributions of animals to the quality of human lives and our acknowledgment of the intense grief their losses may elicit.

We may hold up our animals as beloved heroes, but our clinical attention may not pay sufficient notice to the psychological suffering that may appear upon their deaths. The intensity of feelings will, of course, depend on many factors discussed in greater detail in the assessment chapter of this book and further defined by questions from the Animal Companion Bereavement Questionnaire in Chapter 4.

Assessing clinician perspectives on animal companion loss

It may be helpful to consider your own experiences, perspectives, and beliefs about the value of animal life and any assumptions about what feels appropriate when treating a client who is mourning a companion animal. For example:

- ◆ Do you believe the loss of a companion animal is, on its own, capable of exacerbating a mental health crisis in a previously mentally stable client?
- ◆ If you have experienced a client acutely mourning a companion animal, did you explore it as a primary trigger for their grief, or do you view extended mourning of

companion animals as possibly associated with psychopathology as opposed to the mourning of human companions?

◆ To what extent does species matter in such considerations? Does mourning the death of a parrot or guinea pig feel less valid than that of a canine or feline?

◆ Do you believe the additional stressor of animal companion loss is capable of thwarting a client's recovery – or exacerbating additional symptoms – during treatment for an ongoing mood disorder?

◆ Do you wonder if a primary reliance on animals for emotional nurturance and companionship suggests a client's lack of capacity to appropriately connect with other humans? Or do you view a client's deep connection with an animal as an extended capacity to connect with and benefit from associations with nonhuman species?

◆ Are you aware of which clients live with animals and how many animals they steward? Their species and names? Their ages and health status? The roles they fulfill in family or solitary life?

◆ Do you know which of your clients have experienced animal companion loss in the last year, what their reactions were, and how long their process of healing lasted?

◆ Have you ever discussed the impact of animal well-being on your clients' own sense of safety in the world, including their reactions to endangered species of animals?

◆ If you have not included animal family members during initial intake, is this omission reflective of your perspective on animals' status in family lives? Or did it just not occur to you to do so?

◆ If you yourself are a steward, to what extent does your animal's life join with yours? Would you say your lives are closely intertwined, or are you more an arm's-length observer?

◆ Would you welcome working with those who have suffered the loss of a companion animal as an inclusion or extension of your practice?

Perhaps you have not thought much about these questions but instinctively respond, identifying your own validation and compassion for such losses.

The guidance and healing strategies presented in this book are also intended to assuage the pain of those who care about animals they do not live with, those who place importance on their existence, and those who simply observe animals as part of daily life. Such individuals include shelter workers, zookeepers, pet walkers and pet sitters; those who foster animals and those who attempt to find them homes; those who work directly in the care of animals at veterinary practices. Also in this category are frail elders in assisted living or nursing homes who may become saddened and withdrawn upon hearing that their therapy animal has died and will visit no more.

From the grief following the realization that the therapy canine who visited your hospitalized client has now passed away, to the sudden news that the parrot living in the front window of the neighborhood pet shop has succumbed to illness – the whole range of reactions to the loss of animals merits validation and support in the therapy room with compassionate clinicians wisely affirming the impact of even nondomiciled losses. Proximity and ownership are not the only determinants of grief's degree. The meaning attributed to an animal's life and its integration with our own daily existence are equal factors when gauging the effects of loss and the intensity of grief.

Potential benefits to practice of including animal companion loss

There are many benefits for clinicians willing to include and market a focus on the significance of animals in their clients' lives.

◆ Fostering therapeutic alliance: A client's perception that you value and understand whom and what they value – human and nonhuman – helps sustain the therapeutic alliance. When initial assessment includes all human and nonhuman family members, clinicians demonstrate acceptance of client priorities; clients will then be more likely to share their experience of animal companion grief if it arises. It is not necessary, in my opinion, to create a specialty for grief work associated with nonhumans, but simply to understand the differences and apply theory and intervention appropriately.

◆ Acknowledging client stewardship: It's likely that a significant percentage of your current clients live with animals and that they will experience the loss of an animal companion at least once during their lives. Therefore, not including animal companion inquiry when clients first reach out to us for any kind of mental health treatment may give the impression that we do not treat animal companion loss or view nonhuman family members as significant to our clients' lives and mental health.

◆ Addressing underserved needs: As professionally trained advocates, social workers and mental health counselors are charged with identifying and fulfilling underserved needs. Sensitivity to this issue reflects awareness of how society can disenfranchise the individual experience of marginalized populations whose rights may not be upheld, including the paltry rights of animals. Indicating our attention and willingness to work with animal companion loss is its own form of advocacy.

◆ Developing a closer bond with your community: In working with animal companion mourners, clinicians may also facilitate a closer bond with their communities, not only within private practice or agency-based services but in supporting local veterinary practices overwhelmed by the need for supportive services for their clients and themselves, as well as for secondary trauma interventions.

◆ Facilitating an animal companion bereavement group: Forming a support group – as a volunteer or peer-led resource embedded within a veterinary practice or held privately at your office – signals your receptivity to clients suffering from animal companion losses. Whether virtual or office-based, these groups are generally well attended, in part because there are so few of them. Determining the specifics (the number of participants, age range, length of time since loss, location, frequency, length of meetings) ahead of time is important. Will this be an open or closed group? For a closed group, a clinician may develop a path for recovery that can be applied to new mourners. For an open group, newly bereaved members may benefit from working with those who are ahead of them in recovery; participants further along in recovery can compare their status and feel progress.

Chapter summary

In this chapter, the experience of losing a companion animal is described as an event that – when untreated or invalidated – may lead to severe, unresolved grief reactions depending on the significance of the human-animal bond. This often unidentified and frequently disenfranchised form of mourning may frequently present in clinicians' practice, as the number of animal adoptions continues to rise across the country, and the majority of Americans now live with at least one animal. Such responses are described in four realms: emotional, behavioral, psychological, and spiritual. Questions are proposed to help clinicians locate their own views on animal companion loss and their willingness to more readily identify and include these kinds of losses in their practice. The benefits of including animal companion loss as a treatment focus in your practice include fostering the therapeutic alliance with current and future clients by acknowledging animals as important family members, addressing an underserved need, and forming closer bonds within your community. In this way, clinicians are "starting where the client is," an important value in mental health treatment (McConnell et al., 2019).

2

The impact of trauma on animal companion loss

I should have double-checked the gate. I knew Sammy tended to wander. When I heard the crash and then our doorbell rang, I felt a sickness I've been unable to shake. He died because of me. – Laura grieving her 18-month-old bull terrier, who was hit by a car

Whenever a beloved animal dies, grieving stewards may experience many difficult emotions and potentially negative self-perceptions, depending on the qualities of the relationship and the manner of the animal's death (Goldberg & Brackenridge, 2019; Cusack, 2014; Quackenbush & Graveline, 1985).

The death of any being – human or nonhuman – relied upon for comfort, companionship, love, guidance, support, and social interaction may have traumatic elements, and these may threaten one's sense of safety and the ability to adaptively adjust to the loss. But when trauma complicates grief, it must be identified and treated as an additional issue concurrent with mourning the animal's death.

The goal of this chapter is to describe and explain the role of trauma as a significant amplifier of grieving animal companion death and its potential to prolong or complicate mourning,

DOI: 10.4324/9781003145929-3

potentially leading to symptoms of PTSD. If the traumatic aspects of the loss remain unprocessed, the initiation of normative grieving may not commence, leading to a more complex and isolative experience of mourning (Nakajima et al., 2012).

This chapter will emphasize the importance of a hierarchical approach to treatment planning when trauma exacerbates mourning.

The circumstances of a loved one's death impact our experience of the loss, trigger deep self-reflection, and influence the tasks of grief's resolution. For example, deaths that occur "out of order" – that is, before anticipated life span is reached – can elicit traumatic reactions that may echo through the rest of a mourner's life. Deaths that involve violence or harmful intent, or deaths that a survivor felt could have been prevented (Pearlman et al., 2014), are more difficult to accept and can thwart the initiation of normative grieving.

Unfortunately, animal companion death often involves traumatic circumstances, which can extend grieving or even challenge its initiation (Compitus, 2019; Arkow, 2019, 2020; Schroeder & Clark, 2019). Mourners may feel stuck in the grip of traumatic recall or cognitive dissonance, meaning that their feelings and values associated with animal welfare feel in opposition with the animal's actual fate. Because of the frequency with which traumatic elements occur in animal companion death, it is essential to understand and evaluate symptoms of trauma in those mourning them.

Animal deaths can result from intentional cruelty and deliberate destruction (Arkow, 2019); accidents; missed opportunities for lifesaving interventions; natural disasters from which animals were not protected (Hunt et al., 2008); and estrangement from or abandonment by the original steward. Deaths may also follow a sudden and unexpected realization of advanced animal illness, adding elements of shock and self-perceptions of negligence. When an animal runs away or is kidnapped, its steward may ruminate over the painful mystery of its whereabouts for many years.

Negative impacts of unaddressed trauma

Stewards who experience traumatic animal companion loss can experience significant guilt and marginalization (Russell, 2015). According to Adrian and Stitt (2017), individuals who view their animals with higher empathy are most at risk of developing complicated grief, even when traumatic elements are not present. The additional emotional distress experienced from traumatic loss can result in depressive symptoms, interference with day-to-day activities, and prolonged grief reactions.

While acknowledging the brevity of animals' lives, human stewards are still often shocked to witness what appears to be their rapid aging; a 4-year-old canine, for example, is described as "senior." Their innocence can make their deaths seem out of order. This in itself can feel traumatic. For stewards already struggling with mental health issues, such losses can feel catastrophic. If multiple traumatic elements are present, the likelihood of the development of PTSD may increase.

Triggers of traumatic response following animal companion loss

Circumstances that can trigger traumatic responses (the sudden realization of severe illness, euthanasia, economic euthanasia, lack of verbal communication, abuse and neglect, forced surrender or abandonment, accidents, kidnapping and running away, intentional destruction, lack of health insurance, and the legal status of animals, which thwarts intervention) are described subsequently. All are common, and it is possible for several of these distressing circumstances to occur simultaneously.

The sudden realization of severe or terminal illness: An animal's ingrained and stoic acceptance of pain and discomfort may lead to shocking and sudden realizations of catastrophic illness. Sudden death coupled with traumatic circumstances may evoke a sense of hopelessness and futility.

Euthanasia is one of the most common traumatic aspects of animal companion death. Euthanizing a companion animal is a circumstance up to 40 percent of animal companion stewards will face (Park & Royal, 2020). These statistics do not include unregistered or unlicensed animals or those outside the auspices of veterinary care.

Despite the fact that a dignified, painless, and humane death can be the one final grace bestowed on a suffering animal, the choice to euthanize rarely brings peace to its steward. Many loving stewards who make this decision feel that they "murdered" their animals. Perceptions of themselves as accomplices to their animal's deaths often persist long after the fact. Even when medically indicated, euthanizing a companion animal can leave bitterness, regret, and incredible guilt (Quackenbush & Graveline, 1985; Curtis, 1988).

There is little in mental health research demonstrating euthanasia's direct impact on the development of trauma, but there is much anecdotal evidence of this in clinical work with bereaved stewards, who may report ongoing symptoms that include disturbing flashbacks, depersonalization, and extreme guilt.

Compare this to the circumstances when an end-of-life decision must be made for humans, when there is much reassuring support – even from the dying person themselves or via their advance directive – to guide family members. Animals, on the other hand, have no input, and their stewards are confronted with issues like the expense of treatments, a lack of medical clarity or options, and insufficient time for thoughtful guidance (Savishinsky, 1988).

The results can become an agonizing distraction from the work of mourning. The guilt following a decision to euthanize is perhaps the longest-lasting complication of traumatic bereavement, sometimes revisited years after the animal has died and sometimes resulting in prolonged grieving, self-recrimination, and second-guessing the decision. If family members or medical professionals disagree about the animal's care in such critical moments, schisms can be divisive and long-lasting.

Animal companion stewards often have little preparation for decisions to euthanize. When animals are adopted, endless instructions are offered for their care, feeding, and medical checkups. But consideration of how they will die, and the steward's potential role in deciding that process, are rarely discussed. Often options must be rapidly weighed with the sudden diagnosis of terminal illness; the heightened stress now goes beyond loss to include feeling responsibility for that loss.

Stewards who decide to remain with their companions during this process of euthanization may visualize traumatic images after the animal's death. Bearing witness to what may be perceived as a final fight for life can be deeply disturbing, as animals may vocalize, breathe differently, or tremble.

Persistent flashbacks to such horrifying moments may overwhelm and suppress memories of many years of loving camaraderie. The steward may feel a sense of having failed this creature, instead of allowing a merciful release from pain.

Those who cannot bear to witness their animal's passing may reprimand themselves for their absence, triggering regret that they could not reciprocate the unwavering loyalty the animal had offered them in the past. Such thoughts can become a ruminative form of self-torture.

Given that symptoms of trauma may affect the ability to accurately recollect a situation, the factors behind the decision to euthanize may be misremembered or remain unclear.

After the companion animal has passed away, bereaved stewards may imagine that a different course of treatment might have changed the outcome. They may question their choice and wonder if the animal was truly that ill. Despite medical evidence of the animal's compromised condition, even the most responsible, intelligent analysis may lead to endless self-blame.

Stewards may feel the decision to euthanize was premature or that they waited too long. They may feel they erroneously colluded with the medical recommendation, against the best interests of their animal. Uncomfortable in the position of "playing God," they may assign responsibility for the animal's death to themselves instead of to the illness or event that actually took the animal's life.

Economic euthanasia is a practice (Kipperman, 2010) in which an animal is euthanized due to convenience, an inability to afford treatments, homelessness, or a change in the steward's economic, social, or living circumstances.

It can be a deeply confounding factor in the resolution of traumatic grief and issues of morality, including for the workers who end the lives of healthy animals.

Consider the impact of routine euthanasia on shelter workers (Rollin, 2011). Those who feed, walk, groom, and give affection to shelter residents, sometimes for months or years, are the ones who constantly face their loss, merely because of overcrowding or unadoptability. Ironically, the very love of animals that drives them to do this work can also subject them to the injustice of their needless deaths.

Stewards might believe that dropping off an animal at a shelter is a better option than death. Yet millions of animals awaiting the elusive promise of a "forever home" are far more likely to be euthanized. Of the approximately 6.1 million animals who enter shelters every year, only 3.2 million are adopted.

Lack of verbal communication can confound efforts to maintain animals' health, protect them against abuse, and determine their levels of distress. Most animals are naturally stoic, enduring suffering until it becomes unbearable.

Ill and injured animals will go to great lengths to hide their vulnerabilities (Pierce, 2013). In the wild – from which domestic pets are not that far removed – any display of weakness may attract the attention of a predator. Injured deer or other feral creatures instinctively sense that trailing behind their herd, pride, litter, or covey will lead to exposure or abandonment.

Even healthy animals try to mask their deficits: Birds will puff up their feathers to appear more formidable, mice will leap into a larger predator's face, a turtle will withdraw into its shell for days when confronted with an unrelenting predator.

When illness or disability first appear, most animals, domesticated or feral, will simply rest, taking time off from eating and socializing. Failing to improve, they may attempt to hide. Such changes may be noticed by observant stewards, but without clear signs of pain or distress, it is unlikely a visit to the vet will quickly follow. By the time symptoms become intolerable, and thus more obvious, a terminal prognosis may come as a total shock to the animal's steward.

Accidents can happen with even the most dedicated and well-meaning animal stewardship. Animal deaths can result from the most minor carelessness: the gate left open that allows a puppy's escape from a yard; the unawareness of a cat sleeping under the car; serving expired foods that have become toxic; misreading signs of illness; using home remedies to treat an unwell animal. Ignorance – assuming an animal can swim, allowing predatory creatures proximity within or outside the home, even bathing a fragile creature that results in hypothermia – can be among such dangers.

Accidents are not categorized as abuse when resulting from ignorance or misunderstanding, but their impact on the steward can still result in the traumatic awareness of having caused the death.

Abuse and neglect are unfortunate, and frequent, facts of life for animals (Ascione & Shapiro, 2009). We have all heard stories of puppy mills, animal hoarders unable to maintain basic care and hygiene, cruelty purposefully inflicted, and declining levels of care from impoverished stewards.

The watchful and dedicated agencies charged with protecting animal welfare are often also understaffed and underfunded; neglect and abuse may thus go unreported, while complaints may be set aside, lacking sufficient proof. The evidence needed to prosecute may be difficult to gather in any case, as a steward's rights to privacy and ownership trump an animal's status.

In violent homes, animals may be the first or initial target of aggression by family members – children, adults, and even other animals (Shapiro et al., 2014; Ascione, 2001). When injuries or neglect reach serious levels, veterinary care providers may strongly suspect abuse but be unable to prove it. In cases of domestic violence toward humans, many professions are legally required to immediately report it, and interventions usually follow rapidly. Although much research shows that animal abuse is among the first clues that other family members are also being mistreated, there are not yet legal mandates to report animal abuse or neglect in every state (Arkow, 2020; Ascione & Shapiro, 2009).

Thus, veterinary practitioners and neighborhood observers have limited options when attempting to address abuse – and doing so may result in even worse outcomes. For example, probing questions from concerned vets may lead the animal's owner to withdraw it from care, or even to destroy it. Confronting such circumstances without the power to immediately and effectively intervene is often a component of primary or secondary trauma, which can develop among compassionate veterinarian staff.

The ethical and practical dilemmas go beyond veterinarians. Family members who may have witnessed abuse may feel they can never share this information without a sense of betrayal or fear of retribution. Holding such secrets can result in feelings of complicity. Merely observing such abuse, of an animal or another loved one, can result in trauma, especially when the witness cares deeply for the animal or person but feels helpless or unable to intervene (Herman, 1997; van der Kolk et al., 1996).

Well-meaning stewards may sometimes relegate the care of their animals to people who may not adhere to the usual care schedule. They may be hasty or impatient with their animal charges, managing them roughly, and neglectful of their needs for water and regular opportunities to relieve themselves. Such careless interactions can rise to the level of chronic neglect or abuse.

For example, some temporary caregivers – hired due to a steward's hospitalization or other emergency – may not understand the animal's requirements and may therefore not provide clean water, a warm environment, or human interaction. It is not unusual to find that an animal passed away, or became the victim of an accident, during a steward's emergency absence. While hidden "nanny cams" are now common, animals are still often at the mercy of temporary caregivers. The returning steward may notice signs of distress or injury, but their suspicions cannot be confirmed.

Animals adopted for the sole purposes of fighting, racing, display, entertainment, or guarding the home may also be the victims of abuse and neglect by owners ignorant of their needs and miscalculations about the extent of their suffering. Animals forced to fight, race during the summer heat, or live in stark outdoor kennels without adequate protection from the elements may succumb without notice. Compassionate observers – whether or not they themselves live with animals – may experience ongoing distress due to feelings of powerlessness to stop the abuse.

Forced surrender or abandonment (when stewards must either rehome or bring an animal to a shelter for economic, environmental, health, or social reasons, or other circumstances) can result in long-lasting traumatic reactions, even when such circumstances are beyond their control.

For example, research has shown that animal companion loss during Hurricane Katrina in 2005 was associated with an increase in psychopathology in stewards – even when the trauma of being displaced from their homes was considered. One study showed that forced abandonment of an animal during the associated evacuation intensified the trauma of the natural disaster, which, in turn, increased the risk of post-traumatic stress disorder (Hunt et al., 2008).

On a more mundane level, a family may quickly surrender a puppy adopted with great enthusiasm after realizing how destructive a young animal can be. The arrival of a human infant may end a long-term relationship with an animal, one that may have been brought to the union by one partner. Concern for the new baby's health and safety spurs the other partner to demand that the animal be surrendered. This can lead to incredible distress for the first partner (Stone, 2022).

Sometimes even the steward has no control over such situations. Although some state laws prohibit separating elders and their domestic animals when moving to public or subsidized housing (Pet Ownership for the Elderly and Persons with Disabilities, 2008), some frail elders' moves to nursing homes mean that their animals are left without caregivers.

Some individuals willingly surrender their animal companions to shelters when they can no longer afford their care or when their circumstances have changed. But forced surrender may have a significant impact on stewards who made a commitment to their companion's well-being. If their decision was forced by another family member or partner, resentment may last for years.

Kidnapping and running away have the same outcome and impact on the steward. In both cases, stewards may bear traumatic bereavement, assuming responsibility for the failure to sufficiently protect, suffering without any awareness of their animal companions' fate, and potentially discovering their disposition only after their deaths.

The incidence of animal kidnapping is rising, especially among dogs and exotic species (Ohio State University, 2009). As purebred or exotic animals may be very expensive, there is an underground market for their resale. The expenses that may be associated with exotic or purebred animal ownership can discourage the proper acquisition process – or the person who finds the lost animal may not make an effort to locate its steward, feeling it was somehow "let go" anyway. Certain breeds fall in and out of popularity, making their theft more likely. An animal may be kidnapped as part of a custody battle when separating partners disagree over primary stewardship.

Some stewards, believing that their cat, dog, horse, or rabbit prefers a freer existence, may allow the animal to roam outside, unsupervised. These good intentions may be shattered when the animal follows an intriguing scent, loses its way, and fails to return. Microchipping does not guarantee their return. Frantic efforts to find animals by posting signs and contacting shelters are rarely successful.

In any case, animals that run away are unlikely to be returned – up to 30 percent of dogs may be recovered from shelters, but only 5 percent of cats are (Weiss et al., 2012). In all these cases, stewards are left without any closure or relief; instead, their sense of guilt and abandonment can increase.

When humans run away or are kidnapped, extraordinary efforts are made to locate and reunite them while pursuing their kidnappers. Pictures are posted on social media and in the news, and every law enforcement agency is alerted. The relentless search goes on even during inclement weather and may involve air, sea, and land rescue attempts. Entire communities may join the search. Such efforts may continue for decades. DNA evidence can now bring murderers to justice decades after the loss; social media assists in reunifications that would have once been impossible. Such efforts bring comfort and closure to sorrowing families. But these efforts are rarely employed or available when animals are lost or stolen.

Intentional destruction occurs for many reasons. Animals are regularly hunted, discarded, and killed, sometimes for the inconvenience they present, sometimes for food or clothing, sometimes during the course of domestic violence, for sport, for research.

While most people would not define the intentional slaughter of animals for food or research as murder, many people do experience such actions toward animals as highly traumatic, ethically challenging, and morally unacceptable. This is especially true if forced to witness or participate in intended harm or destruction (as sometimes happens as a prelude to intimate partner violence).

The euthanization of a tiger who attacks an untrained person entering its zoo cage, for example, may bring outrage and sorrow to its caregivers and the public. Decisions to control or manage unwanted populations of deer or geese through sterilization or the destruction of breeding habitat can feel unjust. The torturous confinement of farm animals destined for human consumption has inspired humane laws as well as a growing culture of veganism. Animals used in racing, fighting, or entertaining in zoos or circuses may succumb well before their expected life spans, spurring protests and activism.

Experiencing any death perceived as an unjust or unwarranted loss of life, especially when the animal has no control over its fate, can elicit traumatic reactions among those dedicated to their protection, as well as among the general public.

Lack of insurance affecting treatment choices is a common problem for stewards of ailing animals. Although such coverage is increasing (Napia.org, 2023), only 12 to 24 percent of stewards have purchased health insurance for their companion animals. (These numbers, of course, do not include unlicensed or unregistered animals.)

In fact, according to Forbes Advisor Pet Ownership Statistics and Facts (2023), respondents indicated that a vet bill of $999 would cause 42 percent of pet owners to go into debt, while a vet bill of $499 or less would cause 28 percent to do so. Expenses needed for an animal's health and well-being were among the top four reasons stewards regret their adoption.

The fact that aging animals require more health maintenance does not translate to more frequent veterinary visits. When animals are having an "off day," stewards will sometimes wait to see if the issue corrects itself. Sometimes the delay results in health's restoration, but at other times the steward's efforts to avoid a potentially costly, inconvenient visit to the vet may end tragically if the delay proves to be fatal.

Given that proclivity, catastrophic illness is more likely without rapid intervention – and more expensive to manage. Dental care, X-rays, labs, boarding expenses can further escalate such costs and may be unaffordable. Despite the humane attitude of many veterinary practices that offer discounts for lifesaving services, there is an obvious limit to the extent they can do so.

It's impossible to know to what extent a lack of insurance directly impacts animals' longevity and the extent of their suffering. While some stewards may mortgage their homes to pay for treatments, for others, this is obviously not an option. When caring stewards cannot afford life-enhancing or lifesaving interventions, the resulting traumatic guilt can complicate recovery from animal companion death.

Legal status of animals: Because animals are designated as property – but property that must be licensed or registered to ensure even this fragile status – their sale, exchange, and even deaths frequently fly below the social, healthcare, and insurance statistics radar. As "property," the extent to which legal intervention is possible to protect their safety is minor. A significant percentage of animals are never registered or licensed, be they within the stealthy and illegal exotic animal industry or smaller mammals or reptiles whose fate is never traced once purchased. Animal cruelty laws advocate for their protection and humane treatment but can be difficult to legally enforce. Despite their view as family members by the majority of animal companion stewards, protections for animals have not yet risen to legally reflect this view as full family members. Therefore, the futility associated with their hapless, unprotected lives and deaths may confound grieving or result in secondary trauma when animal caregivers feel powerless to intervene.

For example, when animals are dropped off at shelters, there is no requirement to report their fate to law enforcement or social services. Animals can be purchased, or surrendered at will. Human children and frail adults are protected from such fates, while the indifferent disposition or misuse of animals rarely results in consequences. Human adoptions proceed under the watchful eyes of multiple agencies with ironbound legal protections for infant and parent. The fostering of babies and children follow a similarly legally guided process attempting to ensure that their placement will meet their needs for safety, nurturance, and sustenance. Animals are not afforded any guaranteed protections. They may be disposed of as the current "owner" or steward sees fit. There is little recourse to change their aversive circumstances or hold intentional or ignorant perpetrators accountable for abuse. A steward's awareness of such injustice combined with the helplessness to advocate can contribute to traumatic responses following the animal's death.

Secondary trauma

The earlier descriptions of trauma triggers apply to those who are directly involved in or responsible for an animal's well-being, that is, primary stewards and family members. But other caregivers in an animal's life may also be deeply impacted by tragic circumstances, resulting in symptoms of secondary trauma, which is the experience of having knowledge of, witnessing, or being involved in the harm or destruction of a loved one (Figley, 1999).

Veterinary practitioners and staff are highly vulnerable to secondary trauma and secondary traumatic grieving (Goldberg, 2019). They have little power when an animal's human steward disagrees with or ignores treatment suggestions or emergency interventions. Confronting abusers rarely results in the desired enlightened behavior. For example, a fractured leg on the same cat for the third time strongly suggests abuse; but the practitioner binding it has no power to stop this behavior. Being placed in this untenable situation, understandably, can lead to chronic feelings of helplessness and hopelessness.

Euthanizing animals is almost a daily occurrence within veterinarian facilities, affecting all involved, and practitioners are all too often faced with saying goodbye and humanely arranging the deaths of animals with whom they have formed caring and affectionate bonds. Being asked to euthanize an animal that could be saved through a medical intervention brings an excruciating ethical dilemma, especially when financial issues are involved. Many veterinary practices offer compassionate care gratis, but within practical limits. Stewards may expect fees to be reduced or waived, and sometimes accuse a practice of being uncaring when they cannot comply, further stressing the staff and the viability of the practice (Compitus, 2021).

The lack of appropriate resources to mitigate such distress can lead to burnout, absenteeism, resignation, or suicidal ideation (Hamilton, 2019). The high rates of burnout among veterinary staff – and the significant rates of veterinarian suicide, which may be 2.1 to 3.5 times higher than that of the general population – appear to confirm that stress and heartache without supportive emotional resources can lead to symptoms of PTSD (Compitus, 2021).

Secondary traumatic bereavement can also occur among individuals who are deeply affected by an animal's death, while not being its primary caregiver. For example, others who may develop secondary traumatic reactions to animal deaths include zookeepers, pet sitters, pet groomers, residents in nursing homes where animals visit, and neighbors. Family members who witness animal abuse or neglect may also suffer secondary trauma.

Secondary traumatic bereavement may also extend to people who feel no control over the vanishing habitat of a beloved species or intentional destruction of its habitat. Reports of diminishing numbers of honeybees from gardens, beached whales disoriented by warming seas, and changed migration patterns of spring songbirds, by extension, may bring on uneasy feelings about threats to human existence.

The following case studies reflect the different aspects of traumatic loss described earlier. All are drawn from real experiences, but names of animals, referenced species, and stewards have been changed throughout the book to protect their privacy.

Case study: the nesting drive

Yet another attempt at IVF had ended in miscarriage at 4 months. At ages 40 and 45, Amy and Brad knew their chances of procreation, even with reproductive technology, were minimal now.

Their physician had advised them to consider adoption, but the agencies said they were too old to adopt a newborn. Amy and Brad had waited for career advancement and financial stability before starting a family. Now it appeared that this goal was not in the cards for the loving couple. They felt dejected and struggled to accept a childless life.

Two weeks after their last appointment at the fertility clinic, Amy's sister mentioned that her neighbor's rabbit was pregnant and that she would be unable to care for the expanding family. The neighbor intended to drop off the pregnant rabbit at a local shelter. Amy was distressed by the thought and asked Brad if he would be interested in adopting the mother and her babies.

Neither of them had had animals in their lives previously. Brad was indifferent and left it up to Amy, who felt increasingly motivated. Through her sister, she learned that the mother rabbit had been surrendered to a shelter about 45 minutes away. As if a bomb had gone off in her heart, Amy quickly tracked down the location and drove to the shelter with Brad.

The mother rabbit had died from an illness, but not before giving birth to six bunnies, two of whom had died. The remaining four rabbits were still being dropper-fed but would be adoptable in two more weeks. The shelter workers were delighted to know that Amy and Brad would keep them together.

The second-floor room they had intended to use as a nursery was set up for the bunnies. They purchased every conceivable toy as well as all the necessities. Amy and Brad brought them home two weeks later, naming them Faith, Hope, Charity, and Harmony. They spent hours each day feeding, grooming, holding, and playing with them. Brad built a hut on the house's deck once they were old enough to spend time outside. The couple was thrilled with their animal family.

But when the rabbits were six months old, Faith appeared to be ill, and a vet visit determined she had a serious infection. Not even IV antibiotics could reverse the course of an aggressive upper respiratory infection. She died the following day.

The clinic gave Brad and Amy antibiotics to administer to the other seemingly healthy rabbits, in case they were also infected. Despite careful administration of the medicine, Hope, Charity, and Harmony passed away the following week.

Amy and Brad felt devastated. Brad experienced feelings of anger and disconnect, aggressively dismantling the hut and taking it to the dump, along with all the other paraphernalia associated with the animals. Amy became increasingly despondent, despairing, irritable, and angry, withdrawing into isolation. She felt stunned by the deaths, which reappeared in nightmares and led to a lack of sleep. Unable to function, she took a leave from work.

An underlying depression, which had likely been present for some time, emerged with a vengeance. Amy experienced constant ruminations about Faith's final visit to the vet and frequent flashbacks to the discovery that the other littermates had died. As her symptoms persisted, her doctor referred Amy to a mental health professional for evaluation.

As is sometimes the case, animals may be adopted to bring comfort and facilitate recovery from life events. It is not unusual for well-intended relatives to introduce a grieving family member to a dog, cat, or bird, thinking it will provide soothing distraction.

Amy had already experienced repeated feelings of failure in attempted conception, along with the loss of her family dream. Her treatments involved hormonal therapies, which can sometimes destabilize a fragile emotional balance. Amy's adoption of the bunnies had renewed her nesting drive, providing an opportunity to care for and nurture baby animals. She had allowed herself to bond with the young rabbits and now felt responsible for their deaths. Her self-perception as a competent maternal provider failed in the reality of these further losses.

The sudden realization of acute illness, followed by the rapid deaths of the bunnies, added the dimensions of shock and futility to an already emotionally vulnerable steward. Amy remained in denial, unable to move forward, constantly reviewing every aspect of their care from the day they were adopted.

Amy was ultimately diagnosed with PTSD and referred for treatment of trauma, including eye movement desensitization and reprocessing.

Case study: clinic conflict

Daisy was a 12-year-old beagle brought to a veterinary clinic with multiple health issues. Her stewards could no longer provide the level of care necessary at home, so they decided to incur the expense of boarding her at the veterinary clinic.

Round-the-clock care was required to keep Daisy comfortable and alive. As the weeks went by, her health deteriorated, and it became clear to her team of caregivers that euthanasia was the most humane option for this long-lived, amiable canine. Yet her stewards would not allow it, insisting that Daisy must die a "natural" death.

The dog's comfort level became more difficult to manage. Daisy's stewards stopped visiting, as they could not tolerate witnessing her suffering. She was now deaf, blind, and unable to walk far enough to relieve herself. Her lack of mobility resulted in decubital ulcers, pressure sores that were difficult to treat.

Daisy was depressed and in pain. She rarely ate; her only source of nutrition was a liquid diet and intravenous fluid therapy for hydration. This once-proud and independent creature was now simply existing.

Daisy's vet continuously emphasized the futility of her situation and strongly advised her stewards to allow a peaceful death. Such conversations were futile. Her stewards threatened to take her elsewhere, reiterating that she would die "when her time came." Instead, they called each day in the hopes that she had passed away.

The compassionate vet knew her pain could be better managed at the hospital where Daisy was boarded. But her primary caregiver at the hospital, Monica, began to withdraw from Daisy, dissociating from her own pain in having to witness Daisy's. Faced with the conflict of carrying out treatment orders that would only prolong her suffering, Monica began avoiding or minimizing her interactions with the animal. When Daisy began vomiting, Monica's despair was soon echoed by the entire demoralized staff. When a feeding tube was suggested, many expressed outrage.

Finally, Daisy passed away when her pain-relieving medication was increased to sufficiently ease her suffering.

The following day, several staff members called out sick. Monica was offered counseling by the facility for her grief but eventually left the clinic. A therapist was retained to offer staff support for secondary trauma.

As discussed previously, veterinarians and their staffs are in a difficult situation when they disagree with their human clients, or with one another. But the threat of alienating the steward may mean an animal receives no care at all or receives further abuse.

Those who have spent their careers lovingly caring for voiceless creatures may have little opportunity to intervene themselves. They may be further harmed by their own sense of helplessness.

Chapter summary

The circumstances associated with animal companion death are often traumatic. Without mental health intervention, stressors on human stewards may lead to the development of PTSD or other symptoms of acute distress. Traumatic responses can be exacerbated by sudden realizations of severe illness, euthanasia, lack of animal's ability to verbally communicate its distress, accidents, animal abuse and neglect, forced surrender, kidnapping or running away, intentional destruction, lack of animal health insurance, and the legal status of animals as mere property which prevents/thwarts intercession. Non-primary caretakers may also experience secondary trauma in such situations. Without the provision of mental health services, these individuals may also find themselves struggling with prolonged ruminations about the animal's death and vulnerable to the development of prolonged grief disorders, including PTSD. Untreated symptoms of trauma and secondary trauma may lead to protracted suffering and the exacerbation of other mental health conditions.

Finally, even those who do not take care of a specific animal, directly or indirectly, may find themselves challenged and traumatized by threats to their habitats or their very existence. One does not need to be a steward in order to find animal life important. Many cherish the gifts of animals in the wild and experience symptoms of secondary trauma when their lives and habitats are threatened – and they feel powerless to help them.

3

Considerations of attachment theory in animal companion loss

We were together all day long – so deeply bonded. Logan was everything to me. I don't know who I am without him. – Stephen after the death of his Brittany spaniel, Logan, an agility champion

Whenever you walk through a park, you'll probably notice animals proudly accompanying their stewards. Some are leashed, some little ones are carried in tote bags, some older companions are ferried in carts or carriages. Sometimes it appears that steward and animal are uncannily well matched, with similar gaits, facial expressions, and even coloring.

What accounts for these clear displays of alignment, emotional mutuality, and centrality in each other's lives? And why is it that other animal adopters never reach this level of deep bonding, instead coexisting in a rhythm of more distant caretaking?

Attachment theory, which describes the genesis and resulting styles of how we relate to other humans, is the subject of this chapter as applied to the human-animal bond. But we will widen its perspective to consider three pivotal impacts:

- ♦ The consideration of animals as primary attachment figures, whose own potentially healing or distancing

DOI: 10.4324/9781003145929-4

attachment styles contribute to the attachment style of the created dyad

◆ The attachment style within the human-animal bond as somewhat predictive of how a steward may mourn when the animal dies

◆ The implication of these findings to animal adoption and advocacy

We will then review four case studies that illustrate those considerations.

Basics of attachment theory

Attachment theory has heavily influenced our understanding of the qualities and challenges in human relationships since John Bowlby first described these styles of relating (Bowlby, 1982; Bretherton, 1992). Thought to develop in early childhood and emerging largely from the experiences of reciprocity and/or frustrations in attempting to form our earliest human bonds, attachment styles are understood to continue to influence important relationship qualities and alliances throughout adult life.

Theories further suggest that individual attachment styles may vary depending on the qualities inherent in specific relationships or may even change over time within that same relationship (Krumwiede, 2014; Zilcha-Mano et al., 2011b). Furthermore, one may form different attachment styles to other entities throughout life, including religious figures, institutions, and – as suggested in this chapter – animals.

For purposes of simplicity, this chapter will reference only the three dominant attachment styles: secure, avoidant, and anxious.

In clinical work, moderation of difficult attachment styles within the safety of therapeutic alliance can be an indication of progress, especially in clients whose attachment styles have thwarted their ability to form and maintain healthy relationships.

Bowlby (1988) felt that when the therapist acts as a reliable, secure base, an individual can begin the arduous task of exploring and reworking his or her internal working models of attachment. For example, therapists are trained to titrate levels of closeness with avoidant clients until the client learns it is "safe" and can tolerate increasing levels of intimacy (Sable, 2013).

In such exchanges, the therapist facilitates the experience of secure attachment by remaining a constant figure in a client's life, consistently demonstrating acceptance, and explores their emotional responses until the client develops a capacity for closeness (if avoidantly attached), or trust (if anxiously attached). When attunement is sound, it is thought to lead to a "corrective emotional experience" (Bridges, 2006), in which the therapist's steady presence and consistent support helps heal previous breaches in attachment styles by effecting a different outcome within a close caregiving experience.

Accepting this potential for attachment moderation within the human client-therapist alliance, can we apply this same reparative dance and corrective emotional experience to what is facilitated within the human-animal bond – and attribute any moderations to the contributions of each? That the development of a human-animal attachment style is a two-way street, with both being equal contributors to the attachment style of the dyad, has been repeatedly observed by those who have studied the attachment of human to animal and animal to human (Vanegas-Farfano & González-Ramírez, 2016).

There are thousands of documented descriptions of animals fostering self-esteem in children suffering from insecure, avoidant, or anxious attachment (Parish-Plass, 2008). Similarly, there are plentiful stories of compassionate stewards who rescue fearful, traumatized shelter animals who become loving, responsive creatures thriving under their care. This seems to suggest that these "corrective" or stabilizing emotional experiences may be influenced by the steady response of both humans and animals.

Animals as primary attachment figures

This question of whether animal companions can serve as primary attachment figures is raised in the seminal work resulting in the "Pet Attachment Questionnaire" (Zilcha-Mano et al., 2011a), an evaluative tool that considers a steward's attachment style to their animal as a factor that may influence the intensity and tasks of mourning following the animal's death. It appears that the four elements Ainsworth (1992) associates with primary attachment figures – proximity seeking, secure base, separation distress, and safe haven – are frequently observed within the human animal bond.

Sigal Zilcha-Mano (2012, p. 579) notes that animals do indeed have the ability to "provide a safe haven and secure base." For example, humans and their animals frequently seek each other's proximity, exhibit distress upon separation, and find comfort and safety in this secure base when reunited.

It appears that the human-animal bond may provide another version of the corrective emotional experience, although differently and less intentionally than their clinician counterparts (Sable, 2013). While these conclusions may seem obvious to those who interact closely with companion animals, such considerations have received scant scientific attention.

In one study (Meehan et al., 2017), it was suggested that not only can companion animals serve as primary attachment figures but the perception of their value is heightened within their stewards attachment hierarchy. As the majority of Americans regard their animals as consistent sources of nurturance and comfort, this adds traction to the possibility that animals can also be catalysts of healthier attachment styles.

A further question is whether animals, beyond being primary attachment figures, bring their own unique attachment styles to such relationships.

Shelby Wanser et al. (2019) observed that certain animals display attachment behaviors toward caretakers that can enhance the well-being of both. While such studies do not conclude that attachment styles are thus altered within either being or dyad, they give impetus to the idea that animals equally contribute to the formation of secure attachments.

Similarities in the development of animal and human attachment styles

If we consider that animals may have their own attachment styles, how do they develop? Can we trace their origination, even partially, to their earliest experiences with caregivers, as we do with humans?

In the human infant-caregiver dyad, we attribute the formation of secure attachment to the capacity of both entities to form and sustain reciprocity within the relationship. The simple transactions of caregiving exchange and emotional mirroring (i.e. the caregiver meeting the infant's basic needs and the infant's response to such caretaking with signs of pleasure or contentment) is recognized as a primary factor in this early critical dance, directly impacting the formation of the infant's attachment style (Rappaport, 1999).

Such behavior is also observed between animal babies and their caretakers. We understand that an animal baby's capacity to respond to caregiver outreach can similarly encourage or frustrate attachment efforts, while the caregiver may become indifferent if attempts to feed, nurture, soothe, or bond with its offspring are rejected (Kim et al., 2014). These impasses may result in withdrawal by both entities, creating the potential for caregiver abuse (Brockington, 2008). Birds, for example, may abandon attempts to feed a baby that does not emit a "high-intensity" signal of need in favor of sustaining the survival of its presumably healthier nestmates (Dugas et al., 2016).

A human neonate's response system is focused on receipt of food, facial emotional reciprocity, and response to other caregiving needs (feeding, grooming, cleaning, etc.). Without mature reasoning, the primary function through which the quality of the relationship develops is infant-caregiver emotional and behavioral reciprocity. The infant cries; it is held. The infant exhibits hunger; it is fed. Bowlby himself referred to similarities in the attachment behaviors of primate and human infants, as Carol Tosone and Theresa Aiello (1999) note in *Love and Attachment*.

Next, let's turn to the role of language in forming attachments between humans and animals. Much has been made of the fact that animals do not hold understanding of complicated sentence formation or experience a wide range of emotions, that their reactions seem to be based more on instinct than on true mirroring – a perspective that would render similar comparisons unscientifically inaccurate. Yet animals have been shown to possess a range of basic emotions up to that of a 6-year-old child (Panksepp, 2011a), while human infants' repertoire of expressed emotions is also limited, largely confined to alerts of need and subsequent receipt of that care. Humans do not rely on language to get needs met until their second or third year of life.

As Lorenz (1952) concludes, animals have no need of humanlike language to survive; while dogs have developed an understanding that allows them to communicate nonverbally for a purpose (like being fed or let out), that ability is not true language. Yet "it is incredible, what minimal signs, completely imperceptible to man, animals will receive and interpret rightly" (p. 78).

Another comparison can be found in the biochemical impetus to form attachments. Panksepp notes in his chapter "The Chemistry of Caring" (2000) that the hormonal influences that prepare a pregnant mother for bonding are present in both humans and animals. Feline mothers and their kittens exhibit signs of distress when separated and relief when reunited.

These early impacts have powerful implications for the development of secure attachment between human child and its caregiver (Brockington, 2008; Muzik et al., 2013), as well as its ability to regulate affect (Schore, 2015), an important aspect of forming attachments, so it is reasonable to conclude that the same would be true of a baby animal and its caregiver.

Given that human children's attachment styles reflect their earliest experiences – including trauma from inadequate or abusive caregiving – we can perhaps imagine the same is true for animals. And if that is the case, we must consider that the experience of subsequent abuse and trauma could change the attachment styles of both humans and animals.

It if is accepted that animal and human attachment styles can influence each other and be influenced by life experiences, does the attachment style developed within the human-animal dyad remain constant throughout the course of their relationship, or – as some studies suggest (Sable, 2013) – can it change depending on circumstance? For example, might a role transition from caregiver to care receiver influence or moderate the initial attachment style when a previously independent animal becomes increasingly reliant on its human for care? And can a change in an attachment relationship then influence how a steward will mourn their animal companion?

Finally, drawing on research focused on animals' neurological, emotional, and behavioral capacities and responses – many of which appear to mirror our own (Panksepp, 2000, 2005, 2011b; Alcaro et al., 2017; Bekoff, 2000, 2007; Low, 2012) – we can perhaps add robust scientific justification to consider animals as full-fledged attachment figures, contributing equally to the development of the attachment style within the human-animal bond. Further studies might benefit from Topál et al.'s (2005) argument for the development of novel evaluative tools that do not solely rely on human brain mapping to make such determinations.

Paradoxically, if we consider chatbots as able to provide the basics of secure attachment, through consistent functional and emotional support – that is, "listening attentively, looking at the participant and nodding, being nice and pleasant to interact with, smiling, remembering little personal details about people, for example by using their names, being expressive, for example by using facial expressions, and admitting mistakes" (Heerink et al., 2010; Hermann, 2022) – perhaps we can also accept the attachment influences of animal companions, who do all that, plus the additional benefit of physical touch (Eckstein et al., 2020).

Attachment style influences on animal companion grief

It appears that the attachment style between human and animal can influence subsequent grief reactions (Zilcha-Mano et al., 2011a, 2011b, 2012; Fine, 2019). The "Pet Attachment Questionnaire" concludes that, while secure attachment may result in a more normative course of grieving, other styles may result in more problematic mourning.

For example, Brown and Symons (2016) suggest that a steward's anxious attachment style toward its animal companion while it lived could result in a higher likelihood of anger or prolonged grieving after the animal's death. An avoidant style of attachment was observed to deactivate the grieving process and was associated with decreased post-death anger and likelihood of future animal adoption. Another study (Teo & Thomas, 2019) suggests an association between secure animal companion attachment and reduced psychological distress and conflict upon its passing. That may imply that the steward's secure attachment style within the dyad is likely to result in a more normative course of grieving.

Implications for animal adoption

Learning as much as possible about an animal's previous interactions (as we would when considering adopting a human child) could help determine its potential to meet the emotional expectations of its adopting steward. As Pat Sable (2013) writes, adopted pets "are likely to carry the consequences and difficulties of their previous misery with them, and yet these same pets can flourish if the new pet parent can be helped to understand certain attachment dynamics" (97). From this wise observation, we can extrapolate that an animal's attachment style can perhaps be remediated through its own corrective emotional experience with a human – or vice versa, as anecdotal case studies and research suggest.

Most reputable animal adoption agencies diligently attempt to find a match for the safety and physical needs of an animal by asking about a potential adopter's lifestyle and housing. Breeders discuss the importance of environmental circumstances, willingness to invest in animal health, and expectations of time spent together.

Still, animal adoption may be an impulsive undertaking. A potential steward may simply come upon a community adoption event, become motivated by the plight of a hapless creature, and believe that adopting it will help them or a loved one recover from some adverse life event. Such rapid acquisitions can result in disappointing outcomes when the capacity for both parties to fulfill the other's needs is not considered. Ignoring the requirements necessary for a successful match may result in an animal's being abused, returned, or even abandoned and euthanized.

As Lorenz (1952) writes, "The wish to keep an animal usually arises from a general longing for a bond with Nature. Every animal is a piece of Nature, but not every animal is a suitable representative of Nature to live in your house" (p. 57). The generalization that any animal can provide curative powers – soothing loneliness or participating in cherished activities – could be dispelled by careful pre-adoption exploration.

If such a hoped-for bond does not materialize, each member of the human-animal dyad may become frustrated by the other's inability to meet species or attachment needs. In the book *Solomon's Ring* (1952), Lorenz describes a steward imagining his avian charge happy during his daylong absence simply because his seed cup has been filled and his cage cleaned. More appropriate, suggests Lorenz, would be nocturnal creatures who begin their day just as you arrive home, giving each component of the dyad the interaction and symbiotic companionship they need.

Concluding that animals have their own attachment styles that can moderate the attachment style of their human steward within the safety of the created dyad may also help further legal efforts to elevate their status, based on increased value associated with their sentiency.

The following case studies offer observations that reinforce the ideas referenced in the chapter, that animals have their own attachment styles, which can mitigate and transform human attachment styles and the created animal-steward bond, but also frustrate an alliance when attachment styles between steward and animal are mismatched. Further, the case studies show the impact of attachment styles on how stewards grieve (or do not). They also touch on how scrutinizing expectations could help reduce unsuccessful and mismatched animal adoptions, which often result in more harm to the animal than to the adopter.

Case study: a quiet communion

Larry, a 28-year-old single man living alone in Chicago, was the only son of parents who had not wanted children – he was a surprise pregnancy late in their marriage – and he had no close relatives. Larry's parents were not healthy, nor were they affectionate with each other or with him. His childhood was highly regimented, and he was assigned many household chores from the age of 5. His emotional outreach found no response from his parents, who treated him as a burden who needed to demonstrate appreciation for their support. Larry found emotional refuge largely through his interest in books, especially in the sciences and maths. He excelled as a student, the only achievement that brought recognition from his parents.

As socializing at home was discouraged due to his parents' ongoing health issues, Larry had few friends. By the time Larry was in his teens, he was taking care of his elderly parents, both of whom were now disabled. Accepted into a prestigious engineering school, Larry was forced to live at home to continue his caretaking duties of now-elderly parents.

By the time he graduated, they had both passed away, and Larry was left to manage their affairs and sell the family home. He was offered a great job in Boston, and he moved there to begin a new life and career, leaving behind his one close friend. Work now completely occupied Larry's life. Other than the occasional beer with colleagues, he led a solitary existence. Larry had never dated and was not motivated to do so.

As Larry was walking home one day, he noticed a lizard in the window of a pet store. The pale animal was entirely motionless, attempting to blend in with the wooden stick on which he was perched. Larry stood there, watching and attempting to detect any sign of life. After a few moments, he noticed the lizard blink and turn its head slightly, meeting his stare. Fascinated, Larry entered the shop and inquired about the still, silent being. That evening he pored over articles on the internet, trying to learn all he could about the creature that had so transfixed him. Larry decided to adopt the bearded lizard and purchased the necessary items, intending to pick up the lizard as soon as he set up its terrarium.

In considering the placement of the tank, Larry realized the bareness of his apartment. Only a gray couch, a small round table, a metal bookcase, two chairs, and a computer desk occupied the living room opposite his mostly unused kitchen. His bedroom consisted of a full-size bed adorned only with a comforter, a night table, and a dresser hastily purchased from a thrift shop to hold his spartan wardrobe. Larry decided to place the terrarium between the window and the computer desk, where he often spent long hours working.

Larry brought the lizard home. Once in his new terrarium, the lizard slowly crawled to the carefully positioned perch against the backdrop of cactus, rocks, and sand. Then he stopped, fading into the pale background, his eyes closed. Larry decided to name the lizard "Flage," short for camouflage.

For the first few days, Flage did not eat. While the shop owner had warned Larry this might occur, it worried him. He made several trips to the store to purchase live insects and other enticing edibles. Still the animal did not eat. Finally, one morning Larry noticed that all the insects were gone. Flage had moved to another perch, and his color had changed from a pale tan to a green stripes. That and his bulging red eyes now completely matched the terrarium's blooming cactus flowers.

As Larry spent time coding, he would catch sight of his companion. As they gazed at each other, Larry felt a riveting and calming connection to this vivid presence in his sparse home. Eventually, Flage moved to the side of the terrarium closest to Larry's desk. Although Larry assumed it was in anticipation of being fed, a part of him felt a deep connection to Flage, which filled him with awe.

For six years, Larry and Flage coexisted, an easy alliance in which neither demanded much of the other. Flage outlasted failed attempts at romance, work crises, health issues, and vague depressions that sometimes plagued Larry for weeks.

Most of Larry's days were spent with Flage, as he frequently worked from home. Flage provided a strong and steady comfort, a mystical bond. The fullness of the rich silence between them was both reassuring and stimulating. Larry sometimes felt he could imagine being Flage, existing in his terrarium world yet feeling securely bound to his peaceful life. He believed Flage understood him and that at times they could read each other's minds.

One day when Larry opened the terrarium to feed Flage, the lizard moved onto his arm. His tiny feet attached to Larry's hand, and he seemed to be enjoying the warmth of Larry's palm. Larry marveled at this physical connection with his little friend and felt great satisfaction from the contact, after which Flage moved slowly back onto his branch. Occasionally Larry would attempt to repeat the physical encounter. Sometimes Flage would creep up his arm; other times, he would not respond to the offered interaction.

Larry began speaking to Flage. When he had a problem with coding, he would discuss it with Flage. He felt that Flage helped him consider solutions and build his confidence. With a mere turn of Flage's head or a punctuated blink, Larry felt heard. He felt the kind of reciprocal exchange he had never experienced with any other being, a quiet acceptance of his solitary life, which they now shared.

One morning, Flage was pale, and his usual stillness seemed too still. When Larry removed the terrarium's cover to offer his hand, Flage did not move. When Larry gently attempted to pick him up, Flage's stiffened, cold form fell to the bottom of the terrarium. Was Flage simply playing dead, a response to stress?

Larry became frantic. He placed Flage in a shoebox and brought him to the hospital, where it was determined that Flage had died.

Larry felt disoriented and panicked. He felt a sudden, suffocating rush in his chest – his first panic attack – when arriving back at his empty apartment. Sleep eluded him.

Larry started to display some of Flage's characteristics, becoming less verbal, eating infrequently, and only minimally engaging in human contact. He would sit motionless by the terrarium he could not yet remove, sometimes tearful with despair. While he had rarely cried at times of frustration or disappointment in the past, he was now frequently in tears. After adopting Flage, he had experienced a wider range of new emotions, from quiet joy to contentment. Now he felt extreme sadness and grief. He held a belief that he might somehow reconnect with Flage's spirit.

Larry found it difficult to focus at work and to complete projects on time. He stopped socializing with his coworkers. Concerned about his weight loss and frequent panic attacks, Larry visited his doctor, who initially prescribed antianxiety and sleep medications.

Assessment

As Larry's symptoms persisted, he was referred to a local therapist, who reviewed his history and childhood circumstances in an initial assessment. It was determined that Larry's primary relationships with other humans had been in caretaking, education, or work contexts. He was averse to forming additional human bonds, fearing they would be burdensome, take over his life, and result in further caretaking.

During therapy, Larry confronted his profound sense of loneliness and anger toward his parents. He had been unable to mourn either of them. In keeping with their wishes, neither had a funeral; cremation and immediate disposal of ashes had followed both deaths.

It was determined that Larry's attachment style had been avoidant previous to the adoption of Flage, whose behavior – normative for his species – also reflected a somewhat avoidant style. Over the course of their years together, Larry had come to rely on Flage as an intimate associate. When Flage passed away, Larry lost the first relationship that offered a mutual, even if minimal, exchange of emotional reciprocity. For example, Larry shared that when he returned from a brief evening out, Flage would sometimes display separation distress by moving to the far side of the tank and turning his head away. Once Larry settled down at his desk, Flage would engage in proximity-seeking behavior by moving closer to Larry. When Larry talked to Flage about his evenings, imagining Flage's validating responses, Flage would blink and sometimes tip his head. It seemed that Flage had become a secure base for Larry, who also reflected qualities indicating secure attachment.

As his therapist reviewed questions from the Animal Companion Bereavement Questionnaire (see Chapter 4) with Larry, it was revealed that Flage was the first animal in his life. Although he had adopted Flage with the assumption that the lizard would demand little in terms of caretaking, his developing closeness with the lizard may have represented the most securely attached relationship of his life, including the mutual provisions of a secure base, proximity seeking, separation distress, and safe haven (Ainsworth, 1992). Even Larry's earliest interactions with friends did not include sharing confidences, hopes, or dreams, but rather passive activities like gaming or coding. While Flage did require some caretaking, their quiet relationship had an emotional reciprocity, a nonverbal intimacy that allowed Larry to experience closeness and even enjoy visceral contact with another living being.

After two months of treatment, in which he was able to revisit and understand his childhood's emotional deprivation, Larry's depression abated. He began to socialize again and considered signing up for an online dating site. Ultimately, it may have been the transformational relationship with the animal and the grief over its loss that finally motivated Larry to seek treatment, gain insight into his past, and more willingly explore the external world.

This study demonstrates the meaning of emotional homeopathy, the matching of similar attachment styles to enable a healthier attachment style within a dyad. Matching an avoidant man with an avoidant lizard seemed to soothe the fears of both. Their relationship seems to have fostered a corrective emotional experience for Larry, one that allowed him to finally grieve lifelong losses.

Despite their individually avoidant attachment styles, the relationship between human and lizard appeared to have been one of secure attachment. Undemanding and low in mutual expectations, Flage and Larry's developed relationship was initially avoidant but not disinterested. Their quiet communing built a trust that did not challenge Larry's fear of losing himself. When Larry lost Flage, he reconnected with feelings of loneliness previously repressed throughout his life. It may have been Flage's steady acceptance, which allowed Larry to control and titrate their connection, that perhaps finally provided Larry with a safe haven.

Case study: mutual saviors

The email, received through www.petlosshelp.org, was cryptic and professional: "Please call me, I think I need to talk to someone. One of my dogs passed away, and I am having trouble dealing with it."

The message was from Robert, a veterinarian who had devoted his life to the care of animals. The dog was Sasha, a severely injured, fight-rescued, multibreed canine found caged in an abandoned home.

After stabilizing her medically, Robert knew the year-old pup still needed much care if she was ever going to recover and attain a good quality of life. Minus one leg and one eye, and physically scarred from abuse, Sasha was a full-time job in terms of caretaking. She was not cute or affectionate. She required several weeks of IV antibiotics to combat infection, a specialized nutritional plan to recover from starvation, and monitoring of blood work and electrolytes.

Sasha also needed constant surveillance to minimize chewing on her own bandaged leg. She was sound-sensitive and needed soothing for persistent anxiety and distress. She vocalized constantly and would pace in circles, as if still confined to the horrible cage in which she had been discovered. Any outside movement brought a startle response of aggressive threat.

Robert admired her spunk and was gratified by her slow but steady recovery, fulfilled in purpose by watching his diligent care transform Sasha from a nearly hairless, skeletal apparition to a healthy canine whose main breed now appeared to be some sort of terrier mix.

Four months went by, but no one offered to adopt the strange-looking pup. Handling her required caution, and she could not be around other animals.

One evening, as he was getting ready to leave work, Robert looked in on Sasha. What good did his work accomplish, if she were to spend the rest of her life in a hospital or underresourced shelter? Deciding to adopt the dispirited pup himself, Robert took Sasha home.

Despite long days at work, he consistently returned to her every lunchtime and evening to administer the constant care she needed. In this noninstitutional environment, Sasha's health began to improve, and her anxiety lessened. She enjoyed Robert's small yard, where she would relish lying in the sun or sniffing patches of earth. Initially, she confined her wanderings to a few feet from the back door. But after a few months, Sasha was patrolling the entire yard, now her domain.

With her newly gained freedom, she would now allow Robert's approach and occasional affection. Eventually, she began seeking it, pushing her head under Robert's hand to prompt his stroking of her head and ears. She had become an eager eater, and Robert found great satisfaction in watching her gain weight. Her coat grew thicker and more beautiful, with hints of auburn among the wiry black-and-white fur.

Robert woke up one morning to find her sleeping on the bed beside him. Thereafter, Sasha never left his side when he was home and eventually became sufficiently socialized to accompany him to work. She slept under his desk while he tended to clients and accompanied him on noontime walks.

Sasha began greeting the staff as they arrived in the morning and the clients who followed. She cautiously approached the furry or feathered patients as if to assure them they were safe territory. People and creatures who visited the hospital looked forward to seeing the three-legged, one-eyed dog, whose wagging tail welcomed them and eased anxieties. For eight more years, the miracle pup and her savior worked together, hand in glove.

Never before had Robert felt such a bond with a canine, although he had cared for hundreds.

One morning, Robert felt a lump in Sasha's throat. A biopsy confirmed a stage IV multicentric lymphoma, a terminal diagnosis.

Robert administered an initial dose of L-asparaginase (Elspar) to slow the disease's progression, but he decided not to pursue chemotherapy treatment due to the poor prognosis. Sasha had been through enough in her life; while Robert had clearly extended that life, he rejected the idea of extending her misery.

Robert tried to manage Sasha's symptoms with prednisone, but her appetite continued to decline and her energy level decreased. Once he was unable to maintain her comfort level, Robert euthanized his beloved Sasha.

He insisted on performing the process himself, holding her close as her breathing slowed. While at peace with the decision to end her life before the misery began, Robert was unprepared for the emotional tsunami that followed.

Within five minutes of her death, Robert felt stunned by his grief. He found he had no skills to cope with his utter devastation, a paralysis from which he felt dissociated at times. He found it hard to work and stayed home for several days, but the brief time away brought no relief. His sometimes dark thoughts included a wish to "find" Sasha so he could continue her care.

Robert reluctantly sought treatment with a local therapist, with initial meetings focusing on grief over losing his life's closest companion. Robert, who had never been in therapy before, revealed for the first time the abuse he had suffered at the hands of his alcoholic father, a person he had both admired and feared. When Robert once brought home a stray cat, hoping to care for it as a family pet, his father impulsively shot the animal. As the abuse of Robert and his mother escalated, she finally left the marriage, but his new stepfather was equally dismissive and emotionally remote.

It had never occurred to Robert that his attraction to and adoption of Sasha might have represented the history of his own abuse. Robert had funneled his anxious energy constructively into becoming a caregiver, a protector of the voiceless, an excellent veterinarian – but he had never addressed the mental and emotional anguish resulting from his own abuse.

In therapy, Robert's anxious attachment style was traced to these early instances of abuse, reflected in later relationships in which he failed to develop trust or closeness. As a result of Sasha's abuse, she too was initially anxious in her relationship with Robert.

In reviewing questions from the ACB Questionnaire, their transformation to a securely attached dyad became evident. Robert shared the many names he had for Sasha, from terms of endearment to silly monikers. He felt such alignment with Sasha's plight and safe in their affectionate exchanges. He was able to be physically close to her, having her by his side as he slept.

He now felt a sort of psychic death at the loss of such attunement. Sasha had found her way into Robert's soul, and her loss disoriented him. Sasha may have provided Robert with a corrective emotional experience in which he was able to securely attach to a living being, as well as restoring his sense of agency through saving a suffering creature from the results of horrific abuse.

Robert's relationship with Sasha and his acute grief over her passing brought him to treatment, where he could finally confront and heal the previous abuses in his life, leading to modification of his anxious attachment style. While his securely attached relationship with Sasha was not necessarily predictive of replication with humans, it did allow him a singular experience of secure attachment.

Case study: mismatched partners

Mary, a 51-year-old woman with a lifelong anxious attachment style, was recovering from her most recent depressive episode, which had lasted nearly a year. She had found little solace in her marriage to an avoidantly attached spouse and was encouraged to adopt an animal that could provide unwavering support and unconditional love in order to foster her recovery. It was hoped that a canine's presence in Mary's life would create a regular schedule, motivating her to get out of bed in the morning to care for the animal when Brad left for work.

The couple adopted a 1-year-old apricot poodle from a rescue agency. Mary hoped the poodle would imbue her life with joy, affection, and companionship. Annabelle was a gorgeous standard poodle, intelligent and keenly observant. Not much was known of her puppyhood other than that she had been surrendered by a family who had to move overseas. Annabelle was not an affectionate canine, and Mary's efforts to hold her, stroke her, or invite her onto the bed to sleep were rebuffed, sometimes with a warning growl.

At first Mary refused to accept that Annabelle could not be induced to exchange affection. In her anxiety, she redoubled her efforts to interact with the animal, and ultimately Annabel nipped her hand. Mary began to withdraw from Annabelle, who seemed relieved.

Perplexed by Annabelle's distancing responses, Mary and Brad hired an animal behaviorist in an attempt to heal what they felt may have been an abusive past, but the interventions failed to result in Annabelle's becoming more affectionate toward Mary. She tolerated basic interactions, like being leashed before a walk, but she kept her distance, spending most of her time in different areas of the house.

Mary withdrew her attempts to bond with Annabelle, to whom she now felt indifferent. Her care fell to Brad, who resented the new responsibilities. When walking Annabelle around the neighborhood, Brad, embarrassed, shared with a neighbor that Annabelle was going to be returned to the breeder because she was aggressive.

The neighbor was surprised. When Brad and Mary were out of town, Annabelle had stayed with the neighbor's family, who found her affectionate and warm toward their children, a self-appointed guardian and nanny figure as they played in the yard. The children were welcoming but not dependent on Annabelle. Indifferent to forming a deep bond with her, they were unaffected by Annabelle's avoidant style. While Annabelle could not tolerate Mary's intrusive attempts to attach, she felt no such pressure from the children.

Ultimately, instead of returning Annabelle to the rescue agency, Mary and Brad allowed their neighbors to adopt her. As Mary watched the children playing with their contented canine protector close by, she felt more depressed and rejected.

In therapy, it appeared that Mary's symptoms of depression were exacerbated by difficulties in her marriage. Brad was unemotional and avoidant, behaving in ways that Mary found to be punitive when she attempted to emotionally connect. Annabelle similarly reacted to attempts at intimacy with withdrawal, and she had expressed no separation distress from Mary.

When reviewing the questionnaire with Mary, her therapist found it obvious that a bond had not formed with Annabelle, and expectations of closeness and shared activities remained unmet, furthering feelings of alienation and rejection. But in this case, it was largely the animal's perceived rejection that frustrated Mary's hopes for an experience of closeness. Upon hearing of Annabelle's passing, Mary had no reaction. She never again adopted another animal.

It appears that the mismatch of attachment styles between human and animal was a difficult experience for both. Annabelle and Mary were incapable of serving as one another's secure base, developing emotional reciprocity, or satisfying proximity seeking.

Case study: a tragic spiral

Mazie was a year-old black Labrador retriever trained to be an excellent hunting dog and descended from a long line of successful sporting companions, Mazie was adopted by Hector, a man who hunted infrequently but who wanted a well-trained animal for the times when he was able to engage in this sport. Mazie had an incredibly sweet disposition; she was eager to please, sought affection seeking, and reveled in a close alignment with her human companion – all common attributes of the breed.

Although Mazie fulfilled her steward's goals of responsiveness and expertise as a hunting partner, enthusiastically retrieving his feathered trophies in all kinds of weather, her joy in being with Hector was often short lived, as she was then returned to a local kennel. There, she languished, awaiting the next visit from her steward. Her time alone in the kennel could range from a few days to a month, during which time her basic needs for food, shelter, and exercise were well met but her need for companionship and intellectual stimulation was not.

As Mazie adjusted to this pattern, she became less and less enthusiastic about those increasingly rare excursions, during which she might be crated for several hours as she and Hector traveled to distant destinations. As each hunting weekend drew to a close, Mazie became increasingly anxious, anticipating how she would soon be returned to her kennel for yet another extended, lonely stay.

The change in her personality was not lost on her steward, who became impatient with her distressing vocalizations as they returned to the kennel. Eventually, as Hector lost interest in hunting, his time with Mazie diminished further. Resenting kennel payments for the now-unwanted animal, he surrendered her to an animal shelter. Her developed anxiety, constant vocalizations, and high prey drive discouraged potential adopters. Mazie ultimately became one of the millions of animals euthanized every year.

Hector felt no attachment to Mazie and, therefore, no guilt upon her surrender. He was unaware that she was euthanized. There was no remorse for his purely utilitarian usage of Mazie. There had been no human-to-animal bond, while Mazie's attempts to bond with her steward were met with indifference.

The shelter workers, however, quickly bonded with her, understanding the predicament that had led to her abandonment. They deeply mourned her death, shattered by the need to euthanize this magnificent but damaged creature after she remained unadopted for months in the overcrowded shelter.

Unfortunately, the predicament of animals who exist solely for the fulfillment of human need is not rare. The indifference with which some humans discard their animals may rise well beyond mismatched attachment styles to the undervaluing of animal life in general.

Avoidant or antisocial steward characteristics may be associated with or predictive of animal or even human physical abuse. Research by Ascione and Shapiro (2009), Arkow (2019), and others that associates human attachment and personality styles with the potential for abuse alerts us to consider animal health in family safety assessments; incidence of animal abuse points to a potential for human abuse.

Much like infants who are genetically programmed to bond with caretakers, some animal species and breeds are similarly inclined. When an animal's attachment needs for proximity, secure base, nurturance, and affection are unmet, it may alter their own drive to bond, resulting in personality changes.

Mazie was adopted for one purpose, her emotional needs unconsidered, resulting in reactive changes that ultimately rendered her unadoptable. Careful pre-adoption assessment can reveal potential mismatches in human-animal attachment styles and expectations of the relationship.

It is usually the animal, not the human, who will suffer the consequences of mismatched attachment. Animals can be easily and impulsively surrendered to shelters. But without the multitiered safeguards associated with human adoption, the out- come for surrendered animals will likely be death.

Chapter summary

This chapter focused on applying attachment theory to both humans and animals with the introduced hypothesis that animals can serve as primary attachment figures.

First, by applying accepted attachment theory in humans to animals, we find evidence that animals – similarly influenced by their earliest environments, including biological and emotional components, and the extent that their characteristics are not hardwired within a species or breed – may indeed develop their own attachment styles and are capable of serving as primary attachment figures. While there is no formal research concluding this hypothesis, the same influences that exist in the early formation of human attachment are also present in the development of the human-animal bond. For example, reciprocity, mirroring, and consistency of response are referenced as essential features associated with secure attachment in humans and are also observed in animals. Such exchanges have been observed in the development of human-animal dyads. As such, it is possible that nonhuman creatures may indeed serve as primary attachment figures, reflecting the four elements that Mary Ainsworth (1992) describes as the basis for secure attachment: proximity seeking, secure base, separation distress, and safe haven.

Second, an animal's own attachment style may have considerable impact on the moderation and development of the attachment style of the newly created human-animal dyad, which, in turn, may further impact how a steward grieves when the animal dies.

Third, identifying steward and animal attachment styles, expectations, and needs are vital considerations during the animal-adoption process. When left to chance, as in impulsive adoption, the human-animal bond may be severely compromised, leading to disappointing outcomes and the potential for abuse. In such circumstances, the animal is more likely to suffer the consequences of failed expectations, including the possibility of surrender and euthanasia.

Four case studies were presented to illustrate these concepts, two to demonstrate the potentially healing aspects of mutually supportive attachment styles, and two to demonstrate the difficult consequences, for the human and animal, of mismatched needs and attachment styles.

The considerations raised in this chapter may hold significance in both offering a further basis for what has long been observed: the transformational attachment potential within animal-human relationships and furthering the understanding of the intensity of grief that follows their loss. This may have implications in treatment planning, animal adoption, and, ultimately, animal advocacy, as offering more proof of their sentience may give impetus to elevating their legal status.

4

Assessment strategies for animal companion loss

That cat meant everything to me. She touched me in ways no being ever has. I have felt depressed all spring, but now it's worse. I keep thinking she'll somehow return, even though I know she couldn't have survived the winter outside. – Brenda, mourning her 14-year-old feline, Sparkles, who did not return after her customary surveillance of their property

The mourning experience following the loss of any beloved being is as variable and individualized as the qualities and expectations – fulfilled or unfulfilled – of the relationship itself. Therefore, the tasks of healing and recovery are associated with the complexities, significance, challenges, and strengths of each lost relationship.

In this chapter, we will consider assessment strategies to inform treatment planning. These include formal diagnosis, where appropriate, and the guidance provided by the Animal Companion Bereavement Questionnaire at the end of the chapter.

The ACB Questionnaire can help guide discussion and define significant characteristics of the mourned relationship. This inventory is the result of decades of working with bereaved clients and targeting the most significant aspects of the loss, as they themselves may not appreciate the multiple factors

DOI: 10.4324/9781003145929-5

contributing to the severity of their grief. Without such identification, an effective treatment plan may remain elusive.

When assessing the grief of those mourning companion animals, it is appropriate to begin with the comprehensive assessment that would be conducted for any new client. But beyond that evaluation, it is also important to explore the unique qualities of the relationship within their specific human-animal bond.

Such topics include the circumstances of the loss, noting any traumatic factors that might fuel extreme grief, such as sudden awareness of terminal illness; steward- or stranger-caused accident, and futile searches for an animal who ran away or was kidnapped. When an animal disappears, or is abducted, it is often not possible to determine the circumstances of its death, which can elicit great guilt, the latter fury and outrage. Evaluating symptoms related to trauma at initial assessment is essential, as the steward may underplay the impact of such symptoms, attributing them solely to grief, rather than trauma.

While individuals mourning companion animals will pass through the typical stages of grief – denial, anger, bargaining, depression, and acceptance – described by Kübler-Ross (2014), these stages will reflect additional and more nuanced characteristics that exist solely within the human-animal dyad.

Each stage and its associated challenges require careful exploration for the construction of an effective treatment plan. Working with clients experiencing human loss is a circumstance familiar to most clinicians, but the challenges unique to animal companion loss require additional analysis and identification, especially as stewards themselves may not be aware of the multiple dimensions of animal companion loss.

For example, one of the most important aspects of moving grief toward healing is the validation, of loved ones, friends, and clergy, that what is being mourned is indeed worthy of support. Yet this societal or religious validation may be absent, inconsistent, or perfunctory, potentially protracting each stage of grief, as mourners are left to provide their own validation. If mourners find no commensurate reflection of their grief in their social or even family environment, this process may not result in resolution.

Clients may arrive from various sources. A clinician who has an established affiliation with a veterinary practice will readily receive such referrals. A clinician may list a specialty in animal companion bereavement on their own on other mental health websites. A client's general practitioner or psychiatrist may identify unresolved grief and suggest therapy.

Clients may also be referred from current or past therapy clients. If you included animal family members in your initial assessment, they may return for your trusted guidance when an animal family member passes away, recalling your respect for animal life.

I have often received referrals from a client's primary therapist who assumes they are unprepared to treat this form of mourning. One goal of this book is to encourage clinicians to understand that the guidance offered in these pages, combined with their existing clinical skills, will likely be sufficient to help clients through the healing of these losses.

It's worth pointing out here that clients do not mourn in the same way for every animal, just as they do not mourn in the same way for every deceased human. Many clients express surprise that a specific loss challenges their coping skills and remains unresolved, despite having previously recovered from the loss of a different companion animal. It's important to convey your awareness that grief responses are associated with varying factors, along with qualities innate to a specific relationship, lest they assume this more intense experience is evidence of their defectiveness.

Four common presentations following animal companion loss

There are four primary contexts in which clients present for mental health guidance following animal companion loss:

First, a client may seek treatment for grief following animal companion loss, describing it as the **sole or primary trigger for their acute affective disturbance**. This may often be the case, depending on the extent of the dyad's attachment style or interdependence. Clients who have never previously adopted an animal may be surprised by the intensity of their reaction and ill-prepared for the extent of their grief. However, further clinician questioning may reveal that the client was already struggling with an ongoing affective disturbance prior to the animal's acquisition. For example, the animal may have been adopted to support recovery from another difficult life experience, like the loss of another person or recovery from a catastrophic illness. Therefore, the symptoms of depression or anxiety that were held in check by the animal's presence may have been exacerbated following the loss of the animal's moderating influence.

Second, a clinician may already be working with a client when the **loss of an animal occurs during treatment**. The loss may intensity symptoms, requiring reassessment of affective acuity and expansion of the treatment plan to include a focus on the impact of the animal's death and the replacement of now-missing supports.

Third, a client may show **reluctance to reveal that an animal companion's death is the cause of their depression or anxiety**. They may instead describe vague symptoms of sadness or agitation, casually mentioning the animal's loss without according its death commensurate significance. Most people, believing they should not be so acutely affected and feeling shame at their inability to resolve their distress, attempt to manage it on their own, even while receiving treatment for the associated depression.

Through patient questioning through the ACB Questionnaire, a clinician may determine that the animal's death is in fact its primary cause. But without an understanding of the severe impact such losses may have, the episode may continue as an untreated causative factor, inadvertently prolonging client grief and shame.

Fourth, if an animal is diagnosed with a terminal or chronic illness, the client may be experiencing anticipatory mourning. Treatment, described in detail in Chapter 8, will support the steward through the emotionally challenging caretaking phase and also initiate acceptance of the approaching death. This may help stewards clarify their feelings for the animal, recollect positive memories, and bring attention to the steward's compassionate investment in caretaking, potentially avoiding or reducing feelings of guilt and creating important groundwork for legacy creation.

In all cases, clinician validation, along with interested, consistent inquiry, helps both therapist and steward place loss in the context of other life stressors. The gathering of information about a client's living situation, other relationships, supports, physical health, and other life circumstances goes a long way to developing understanding of grief's intensity.

As we have discussed, a steward's mental health prior to an animal's adoption, during their time together, and at the time of the animal's illness or death are important aspects of assessment to better define the timeline of affective or attachment disturbances or changes within the relationship or the steward themselves. Awareness of all these time frames gives critical information about the status or changing role of the animal and steward in each other's lives. It also identifies life events that may be contributing to the client's affective experience.

Elements that may complicate grief's resolution

The following six challenges that may be associated with animal companion loss benefit from exploration, as they can greatly impact the course and tasks of mourning. These elements may not be recognized or given appropriate significance by mourners themselves; therefore, clinician evaluation of each helps identify associated tasks for treatment planning. These factors are

- ◆ the trauma associated with animal companion death,
- ◆ the persistence of guilt that may follow animal companion loss,
- ◆ the impact of shame as a result of societal invalidation of the steward's mourning,

- ◆ the paucity of social support and rituals as challenges to normative grief resolution,
- ◆ identification of the roles fulfilled by the animal, and how those roles will now be filled, and
- ◆ the steward's assessment of their caretaking while the animal lived.

The Animal Companion Bereavement Questionnaire

The ACB Questionnaire, meant to be a clinician-administered inventory, was compiled based on 20 years of conducting animal death-related assessments and interviews; facilitating an animal companion bereavement support group; gathering experiences from individual clients and veterinary staff; feedback from www. petlosshelp.org; and general inquiries from humans mourning animals around the world.

These questions were also informed by decades of clinical experience working with loss and bereavement, specifically the understanding of how roles and qualities lost in such relationships impact grief and the resumption of normative life.

The ACB Questionnaire delves into psychodynamic and relational expressions of the lost steward-animal relationship, including the extent and qualities of attachment, shared activities, and the significance of the relationship.

Responding to the questions may prove to be enlightening, joyful, or satisfying for the client. Or – if the relationship was plagued with disappointing exchanges, constant illness, behavioral challenges, or caregiving needs beyond the steward's capacity – such revelations can help identify recovery tasks, a process similar to identifying complicating factors in lost human relationships.

Many individuals in both group and individual therapy have expressed appreciation for the directness and specificity of these questions as they helped clients elicit, recall, reflect, and define their own experiences with the animal that may be temporarily forgotten amidst the grief of loss. Ultimately the questions help develop a narrative, a story of this particular human animal relationship from adoption to death. By describing the degree of companionship achieved, and its impact on mental health and functioning, clinicians gain a more complete understanding of what has been lost.

These questions can also help support exploration in those experiencing secondary trauma and those who do not live with companion animals but who are deeply affected by their absence as therapy or observed animal citizens.

Finally, the included questions also emanate from an appreciated understanding of bereavement related to aspects of environmental or legal threats to the very existence of innocent sentient beings, including grief over loss of life-sustaining habitats or the continuance of cruelty due to their lack of legal status and protections, both of which present threats to our own social, environmental, and ethical health.

The ACB Questionnaire is meant to be facilitated by the treating clinician, not by the client independently. Not all questions may be relevant, and some may be inappropriate – especially for stewards who may have, intentionally or inadvertently, caused the animal's death. Many clients, if left to complete such a survey on their own, may minimize their responses, feeling too vulnerable or embarrassed to acknowledge the extent and depth of their sorrow, or they may forget memories that a patient therapist could help recall. The encouragement of a clinician's guidance can extend this important informational exchange.

1. *How did this animal enter your life?*

Adopting an animal can be a carefully considered or impulsive decision. The factors that prompt it – for example, the timing and choice of species or breed – often reveal what the adopter was hoping to achieve or experience from their alliance with this animal. If it was an impulsive decision, there may have been little consideration of required caretaking, potential disruption to lifestyle, ignorance of the animal's needs, or consideration of required investment in the animal's health maintenance.

Impulsive choices may lead to reversals or resentment, which may, in turn, lead to abandonment at shelters or sub-optimal rehoming. Sometimes, though, impulsive choices result in more joy than was initially anticipated. For example, being left with an adolescent's hastily adopted cat when they go off to college may result in the most significant human animal bond of the substitute caregiver's life. Or perhaps the goal of adoption was initially utilitarian based on expectations of comfort, but the animal's exuberant gifts elevate the dyad beyond expectations. If the animal was not domesticated, this question can be rephrased (i.e. "When did you first start noticing/observing/feeding bats/whales/hummingbirds?").

2. *What names did you give this animal? Where did the animal eat and sleep?*

It is common for stewards to have multiple names for their animals, domestic or feral. Within the animal companion bereavement group, this question was one that often prompted smiles as various names were fondly recalled. Sometimes secondary names were reflective of the animal's favored activities (Catcher, Foodie, or Circus Syd for a particularly skillful border collie). Sometimes the names were loving (Cuddlebug, Baby, or Precious). As animals respond to tone of voice as much as phonetics, those names gave evidence of a deeply shared emotional connection. (Conversely, it does not seem to matter in what tone "walk" or "dinner" are stated, as animals recognize words associated with preferred activities even when neutrally stated.)

The location of the animal's sleeping and eating quarters (even if feral) may vary over the course of its life. Some stewards initially forbid an animal to sit on a couch, or confine its sleeping to a cage, but over time these creatures find their way onto that forbidden furniture. Animals who are caged, like birds or small mammals, may eventually delight their stewards with a flight around the room or a seat at the table. Other stewards maintain spatial boundaries, reflecting a more arm's-length approach to life reflective of their attachment styles and/or capacity for connection.

> **3.** *How was this connection or relationship different from past stewardship of other animals?*

If a client has lived with animals before but did not experience the depth of mourning elicited by this specific loss, it is helpful to acknowledge and clarify such variations. Were the steward's needs and life events different when the animal was adopted? Past stewardship may have been of another species or breed that did not foster the same level of attachment.

> **4.** *What special qualities did this particular animal have? What qualities did this animal bring out in you?*

This question can evoke anthropomorphic responses, responses that project human qualities onto the animal that sound unrealistic until the steward offers examples of such observed or felt attributes. It also gives clues to the steward's perceived value and characteristics of animals such as loyalty, honor, stoicism, forgiveness, and unconditional acceptance.

What was it about this particular animal that captured its steward's imagination and allegiance? What qualities in the steward were experie ced when interacting with this animal? For example, someone who may not consider themselves a playful person or a concerned caretaker may be surprised to find great joy in endlessly playing ball or administering ear drops. Finding in themselves qualities of mindfulness or compassion can increase self-esteem, as their capacity to give finds expression.

> **5.** *How much time was spent with the animal? All day, evenings, weekends? Did the animal travel on vacations with you?*

Determining the amount of time spent together offers perspective on potential disruption to daily functioning, as well as how and when the loss may be most acutely felt. Was the steward a remote worker who spent most of their day at home with the animal, or was the animal alone much of the day, sharing only evenings with its steward? Was the animal kenneled or left at home to be cared for by others or by itself during vacations, or was the animal brought along? This question can help establish an animal's priority as a family member as well as help elicit fond memories of shared travels – or it may provoke discussion of regrets, which can be placed in appropriate context. For example, the animal was too anxious for air travel, or could not tolerate riding in the car.

6. *What activities did you do with the animal? Did the animal structure your day?*

The responses to this question further define shared aspects of the relationship. Was this magnificent equine a champion jumper with whom a steward traveled to shows? Or were their shared activities more homebound: a petulant feline walking over their computer keyboard and demanding notice during the workday? What was the extent of their reliance on a service or emotional support dog? Did they share walks with their canine twice a day, sing with an avian companion, or make daily trips to the pet store for specific foods? Did the animal awaken its steward in the morning, decide on mealtimes, or initiate affection? Did the steward socialize with the animal on walks, facilitating other relationships with other human-animal dyads? If the animal was a K-9 or therapy partner, how has that partnership been affected? If charged with the care of an animal at veterinary clinic, zoo, or shelter, how and with whom will they mourn?

7. *How long was this animal in your life? What important life events occurred while the animal was with you?*

While the duration of the relationship is not always associated with the length of mourning, longevity suggests that the animal may have been present for many seminal life events. What were they, and how did the animal's presence affect or support these changes or events? Was their presence comforting, or was it another commitment that needed to be accommodated? For example, if the animal's primary steward passed away, how was their caretaking reallocated? Was it resented? If a new baby came into the home, was the animal perceived as an additional care-taker or a danger to the infant's safety? If an adverse life event (such as unemployment) became a stressor, did this impact the animal's care? Did their death demolish a bridge to other important lost relationships?

> 8. *Did you talk to the animal? Share experiences of your day? Do you think the animal knew what you were thinking or feeling? Do you think you knew what the animal was thinking or feeling? Throughout its life? Just before it died?*

The answers to these questions help indicate the depth of emotional bonding, reliance, and perceived or actual communication between the steward and animal. They can reveal the steward's perception of the animal as friend, confidante, even soulmate.

Did they share thoughts and fears? Verbalize moods, love, and hope? Share decisions to be made? Did they imagine that the animal's responses mirrored their angst, joy, or sadness? Were there behavioral indicators that reinforced this sense of being heard?

Conversely, did they feel able to interpret the animal's wordless responses? Did they feel their ability to communicate was present in the days approaching the animal's death? Do they imagine they knew what the animal was thinking and feeling? Were decisions about treatment or euthanasia influenced by such exchanges? If they felt disagreement or sadness regarding their choices, the therapist can help explore guilt-driven or disappointed thoughts.

> 9. *How did the animal die? Was it sudden, or was it the result of a chronic illness, an accident, or an unrecognized health issue? Was the animal healthy or ill most of its life? What was your degree of caretaking?*

The circumstances of an animal's death are a major factor in experiencing grief (Rando, 1993), and clarifying that context aids in the understanding of response. Was it traumatic? Accidental? Was the person suddenly confronted with end-of-life decision-making?

Did months or years of caretaking precede the death? Some research suggests that caring for an unwell animal may strengthen the bond between animal and steward but lengthen the grieving process (Davies, 2000; Attig, 2000).

Conversely, the impact may be destructive if stewards are not prepared to devote the time, energy, and economic resources to lengthen or improve the animal's life. If great investment was required, describing the sacrifices made can help reduce guilt.

10. *Are you surprised by the extent of your grieving, the degree of pain you feel, and its persistence?*

Many stewards are taken off guard by the devastation of animal companion grief. Even those who have previously lived with or adopted animals may not have experienced the pain they now feel. To this one animal, they may have felt a different and more profound connection even though still living among multiple animals of different species and breeds. Stewards whose animals were their only source of companionship may find it especially difficult. The routine and structure provided by caring for an animal – even one who is extremely ill – can leave a steward feeling deserted, a busy schedule empty, and a shared home lonely.

11. *How much time are you spending mourning the animal? Is it interfering with sleep, eating, work, daily activities? Are you isolating because of this loss?*

The loss of a companion animal can negatively impact all aspects of health, functioning, and daily life. Sleep and nutrition may be disturbed, emotions dysregulated, social involvements reduced or ceased. Some stewards find they need to take personal or sick days from work due to insomnia, severe suffering, and feelings of alienation.

12. *Did you communicate your grief to others? Who did you tell, and what were their reactions? Are other family members mourning the loss with you? Are other animals also reacting to the loss?*

Those grieving companion animals may share the loss with close friends and family. Sometimes responses may lack sufficient empathy or minimize the significance of the loss. Variations in such reactions, even within the same family, partnership, or close friendships, may cause breaches in those relationships.

In some cases, one partner or family member may blame the other(s) for the loss of the animal's life or may disagree with decisions made around the time of its death. This can lead to withdrawal of support, furthering grief's persistence.

The reactions of other animals in the household may require additional attention to their needs, as they too have experienced a loss.

13. *Has your view of [cats, dogs, horses, small mammals, fish, reptiles, birds] changed as a result of your experience with this animal? What is your view of the natural world and human responsibility to protect it?*

If their view of a particular species or breed has changed, how has it changed? On a specific level, did they find the unfairly stigmatized bull terrier to be the most lovable mush ever? On a more general level, did their bond with this animal surpass expectations in depth or significance?

Was the clear display of animal emotions revelatory? Were they captivated by their experiences with wilder creatures in the seas and skies? Incredulous about the survival strategies of a colony of feral cats?

Do they feel that this animal catalyzed transformations within themselves and others? How will this new or renewed fascination with the animal kingdom impact their expanded perspective of life on this planet? Change their view of animals' position in the world? Consider an intention to protect voiceless creatures?

14. *If you chose to euthanize your animal companion, were you present? What factors influenced your decision? Are you at peace with that decision? Do you have memories of that experience that feel difficult to manage?*

Discussing euthanasia-related experiences will reveal much about the emotional tasks ahead, especially if also addressing feelings of guilt and symptoms of trauma. Some stewards experience guilt if they were unable or unwilling to be present during the procedure. Sometimes, the process is not peaceful, and stewards may experience ruminations or flashbacks of the animal's death.

While many stewards self-blame for having made the medically sound and compassionate choice, their hearts remain at war with their decision, questioning its necessity or feeling it was premature. At other times, a steward may regret that the choice was not made sooner. Discussion of these thoughts and feelings is an essential aspect of healing from animal companion loss.

15. *Do you feel you gave the animal a good life? Do you have any regrets about the experience? What do you imagine the animal felt during its life with you?*

Carefully listening to a mourner's retrospective self-assessment of their competency, successes, and failures as a steward can also help guide the formulation of treatment planning. Is their conclusion that they provided the animal with a good life, that the animal felt cared about and was given all it needed to maintain optimal health and quality of life? Or do they feel they should have spent more time with the animal, or that their caretaking was suboptimal? It is useful to remind stewards that the circumstances of the animal's death are not representative of the entire relationship; that throughout their association, there was much mutually fulfilling reciprocity of love, affection, and companionship.

One common area of self-recrimination is not having spent enough time with the animal. A review of life's many responsibilities may help reduce this feeling. If the steward was truly neglectful in offering sufficient companionship, such feelings can be objectively reviewed and processed. What might the person want to say to the animal about the imagined or actual neglect?

> **16.** *How have you coped with past losses of animal companions or important figures in your life? Have you engaged in destructive behaviors to moderate grief?*

This question helps clinicians survey client strength and skills for coping with significant loss. Reminding stewards of the internal and external resources they utilized in the past when encountering aversive life events can build confidence that this loss too can be managed. If past encounters with significant loss or challenging events have triggered negative thoughts, emotion dysregulation, destructive impulses, or substance abuse, the potential for reoccurrence must be assessed. If the client is already in treatment for depression, anxiety, or substance misuse, reassessment of symptom severity or watchfulness for emergence risky behaviors is warranted, along with practicing coping strategies that helped in the past. This may be especially true if guilt or symptoms of trauma remain unaddressed.

> **17.** *Have you felt as if you did not want to live since the animal passed away? Do you have a wish to join the animal? Does your heartbreak include other hopeless thoughts involving threats to animal life on this planet?*

All expressions of suicidal urges require immediate assessment and, in some cases, protective action. Has the client experienced suicidal ideation in the past relative to stressors or losses? Has there been a previous suicide attempt? Questions related to suicidal urges are important to explore even when the steward has no history of suicidal thoughts. This is especially true for those who experience repeated secondary trauma such as veterinary staff or others whose professional or volunteer experience is directly associated with animal welfare. The cumulative effects of secondary trauma may require intensive intervention.

Discussing the client's remaining attachments to life can help identify important supports, highlight areas in which significant rebuilding must occur, or reveal cherished but unattained goals. This may help clients envision a life that still holds meaning, especially if such goals now include advocacy for animals.

Clients who are already suffering from affective disturbances may be further separated from their will to live if the animal was their only resource for comfort and companionship. While an expressed wish to join the departed animal is not always indicative of suicidal urges, it must be explored, even as a transient expression of acutely felt absence.

> **18.** *How has your perception of afterlife or spirituality changed as a result of the animal's life or death? Have you had any experiences in which you thought you felt the animal's presence, saw it, or heard it?*

It is common for those mourning companion animals to revisit the idea of an afterlife, even when agnostic or atheist, so intolerable can be a conclusion of permanent loss. Changes in belief systems or renewed spirituality are not uncommon reactions following animal companion loss, as the mourner attempts to imagine where the animal went, or in what realm it now exists.

Does the thought of some sort of animal heaven bring comfort? What about the idea that the animal is now reincarnated in the cardinal outside their window, or that the apple tree blooms are more plentiful for having subsumed their animal's spirit? Do they imagine a place in which a reunion is possible?

Many mourning stewards report dreams or transient experiences in which they feel they saw, felt, or heard their departed companion. This is not necessarily evidence of a psychotic reaction, but an intense wish to stay connected, to feel that the animal still lives in some form. Mourners may seek the counsel of animal communicators in an attempt to ascertain the whereabouts of their animal and confirm it is at peace. Exploring such thoughts can help mourners find even transient comfort in imagining that the animal is not completely lost to them.

> **19.** *How have you memorialized the animal, or do you plan to do so? Are you interested in exploring rituals to mark its life and death? What do you feel is the legacy of this animal's presence in your life?*

Given the minimal availability of formal rituals for mourning animals, memorials must often be constructed and facilitated by mourners themselves. The assistance of others can help support this bridge to healing, this reverence for the life of a sentient being.

Has the steward begun this process or reflected on the animal's overall legacy? The two processes can be reinforcing, as they combine active memories with internalizing the animal experience, an essential part of healing. For example, if much time was spent in shared activities in nature, planting a tree could be a meaningful gesture both honoring those cherished activities and reinforcing a legacy of respect for nature.

If end-of-life decisions had to be made quickly, thoughts of memorializing are often not considered, limiting the options once the death has passed.

Legacy may also be reflected in the steward's newly gained compassion, spirituality, or respect for the natural world. Memorializing deceased animals through legacy creation can be the linchpin that moves grief into healing. Internalizing the wonder and gifts of the created bond is transformed into an accessible and comforting resource for the surviving steward.

Mourners can donate to animal-related causes in the deceased companion's name, volunteer with an animal organization, or journal about their lives for online websites or their own reference. Writing about some of the most transformative or fondest memories can help stewards define the qualities they wish to internalize and demonstrate in their lives.

Stewards may send out death announcements to local news outlets or create a remembrance holiday card. Assembling video or photo albums can be easily accomplished. Clothing or jewelry bearing the animal's image, or even containing some of their ashes, may be created.

Mourners may be moved to create a garden or create a home altar to display pictures and mementos throughout the period of mourning. They may wish to hold a funeral or memorial service to acknowledge the loss formally, religiously, and publicly. Cemeteries for animal burial offer a peaceful resting place, which stewards can visit. Some stewards express wishes in their wills to have the animal's ashes buried with them when they die.

While these options are commonly used in mourning humans, grieving stewards may not consider them unless such discussion is encouraged.

> **20.** *Have you attended bereavement groups in the past? Would you be interested in attending an animal companion bereavement support group? Have you sought counseling services in the past?*

Determining a client's experiences with mental health support in the past requires review, especially if the current symptoms are severe and/or reflective of trauma. If stewards have reached out for bereavement or other mental health services in the past, what was their experience? What were some of the aspects, helpful or not, of the support offered?

It's wise to research options for mourning animals (like the existence of animal companion bereavement support groups) beyond your practice in case the need arises. Are the resources in person or virtual? Might the client benefit from group activities? Some mourners, still feeling a sense of shame over the intensity of their grief, may avoid any kind of group interaction and instead prefer individual support.

In summary, the responses to these questions, gently posed and guided, can help create a road map to recovery as well as bring validation to the loss. The important clinical information gleaned from this inventory can also help direct clinicians toward the appropriate selection of interventions and treatment approaches.

DSM diagnoses associated with animal companion loss

Common diagnoses that may be appropriate for animal companion bereavement are included in this section, although it is far from a complete list. Note that concurrent diagnoses for depression, anxiety, and other disorders may also be required when assessed, depending on a client's clinical condition and symptoms.

Uncomplicated Bereavement Z63.4 (American Psychiatric Association, 2022, p. 834) may be appropriate if clients present with distressing, but normative, symptoms of grief. This diagnosis is applicable to those mourning companion animals, as long as symptom criteria are met, that is, grief steadily resolves over days and weeks, and the person is able to continue daily routines without serious interruption.

Symptoms of uncomplicated bereavement may include

- ◆ waves of sadness and low mood associated with the lost animal,
- ◆ transient feelings of guilt,
- ◆ lack of appetite, and
- ◆ insomnia.

Adjustment Disorders F43.20 (unspecified) (DSM V TR American Psychiatric Association, 2022) may often be an appropriate diagnosis when a new client first indicates that loss of the companion animal is the sole reason for seeking mental health services. As therapy progresses, other issues may become evident that alter that initial diagnosis.

Symptoms of an adjustment reaction following animal companion loss may include

- ◆ having emotional or behavioral symptoms within three months of a specific stressor occurring in your life (and once treated, those symptoms do not persist for more than an additional six months);
- ◆ experiencing more stress than would normally be expected in response to a stressful life event and/or

having stress that causes significant problems in your relationships, at work, or at school;

◆ not being representative of "normative" grieving; and
◆ not being the result of another mental health disorder.
(American Psychiatric Association, 2022)

If clients are already in treatment when the loss occurs, the initial diagnosis may still be appropriate, and additionally noting the added stressor of loss is sufficient. If the initial affective disturbance resolves but grief over the loss of the animal remains or intensifies, review of that diagnosis is warranted.

Prolonged grief disorder F43.8 (DSM V TR American Psychiatric Association, 2022) – which replaces/incorporates persistent complex bereavement – is the newest disorder added to the *DSM* after studies found that many people continue to experience persistent bereavement difficulties beyond culturally expected norms. When the primary trigger for the prolonged affective disturbance continues to be attributable to the death, this diagnosis may apply to those mourning companion animals.

Such symptoms will cause substantial distress for the sufferer or impact significantly on areas of functioning and cannot be attributed to other causes.

Those more likely to develop prolonged grief disorder include those with a previous history of a mental health disorder and/or those who have suffered from substance addictions (American Psychiatric Association, 2022)

Symptoms for prolonged grief disorder may include

◆ feeling shocked, stunned, or numb since the death;
◆ disrupted identity;
◆ continued denial or inability to accept the loss;
◆ continuing rumination about the circumstances or consequences of the death;
◆ ongoing anger or bitterness about the death;
◆ experiencing the pain that the deceased suffered;
◆ hearing/seeing the deceased;
◆ difficulty trusting or caring about others;

◆ intense reactions to memories or reminders of the deceased;
◆ avoidance of those same reminders; and
◆ lasting at least twelve months.

If symptoms of trauma are part of a distressing presentation along with, or emerging from, any of the diagnoses given earlier, an additional diagnosis of **PTSD 309.81** (DSM V TR American Psychiatric Association, 2022) may be added to ensure that all aspects of the client's presentation are treated and resolved.

Common symptoms continuing beyond one month may include

◆ having witnessed or been exposed to death;
◆ recurrent distressing dreams and memories;
◆ dissociative reactions (flashbacks);
◆ prolonged psychological or physiological distress;
◆ negative beliefs about the self (expressed as guilt); and
◆ alterations in arousal and reactivity manifested as irritability, insomnia, hypervigilance, reckless or self-destructive behaviors, and problems concentrating.

Regardless of diagnosis, treatment will always focus on symptom reduction and return to functional homeostasis through the application of appropriate evidence-based modalities. The presence of traumatic symptoms and potential for suicidality requires continuous vigilance throughout treatment. Disenfranchised forms of grief often result in an alienated isolation, in which symptoms can persist and worsen as the significance of the event remains unrecognized, unvalidated, and without the ritual and community support that facilitate grief's resolution.

As with any loss, assessment and treatment planning will include developing an understanding narrative of the lost relationship, building coping skills to moderate difficult emotions and social and personal supports to replace what was lost, and, ultimately, the creation of a legacy, offering a resource for healing.

Chapter summary

This chapter emphasizes the importance of thorough assessment when working with clients experiencing animal companion loss. Elements of loss often associated with animal companion death include the frequent presence of trauma, societal invalidation, the need to make sudden, shocking, end-of-life decisions, the ethical challenges of euthanasia, and the lack of social support and rituals to process animal companion mourning. Some stewards may delay seeking treatment despite acute distress because of shame and the erroneous belief that they should be able to recover on their own. Therefore, the time frames between the loss and treatment seeking may be months, and in some cases years, when it is mentioned amidst another acute mental health issue.

The Animal Companion Bereavement Questionnaire, an author-designed survey, is introduced to help guide clinicians and mourners alike in considering the multifaceted aspects of the steward-companion bond. Such an inventory may help correct cognitive errors related to guilt, elicit positive memories, define qualities in the lost relationship, and identify tasks of recovery. The potential for immediate response to suicidality and/or acute symptoms of trauma is suggested as post-death outcomes from animal companion loss require ongoing, vigilant assessment.

A brief overview of DSM V TR diagnoses that may be applicable for animal companion bereavement concludes the chapter, with the understanding that it is also important to assess for concurrent or previous mental health disorders that may be exacerbated by this loss.

5

Psychodynamic approaches to healing animal companion loss

Even though I didn't want a dog, Myrtle brought out the best in me – a willingness to play, to give, to remember. – Barb, who assumed the care of her father's 10-year-old dog after his death

Psychodynamic theory, or "talk therapy," focuses on healing maladaptive relationship patterns and aspects of attachment as reflected through our most intimate or significant connections. Styles of relating and perceiving – adaptive or maladaptive – may remain consistent across relationships or manifest differently within specific important relationships. The changing interpersonal dynamics or external stressors associated with loss may trigger previously unresolved relationship experiences, resulting in psychological distress.

As the bereavement tasks associated with animal companion loss can be greatly influenced by the relationship qualities and attachment styles of the created dyad, psychodynamic approaches may offer needed perspective in exploring related patterns, helping to identify attachment breaches that may thwart healing (Archer & Ireland, 2011; Ucceheddu et al., 2019; White et al., 2017; Parthasarathy & Crowell-Davis, 2006; Zilcha-Mano et al., 2011a; Zilcha-Mano et al., 2012).

DOI: 10.4324/9781003145929-6

Psychodynamic theory forms the basis of many evidence-based therapeutic approaches, and when enhanced with interpersonal theory, it can strengthen application to problems that may emanate from the external environment but that trigger internal crises and affective symptoms. Psychodynamic approaches – with their attention to ego strengths, defensive structures, attachment styles, and associated human drives – are designed to assess these related capacities.

In this chapter we consider two interpersonally focused psychodynamic models for application to animal companion loss: interpersonal psychotherapy (IPT) and narrative therapy (NT). Both approaches are based on a humanistic, client-centered perspective that positions the client as the expert on the current stressor; are effective for the relief of symptoms associated with depression and anxiety; include established interventions and hierarchies for managing the current crisis; encourage identification, articulation, and rebuilding of what has been lost; are relatively short-term in format; and provide flexible theoretical frameworks that adapt to a variety of concurrent issues that are external to or associated with the loss (Frank, 2014).

Cultural competency

Perhaps most importantly, these models were chosen because they encourage and support the client's perspective, interpretation, and experience of their loss's significance, accepting a wide inclusion of what and how humans grieve. This humanistic foundation supports the cultural and diverse complexity reflective of steward demographics in this country. The flexible framework of both IPT and NT allow adaptation to different cultures and populations without the loss of rigorous efficacy (Mufson et al., 2014; Seponski et al., 2013). Because of this perspective, IPT and NT can be effectively adapted to many social or life problems in clinical work (Allan et al., 2016). There is no form or expression of grief either model would disenfranchise, including the loss of animal companions.

IPT's cocreator, Myrna Weissman, acknowledges (Weissman et al., 2017) that the loss of an animal companion may cause acute grief. Leonhardt-Parr and Rumble (2022) address changing the narrative as an essential aspect of pet bereavement counseling. Neither IPT nor NT has a built-in assumption about which losses can devastate human lives. Instead, both IPT and NT focus on validation of the experience, reduction of associated symptoms, articulation of its meaning, and rebuilding lost supports.

Adaptability

Both IPT and NT are foundationally well equipped to incorporate other concurrent stressors that may arise within therapy for bereavement. Both models work well in terms of helping clients manage changing roles, communicating the importance of the experience, rebuilding essential elements that have been lost, and offering unique skills and interventions to return clients to normative or enhanced functioning. For example, recovering from the death of an animal that was central to the steward's daily schedule of walks requires not only grief's resolution but a review of all aspects of the steward's life that have been altered and need to be rebuilt – emotionally, practically, and socially.

It may be that the deceased companion animal offered sufficient support, socialization, and affection to contain other "subclinical" disturbances – for example, holding and healing grief from previous losses or helping facilitate a secure attachment style – but the animal's death has now removed an essential emotional support from that homeostasis. This can be particularly true when the level of interdependence was intense, as in a relationship with a service or emotional-support animal, a professional K-9 partnership, or a companionship that mitigated an otherwise isolated steward's life. In addition, other feelings of depression related to threatened losses or extinctions within the natural environment may be supported by IPT due to its flexible perspective of allowing the client to determine the factors associated with affective disturbances.

Therapist's role

Both IPT and NT conceptualize the therapist's role as that of supportive advocate and guide who helps clients articulate and express their feelings around the loss, while identifying coping skills and strengths relied upon to relieve past losses (Weissman et al., 2017; Laube, 1998). Both of these humanistic models rely on a strong and active therapeutic alliance to facilitate psychological healing.

Multiple studies across many therapeutic modalities consistently reflect the association of client progress with strong therapist-client attunement in achieving the corrective emotional experience (Langston, 2019; Milot-Lapointe et al., 2021; Constantino, 2017). As therapist validation of animal companion loss is pivotal to initiating a strong therapeutic alliance, expressing understanding and support for the client's experience helps build this alliance. Clients may fear and expect minimization of their acute grief to animal companion loss, especially if caused by the loss of a less appreciated or exotic creature such as a gerbil or reptile. A therapist's immediate and genuine condolences can strengthen the client's perception of their acceptance. Conversely, a reserved response may result in the client's abandoning hope for such an alliance, as their self-invalidation or shame may be inadvertently reinforced.

When the acuity of grief-related symptoms is the initial focus of psychodynamic treatment, prompt validation of despair associated with the loss can, by itself, often reduce the intensity of initial client suffering. When I facilitated an animal companion bereavement group, the relief expressed after a single 90-minute session was primarily related to the validation of sharing their story with similar mourners. They saw that their grief was not evidence of pathological defectiveness, but rather their capacity for deep love.

Combining with ACB Questionnaire

Following the initial clinical assessment, posing questions from the ACB Questionnaire will supplement the understanding of both therapist and client as to what specifically is being mourned.

The very existence of the ACB Questionnaire can be validating; if such an inventory exists, stewards might reason, their grief must be normative.

Both IPT and NT encourage exploration of all aspects of the grief associated with loss. As unexplored, cumulative grief reactions may underlie this loss, clinicians are presented with a rich opportunity to intervene and treat previous unresolved losses (Boelen & Smid, 2017; Weissman et al., 2007, 2017). Without extensive review of all facets of animal companion loss, the reverberations of death may remain unresolved, causing the steward to linger in unresolved bereavement associated with more complex, longer-lasting grief experiences (Iglewicz et al., 2020).

Interpersonal psychotherapy

IPT, with its person-in-environment focus, conceptualizes clients' affective disturbances in an interpersonal context (Klerman & Weissman, 1993). The interpersonal triad that forms the basis for IPT proposes that external stressors or events can cause psychological symptoms in those with attachment vulnerabilities and low or absent social support (Weissman et al., 2007). Its four key target areas experienced by all humans are grief and loss, role transition, interpersonal disputes, and interpersonal deficits. This commonsense perspective, combined with IPT's client-centered approach, helps avoid pathological interpretations of universally experienced human challenges, while identifying and remediating lack of social support, skills deficits, or problematic communication styles that maintain the distressing symptoms (Stuart & Robertson, 2012). With its focus on a humanistic understanding of life's stressors, IPT, along with the ACB Questionnaire, can help clients mourning companion animals, or the natural world, more specifically define the qualities of their grief.

IPT draws its theoretical basis from Bowlby's Attachment Theory, Sullivan's Interpersonal Relationships Theory (Rajhans et al., 2020), Kiesler's Communication Theory (Kiesler, 1996), and Bandura's Social Learning Theory (Wulfert, 2015). It gives evidence of both psychodynamic and cognitive behavior therapy influences; Beck's CBT manual provided some initial guidance (Markowitz & Weissman, 2012).

IPT can be applied internationally because of its capacity for cultural adaptation. By identifying sources of client distress as also emanating from societal and interpersonal realms, it provides a socially just lens through which such impacts are considered to be the problem, rather than a client's appropriate response to ongoing social invalidation and hostility.

IPT reviews all facets of a client's life, including the environment in which they live, as capable of frustrating attempts to negotiate grief and loss, role transitions, interpersonal disputes, and reparation of interpersonal deficits. IPT is therefore also an excellent therapeutic choice for other losses that may fall into the category of "disenfranchised grief," meaning losses for which society does not have formal mourning protocols and tends to invalidate, like miscarriage, loss of capacity, social status, country of origin, and gender transitions (Barbisan et al., 2020). This could also include mourning of loss of animal habitat, threatened extinctions, and other environmental threats.

Grief and loss

Since IPT interprets loss through the client's lens, this category may therefore include losses of mental or psychological capacity, social status, income, physical health, identity, mental acuity, relationships, family involvement, employment, independence, country, feelings of safety, in addition to the death of loved ones. Therefore, the loss of a companion animal holds equal status to any other loss and will follow the same recovery blueprint. And through the exploration of the presenting loss, other losses may be incorporated into treatment as well.

For example, when I once treated a client who initially presented with acute grief following the loss of her dog, another significant loss was identified. The client had once been a concert pianist, but following a mastectomy that robbed her of sensation in one arm, she lost the ability to play with her trademark perfection. Demi, her standard poodle, had helped assuage this sorrow. But after his death, she experienced this new loss as a damaged self-image; she felt worthless and directionless. Music had once been her entire life, but she would not have sought treatment for her disability, as she felt her survival precluded her right to mourn. It was the death of her companion that brought her to treatment, in which both losses could be mourned and healed.

Role transitions

Every human being will experience multiple role transitions throughout their life. By making role transitions a second target of exploration, IPT brings attention to the fact that every transition yields rewards and challenges, losses and gains. Adopting a baby bunny may bring the rewards of engaging in playfulness, the chance to love and be loved, and the responsiveness of a warm, affectionate being. But it also requires commitment and vigilance (Corcoran et al., 2019).

When the animal dies, the transition from steward to mourner has the potential for alterations in identity. IPT's objective review, combined with questions from the ACB Questionnaire, may bring additional awareness of what has been gained despite the loss; for example, the death of an unwell animal releases its steward from caretaking responsibilities and financial outlays. In its attention to both reward and losses inherent in every role transition, IPT validates potential difficulties even when it would seem that gains clearly outweigh such challenges, for example, becoming a steward to an adopted animal, which is likely a time of great joy, yet balanced with the assumption of caregiving needs.

Interpersonal disputes

Dealing with conflict presents in the human-animal bond and also among family members or partners who may not share the same attitudes about animals in the home (i.e. sleeping on the bed or keeping a cage in the kitchen). Animal companion loss may have been preceded by disagreements about its care and associated costs, causing breaches in formerly strong relationships. Family members may mourn differently, invalidating the experience of those who take longer to recover. IPT brings attention to such problems in terms of looking for ways to negotiate, remediate, or acknowledge impasse (Murray et al., 2017).

Interpersonal deficits

For someone reliant on an animal for practical or emotional assistance – for example, a disabled steward with a service animal – the loss of their companion may highlight the difficulty of managing tasks on their own. IPT can help guide the mourner to regain that lost independence by focusing on considering adoption of another service animal or creating opportunities for emotional support through new social networks.

Case study: a harmonious connection

Irma motioned for her neighbor to stop shoveling. The hole beside the flower bed was now more than deep enough for the box that held the body of Misty, the gray canary who had lived with her for five years. Irma, 83 and white-haired, could not easily bend over, so her daughter took the box, covered with loving inscriptions, and placed it tenderly in the tiny grave. "Please be careful, he was so fragile," Irma murmured, her voice breaking. She held onto her daughter, faltering, as the neighbor replaced the soil. "How will I go on?"

Irma would repeat this question every day for weeks to her son, her daughter, the neighbors who came to check on her, and the doctor who prescribed sleeping meds for her persistent insomnia. Ultimately, her physician referred Irma to a local therapist, believing she was experiencing major depression.

Irma initially resisted the idea. When presented with the option of IPT, with its short-term focus on the loss of Misty, she decided to engage, as she longed to talk about Misty and how his death had changed her life.

Assessment

In the initial encounter, it was determined that Irma had no history of mental health issues, although both her parents had abused alcohol. Her current health issues were related to mobility, including a recent hip replacement, but she was able to continue life in her small home.

Irma, who had married at 18, had two children and described a solid marriage lasting 45 years. She'd been a singer in her youth, enjoyed concerts, and possessed an extensive record collection of classical music. Her husband, Matthew, had played the French horn for a regional orchestra, and they'd met at a reception following a concert. They loved to play canasta and had a regular foursome with neighbors who had now moved.

Matthew had passed away eight years ago. Her children and grandchildren were somewhat attentive and lived fairly close by, but with his death, she also deeply felt the loss of a cultured social life, a fellow music appreciator, and intimate confidant. Satisfied with her married life, Irma had not developed an extensive social network, which now consisted of her family, two neighbors with much younger children, and a few friends who lived far away. Her closest friend had passed away two years ago.

After establishing Irma's history, the therapist moved on to the ACB Questionnaire in order to better understand all aspects of Irma's relationship with Misty. Irma enjoyed answering the questions, which brought back cherished memories and allowed her to expound on how the bird's simple life had enlivened her own.

Irma had never before lived with an animal. After her husband's death, she rejected her daughter's suggestion of adopting a cat or dog. One day, when she stopped to purchase a toy for her daughter's cat, she heard birdsong from the rear of the pet shop. The store owner led her to a canary, the only bird remaining from the spring shipment. Most people preferred yellow or multicolored birds, so its pale-gray feathers had not attracted much buyer enthusiasm. But he was quite the musical virtuoso, entrancing Irma with the trilling clarity of his song.

Still, she spent several anxious days considering what the adoption would entail. Several calls to the shop owner encouraged her to believe she would be able to care for it, and she finally brought the canary home. She set his large cage by a bay window in her living room, so that he could see other birds outside and be present in the room where she spent most of her time. The bird's coloring reminded her of a foggy dawn, so she decided to call him Misty. Irma's caretaking included ensuring he had nutritious seed, water, and occasional treats and replacing the paper that lined his cage. She ordered the highest quality of supplements and sustenance. Once a month, she enlisted her daughter to help move Misty to a smaller temporary cage so his primary dwelling could be completely cleaned.

Misty thrived in the new home, reciprocating this dedicated caretaking by entertaining Irma for hours, especially in the late morning or close to dusk. She soon discovered that if she played Bach or other music that featured wind instruments, harpsichord, or organ, Misty quickly attempted to surpass the concert, in both volume and complexity, with his own astoundingly original variations.

Irma was thrilled with her new avian companion, her heart full of his presence and music. She would talk to Misty about her family and her day, call him by many endearing names, including Pavarotti, Scene Stealer, and Mystical Misty. No longer feeling alienated or isolated, Irma felt that living with Misty imbued her life with joy and camaraderie. Friends and neighbors knew to inquire about Misty if they expected an enthusiastic conversation.

At 8 o'clock each evening, Irma would cover her songster's cage and go off to bed. Each morning at 6:30 a.m., she would remove the cage cover and delight in Misty's excited greeting. For five years, Irma and Misty made the most of their simple lives, content in the other's presence.

Misty sang right up until the morning he passed away. He died suddenly, his reduced appetite having given the only suggestion of illness. Irma found his tiny body on the bottom of his cage. Despite his lifeless appearance, she rushed him to the animal hospital, where his death was confirmed. He had developed an infection that rapidly overtook his delicate system. Irma was haunted by guilt, that she had not noticed or inquired about the significance of his appetite change.

Following Misty's death, Irma became increasingly uncommunicative, and her sleep and appetite suffered. She could no longer listen to classical music without tears. Misty's absence felt unbearable. Irma expressed that she felt like her own life was now over. She found no solace in her adult children or grandchildren and withdrew from them.

In reviewing IPT's four targets, the therapist found that grief and loss appeared to be the primary issue. This included the emptiness that retriggered the grief associated with her husband's death, for which she had not pursued bereavement support. Misty had become a conduit to her deceased husband through their shared love of music.

The loss of Misty magnified Irma's sense of alienation. Her mobility decreased further, as she was no longer motivated to walk around her home. Thoughts of her own death were now prominent. She found such thoughts comforting, associating them with the potential to rejoin both her husband and Misty. She was, therefore, less diligent with her own self-care and nutrition.

Irma had not adjusted to the loss of her husband or Misty by expanding her social circle to include others with whom she might enjoy music. This deficit, in combination with both losses, had led to a persistent, low-level depression that kept Irma isolated and, per her own description, "seeing the glass half-empty."

When Misty entered her life, Irma felt renewed, connecting to another living being who didn't mind her declining age, reduced mobility, or quiet moods. Irma had now lost her day's anchor, the daily rituals of caretaking.

The treatment component of interpersonal disputes was discussed in only one context: Irma refused to consider her daughter's suggestion of adopting another animal. She felt her age could be unfair to a companion who might outlive her. Despite her daughter's promise to take over the care of any animal she adopted, Irma continued to protest the idea, citing her worsening disabilities and advancing age, which caused dismay and disharmony with her daughter. She also rejected the idea of spending alternate weekends at her children's homes, arguing that she was not "good company" and resenting the implication of waning independence.

As an identified deficit in Irma's life was lack of social interaction, creating new social networks consisting of previously enjoyed activities was identified as an important treatment goal. Another was learning the basics of operating a computer to facilitate such connections, more regularly communicate with friends without dependence on mobility, and to find local cultural events. Additionally, her doctor reminded her therapist that physical therapy could greatly improve her mobility if only she would agree to participate.

Treatment plan

Irma would continue supportive therapy until she had successfully transitioned to an acceptance of the dual losses of Matthew and Misty. This transition would involve reviewing the relationships with her husband and canary, with all aspects of each loss explored. Specific treatment targets included remediating Irma's guilt over not having perceived Misty's illness. In addition, discussion of her own mortality was undertaken to identify enjoyable aspects of life in which she could still participate.

Irma would also commit to better self-care, including participation in physical therapy to improve mobility, as well as adherence to a nutrition and sleep routine to help rebuild psychological and physical strength. More frequent visitation with her family was recommended until her tolerance for socializing increased. Finally, she would take a computer class to help discover interesting local events, with the long-term goal of creating new friendships and social connections.

To help achieve the treatment goals set for Irma, several IPT interventions were utilized, all unique aspects of the model associated with its success (Weissman et al., 2007).

One IPT intervention is doing an **interpersonal inventory**, which helps clients identify all the key relationships in their lives. Genograms have been used for this purpose, but they include only biological relatives. An interpersonal inventory, by comparison, avoids focusing only on relatives – many of whom will have already died, the unavoidable, and potentially isolating, reality of the lives of elder clients. Instead, it focuses on inclusion of other relationships that may be present in the elder's life.

Irma's interpersonal inventory included Misty, of course, but also her son, daughter, and grandchildren. The expanded version took note of neighbors, telephonic friends, and service providers. Irma was surprised to contemplate that her UPS driver was a constant in her life, providing moments of socialization and connection every time a package was delivered. Frequent trips to the post office featured the elderly clerk who sold her stamps and told jokes. At the bakery she had visited weekly for 25 years, the lady behind the counter regularly took note of how their hair had grayed in lockstep. Also on the list were her neighbor's teenage son, who helped with yard work and snow shoveling, and the pet shop owner, with whom she still communicated regularly. While not significant in depth or overreliance, these social bonds brought a satisfied smile to Irma's face.

Another intervention, that of **communication analysis,** helps clients improve effective communication. The analysis revealed that Irma either passively awaited an invitation from family or had trouble saying no when her preference was for alone time or because she recognized how busy their lives were. By practicing articulating her wishes, Irma felt more confident in her ability to say what she actually wanted. For example, rather than a vague, open-ended suggestion ("It would be nice to see you"), she was able to make more specific requests ("I am wondering if you could come to dinner next Sunday at 2 p.m.").

This third intervention, **role-play,** helped Irma practice how she might make new friends at the senior center's cultural events. Irma practiced saying hello and introducing herself as a beginning strategy. After several awkward rehearsals of this skill, Irma said she felt confident that she could at least say "Hi!" to one person and perhaps seat herself near them.

In the IPT intervention of **interpersonal incident**, the client describes a challenging event, which is then analyzed for alternative options that might be employed in the future. Irma described attending a social event and finding herself sitting alone. She had introduced herself to another woman, who was also sitting alone in the row behind her. But another person joined the woman and they ignored Irma, who felt rejected, a discouraging outcome. But Irma agreed to persevere, and she decided to sign up for a canasta tournament that would automatically match her with others. Irma was encouraged to enroll in a computer class to learn basic internet search skills. Finally, it was suggested that Irma select orchestral pieces that particularly represented the highlights of her musical communion with Misty and Matthew.

Outcome

After 16 IPT sessions, Irma's depressive despair began to wane. While she still could not imagine adopting another bird, she would walk to the park, engaging with or observing animals accompanying other stewards. In this way she was able to maintain a connection to the animal world. She created scrapbooks for Matthew and Misty, including pictures and recollections of significant memories. She planted a burning bush next to Misty's grave, as well as a bench where she would sometimes sit and listen to her portable radio, imagining that Misty could hear it or that Matthew might critique it. She joined an online hummingbird forum and followed their annual migration from Costa Rica to northern New England. She began hanging hummingbird feeders in her yard, ultimately attracting several of the birds. She donated to a nonprofit canary rescue organization in the name of Misty.

Because IPT neither patronized nor pathologized her grief, Irma was able to fully engage. She appreciated its focus on the practical rebuilding of her life. She appreciated its strength-based attention on what was still possible for her, rather than focusing on deficits associated with her stage of life. Improved mobility from physical therapy also enhanced her mood and extended her independence.

Her canary's death – leading to attention to other long-ignored deficits in Irma's life – resulted in improving the quality of her life, another significant part of Misty's legacy.

Narrative therapy

Narrative therapy (White, 2007) is another psychodynamically based approach to aversive or challenging life events that engages and heals clients through the creation of stories or narratives.

NT encourages the articulation and expression of an experience, including all of its impacts, themes, behavioral and emotional manifestations, and (when possible and appropriate) the inclusion of other stakeholders or witnesses in order to ensure that all dimensions are considered.

The therapist, through a series of questions about client reactions, conclusions, thoughts, and the significance of an event, helps the client move from a potentially negatively weighted perspective (which may represent a series of cognitive errors) to a wider, fuller understanding of the event. In this way, self-blame, or internalization of the problem as indicative of personal deficits, is reworked to create a more accurate story. In addition, this process can help identify the tasks and coping skills needed for healing.

For example, dedicated animal stewards often place inordinate amounts of blame on themselves when an animal dies. NT's Socratic approach can help consider all aspects of the steward's life with the animal, potentially moderating guilt and turning the client's mind to the equal joys of the lost relationship. This achieves another goal of NT, which is the separation of the problem from the person, changing their relationship with the problem from one of passive reaction to one of self-agency or self-advocacy (Morgan, 2000; Heywood et al., 2022).

In this way, a more objective alternative narrative may be developed through respectful, interactive, collaborative questioning to elicit more detail about the stressful event or loss. Questions from the questionnaire may also supplement this process by considering aspects of the relationship unique to the human-animal bond.

Stewards mourning animal companions may have great difficulty accepting and understanding their own intense grief, erroneously interpreting it as the primary problem (i.e. "Why am I mourning this animal so intensely? What is wrong with me? This can't be normal").

Developing a narrative that includes consideration of the steward's life before, during, and after the animal's adoption and death reveals the impacts and fulfilled needs of the relationship. This expanded view helps the client see what aspects of their lives were fulfilled by their relationship with their animal companion. It can then help identify what is now lost, missing, or in need of repair. Treatment can thus focus on what the mourner needs in order to regain emotional and social equilibrium.

For example, a steward experiencing excessive guilt because they could not afford medical treatments might be encouraged to consider the view of the animal. Would the animal have even wanted to endure invasive treatments or the diminished quality of life that might have resulted from chemotherapy? Perhaps the animal's health was deteriorating overall, and treatment would not have provided significant longevity or quality of life. Including veterinary professionals who had a stake in the animal's welfare as witnesses could also impact the client's guilt-laden perspective.

Stewards whose initial narrative concluded that they did not spend enough time with their animal might be encouraged to balance this belief with recollections of the stellar care provided to the animal and its happiness while it lived. Recalling family vacations and weekend hikes, for example, could moderate the experience of guilt amidst the sorrow of loss.

On the other hand, if the steward neglected an animal or somehow contributed to its death through ignorance of its needs or illness, it can be equally relieving to explore this reflection, validating those regrets within the developing narrative. Such objective review can lead the client to taking action to repair past mistakes, make amends through volunteer work, or become a more diligent, knowledgeable steward in the future.

With its focus on inclusion of all possible stakeholders, the animal itself can be given a voice through the projection of its steward. By imagining what this creature might have thought about its care or the end-of-life decisions made on its behalf, NT can help correct skewed assumptions. Stewards might conclude that their animal would have agreed and appreciated actions taken to end its suffering or better its life. Such discussions, guided by the therapist, can moderate the tendency of grieving stewards to recall only their failures within the relationship.

The use of the ACB Questionnaire can further the process of eliciting specific recollections of shared activities and mutual caretaking. For example, to begin creating a narrative that ends with the animal's loss, it is imperative to start with the circumstances of adoption. What were the goals or expectations realized within the dyad? How was the steward's life transformed or enhanced by the animal's presence? If life with an animal was not their initial choice (i.e. a young adult steward leaves for college while their feline remains at home), how did that story evolve?

Through its emphasis on stakeholder inclusion, NT is also an effective treatment approach for situations in which the animal lived within a family or group. Each contributing stakeholder has the opportunity to enrich the narrative with their own version of the experience. The completed story, an accumulation of all witness "chapters," can help unite family members in their grief – even if they are mourning differently – by recalling aspects of the human-animal bond that other people may not remember.

Case study: a family of witnesses

Members of the Sanchez family recently arrived from Mexico and lived in adjacent apartments in a third-floor walk-up in East Harlem. The family consisted of two brothers and their wives, an elderly aunt, a grandmother, and four children ranging from 10 months to 9 years old.

The brothers were diligent in their attempts to find work, but without documentation, they were only sometimes successful. Initially, the family was largely supported by the women, who cleaned homes or cared for neighborhood children. On a good day, there would be opportunities for work, a full refrigerator, and enticing aromas coming from the busy kitchen; during difficult times, the grandmother and aunt would visit the local food pantry that the men were too proud to use.

The family's arrival in the States had been laden with difficulties. One child had become very ill on the journey, and there was now no access to healthcare; a third brother had to turn back to care for an ailing grandfather. Finding housing was wearisome, as much of their cash was needed to pay off a landlord who would not offer a formal lease. Only the aunt spoke fluent English, meaning she had to serve as the family interpreter and spokesperson.

Once finally settled, the family noticed a stray dog scrounging for food in the alleyways, quickly running away if approached. Neighbors had begun feeding it, throwing scraps out the window if they saw him lingering. During one weekend block party, the street-savvy canine gobbled down a plate of flautas while a distracted family member spoke with a friend. The dog was thereby christened Federale, reminiscent of a scoundrel who could be bribed with food.

Federale soon recognized this dubious moniker, warily approaching when called. He was a small dog of maybe 35 pounds, multicolored, with wiry fur and deep-brown eyes, fast as lightning. He'd launch himself into the air and spin around like a whirling dervish. He was amusing and socially responsive.

Through the weeks that followed, he allowed the Sanchezes ever-closer proximity. One day, the grandmother noticed her 5-year-old granddaughter petting him in the tiny backyard, but she had no idea how Federale had managed to get in. She shooed him away, but Federale was calmly sitting on the front stoop, ready to accompany them on a walk when they ventured out again.

Within another two weeks, Federale had wormed his way into the building and was given a makeshift bed in the hallway between the two apartments. As if understanding the precarious nature of his new shelter, Federale never barked, patiently waiting to be let outside. But if anyone approached the third-floor landing, Federale would growl softly until he was told, "It's okay, boy."

Federale became the family's anchor, entertainer, and support giver. If someone was having a tough day, he would lie beside them, staring into their face until they looked back. Then he would slowly wag his tail as if to say, "Things will get better, we're all still here." When the little ones were outside, Federale was never far behind; when the school-age kids made their way to a local playground, he was there as their supervisor and self-appointed babysitter.

The family spent two difficult years living on the community fringes, fearful of discovery and deportation. While they heard of legal services, they feared that accepting help could risk exposure – and they had no money to pay for it anyway. When life was especially difficult, they discussed returning to Mexico and how they might take Federale with them.

Throughout this time, Federale was steadfast in his role as family member, shepherding children from one apartment to the other, soothing weary workers by lying on their tired feet, and eagerly jumping onto any available lap. Federale was polite and respectful, appearing to reflect the cultural values of his adoptive family. The Sanchezes adored him. When he cut his paw on a piece of glass, the grandmother made poultices for his foot, wrapping it tenderly and bathing it each day. Federale now allowed attention and handling, seeming to understand their good intentions.

Unfortunately, a new downstairs neighbor did not want animals in the building and reported the growling dog on the third floor to the landlord. Within a few days, Federale was picked up by animal control officers as he lay on the front sidewalk. The family members who were at home during his capture watched, horrified, as Federale was chased, harnessed, and loaded into a truck. Due to the potential consequences, the family felt unable to intervene. They were haunted by his frantic barking as he was driven away.

The officer had told a neighbor that they could claim him at the pound if they were willing to pay for shots and a license, which would require an official ID bearing the name and address of the owner.

For weeks, the family was plagued with distress. But there was no solution that would not jeopardize their fragile finances and legal status. They approached a sympathetic neighbor who might find and adopt Federale on their behalf. But the search proved futile.

The loss of Federale was the last straw for this fragile family. As their social and economic circumstances deteriorated, the Sanchezes became dejected and unmotivated to further invest in their new life. Noticing that the children were also in distress, the despairing family approached a trusted physician, who referred them to a local mental health clinic. Although they were initially hesitant to present for treatment, the agency, called The Door, was reliably regarded as protective of immigrants, offering or locating free services regardless of documentation status.

Assessment

Narrative therapy was selected as the appropriate modality for this family's treatment, for several reasons:

First, the therapist was aware that many Hispanic families are likely to regard their animals as true members (Schoenfeld-Tacher & Kogan, 2019). Reinforcing cultural norms is emphasized within the inclusive, socially just philosophy and framework of NT, which has been therapeutically adapted across many cultures, ethnicities, and identities, including among immigrant children.

Second, NT's flexible structure would allow all members of the family to participate despite varying time and work commitments. NT encourages the participation of all "witnesses" in creating the new narrative, with each family member's experience receiving equal weight in story construction. Through this process, a multidimensional version of Federale's brief presence could be constructed from a collective process that would capture the sense of loss as well as the joy of his loyal camaraderie. As not all family members could be present at every session, recordings or written accounts of their experiences were encouraged, which were then conveyed to the agency and translated as part of the story. As not all their words and feelings had equivalency to English counterparts, the ultimate narrative was created in Spanish to better capture the family's experience.

Third, it was clear to the therapist that the overwhelming guilt and self-blame the Sanchezes professed for the dog's removal failed to give sufficient context to the many challenging circumstances that led to their inability to protect him.

In addition, to help further define and recollect specific experiences for the development of a new narrative, the questionnaire was used to add detail to each person's experiences with Federale.

The assessment began with the reasons for the family's journey to the U.S., the events that occurred during that journey, and the elements of trauma associated with their relocation. Interviews were conducted with all members of the family, in person or via phone, about their experiences during the immigration, as well as the relationship of each to Federale. For example, the children focused on the activities they had shared with Federale, and the adults felt his absence as that of a friend and protective spirit. The grandmother, who had spent the most time with Federale, expressed how he had tethered her days, providing structure and companionship.

Treatment plan

The primary goals of NT were to support the family through their grieving of Federale and to create a realistic narrative that externalized their inability to save him as a social problem rather than a family problem. For example, the stark realities, including deportation, of any attempt to claim Federale were emphasized.

Instead, the narrative would include the fact that they had rescued Federale as much as he had rescued them; his life on the street would likely have been shortened if not for their intervention. Federale had received shelter, care, and affection, which had enhanced his life.

The narrative would also emphasize Federale's alignment with their plight and culture. For example, the dog's "personality" seemed to mirror important values – he was not a "one-man dog," but belonged to the entire family. He was respectful, polite, and concerned about all of them.

Additional treatment plan recommendations included

◆ continuation of family therapy and further assessment for symptoms of trauma;
◆ continuous reinforcement with each other that the risk of exposure through attempted adoption of Federale could

have had dire consequences, including deportation and family separation;

◆ initiation of family involvement with supportive services available to immigrant families, including those for financial assistance, medical treatment, educational opportunities, legal services, and safe social interaction through community activities; and

◆ the creation of a legacy for Federale, which would draw upon aspects of the created narrative and internalize his continuing presence in their lives.

Outcome

Creating the family narrative of Federale's life within the guidance of NT helped relieve the Sanchez family of excessive feelings of culpability. Identifying the aversive circumstances that led to his removal as beyond their control led to pivotal modifications in the narrative.

For example, the eldest child's self-recrimination – had she let him sleep on her bed that day, he would not have been outside – was placed in a new context of the animal's need to relieve himself, just as her own family had to expose themselves to find economic opportunities. In addition, the animal control officers would have continued to search for Federale as long as the complaints continued, just as federal agencies would continue to identify undocumented families. In other words, Federale's circumstances were emblematic of their own.

The family created a legacy for Federale. A corner of the apartment was reserved for his bed, picture, ball, collected fur, and a candle. Dominating this legacy was their perception of Federale as not only an important source of support throughout the early months of their immigration but as a hero for what he had contributed to family life.

Their new view was that the dog's story was a metaphor for their own arduous journey to establish a new life. Federale's "feral" status made him a target for societal marginalization and the abuses of undocumented life – much like his adoptive family.

Chapter summary

In this chapter, we explored and applied two humanistic, client-centered, effective, and adaptable psychodynamic models, interpersonal psychotherapy and narrative therapy, to the experience of animal companion loss. These approaches were chosen because client authority is emphasized in defining the problem – in this case, the loss of the companion animal – with goal establishment related directly to problem definition. In addition, both IPT and NT are culturally adaptable to a variety of racial, gender, and ethnic identities.

As person-centered approaches, they do not approach human problems from a primarily diagnostic or pathological perspective, but instead focus on articulation of the experiences, symptom relief, and tasks of recovery.

Interpersonal psychotherapy focuses on shoring up social support and paying attention to the quality of interpersonal transactions, attachment, and communication styles that may thwart progress of reintegration after a loss has caused disequilibrium or symptoms of depression or anxiety. It focuses on four key areas: grief and loss, role transitions, interpersonal disputes, and interpersonal deficits. The impact of each area is evaluated and defined by the client's experience of its significance, guided by the therapist.

Narrative therapy emphasizes creation of a narrative infused with the input of all stakeholders, widening the client lens to create a more representative, adaptive, and objective version that corrects cognitive distortions or the over-assumption of blame. As NT's inclusive perspective encourages the participation of all "witnesses," it is an excellent choice when animal companion loss affects families or groups. It helps the client or group to reconceptualize the experience of loss through the consideration of alternative perspectives.

These two psychodynamic models may also be helpful in treating grief when an individual's depression includes mourning for lost or threatened aspects of the animal kingdom or natural world. For example, concerns about diminishing animal habitats, species on the verge of extinction, animal abuse, climate change, and other societal problems relating to the natural world can be significant components of client depression and anxiety, even when not the primary target of treatment.

The inclusion of the ACB Questionnaire was again emphasized as helping to define the qualities and impact of the lost animal and to identify aspects of the lost relationship, which may need to be rebuilt. In addition, including the ACB Questionnaire during assessment may help validate a steward's experience of despair as a normative response to the significance of animal companion loss.

6

Cognitive behavioral approaches to healing animal companion loss

I didn't give Odie a very good life. It took so little to make her happy, and yet work was always my priority. – Nancy after the death of her miniature pet pig

Cognitive and behavioral therapies can clarify and moderate distorted cognitions, like the one earlier, in which the steward erroneously concluded she failed her animal companion. Distorted thoughts that may emanate from depression can result in negative ruminations (Beck, 1995), difficult emotions, and potentially destructive behaviors (Malkinson, 2006). Cognitive behavioral therapies have their theoretical basis in the assumption that our thoughts and beliefs about a situation, our role in the outcome, and our interpretation of its meaning greatly impact the emotions and behaviors that follow (Spiegler & Guevremont, 2010).

In particular, cognitive behavior therapy (CBT) and dialectical behavior therapy (DBT), its emotionally focused cousin, are presented as potentially efficacious models for the treatment of depressive or anxious grief, which results when cognitive distortions dominate feelings, leading to persistently negative emotions that then influence behavioral choices. Both approaches are evidenced for the treatment of depression and anxiety (Falabella et al., 2022), while DBT adds focus to the management

DOI: 10.4324/9781003145929-7

of emotional lability through specific skills helpful to restoration of affective equilibrium.

Both CBT and DBT explore and objectively evaluate client thoughts associated with negative emotions, self-invalidation, and maladaptive behaviors. Both approaches focus on symptom reduction through cognitive restructuring, as well as the introduction of skills and interventions that can help reduce psychological distress. Both models also emphasize shared responsibility for healing within the therapeutic alliance via commitment to behavioral homework (Neimeyer & Feixas, 1990) to better generalize skills to the client's external environment.

A steward's belief that they were somehow responsible for their animal companion's poor quality of life, or even for its death, could be a form of "undoing." Mourners may assume if they had taken another action, the result would have been different (Butler & Northcut, 2013). Imagining themselves as having so much power can protract denial while self-blame continues (Davis et al., 1996).

Cognitive behavior therapy has partial roots in behavior therapy, which relies primarily on the reinforcement of desired behaviors through rewards or extinguishment of unwanted behaviors through negative consequences to achieve behavioral goals. *Don't Shoot the Dog* (Pryor, 2002), a primer on training animals based on classical conditioning and consistent reinforcement of desired behaviors, is an example of a purely behavioral intervention. In humans, behavior therapy was most often utilized in a medical context for recovery from physical ailments, that is, encouragement of walking on the treadmill after cardiac events or ensuring medication compliance for chronic health issues like diabetes (Lin et al., 2010) Behavior modification, on the other hand, was historically associated with coercive efforts to control unwanted behaviors in institutional life through various forms of containment, punishment, or withholding of rewards (Bandura, 1975). In the past this also included the use of pharmacological agents, or even surgical interventions like frontal lobotomies (Kucharski, 1984), designed to increase passive compliance. However, the application of such extreme methods to induce behavioral compliance among populations who lacked the autonomy to consent brought ethical concerns.

The idea of thinking as a behavior, and thoughts as primary prompts leading to specific emotions and behaviors, is attributed to the work of Aaron Beck, considered to be the father of CBT. Beck's conclusions – that exploration of negative thoughts can be an essential catalyst to modification of the emotions and behaviors that follow – found acceptance in the therapeutic community once initial skepticism of this manualized approach was reduced by repeated studies demonstrating CBT's efficacy in reducing psychological distress (Beck & Fleming, 2021).

While Beck agreed that humans can be induced or coerced by external factors of reward or deprivation to perform behaviors (both positive and negative) that they might ordinarily reject, such considerations first pass through our "meaning making systems." That process is further influenced by the schemas we have developed about ourselves and the assumed outcome of behaviors that follow (Beck et al., 2006). Such beliefs represent a person's general perspective about themselves, others, and the world (Otani et al., 2018). This can result in a vicious cycle; the higher the degree of distress, the more likely such thinking patterns may be triggered, continuing a ruminative cycle of negative conclusion and heightened affect.

Self-schemas can be triggered by many life events. With the intensity of grief associated with animal companion loss, the influence of such beliefs may result in distorted recollection and useless, self-blaming conclusions about the animal's care or its death. Thinking and behavioral outcomes can be further influenced by social cues.

Albert Bandura's social learning theory posits that humans tend to engage in behaviors that enhance their position in the social hierarchies to which they seek affiliation and proximity (Hammer, 2011). Many species – including primates, mammals, and some reptiles and insects like bees and ants – also appear to engage in behaviors that support their affiliation and species survival within predetermined communities of established hierarchies (Lahn, 2020).

Animals, apparently less distracted by the intrusion of emotion, appear to more readily adopt behaviors that reliably fulfill survival needs, which then become the behavior's own reinforcement. Even under the care of responsible human stewards, there is no guarantee that animals will have their basic needs for nourishment, shelter, and affection met.

Animals rarely make behavioral errors associated with survival and procreation; could their behavioral consistency be the result of their historically more tenuous existence? We often regard their behavioral consistency as pure instinct, an assertion worth challenging when we consider animals' exhibiting new and successful problem-solving skills. There are many instances of animals appearing to alter behaviors when dominated by situations triggering fear, anger, life-threatening confinement, or hunger (Rowell et al., 2021)

Clinical research posits the question of behavioral choices being based on fear or survival assessment in both humans and animals (Mobbs et al., 2015). Humans appear to stand alone among sentient beings in understanding that a behavioral choice is maladaptive yet continuing to choose it (Carucci, 2019).

Another contribution of CBT to the therapeutic process is its scientific focus on symptom evaluation throughout therapy in order to assess client progress and inform treatment planning. This can be especially helpful when evaluating symptoms of grief over weeks and months. For example, the Beck Depression and Anxiety Inventories, and the Beck Hopelessness Scale can be effectively utilized to monitor emotional states and response to treatment (Spiegler & Guevremont, 2010)

Cognitive behavioral interventions, then, do more than scrutinize disturbing or negative thoughts related to a specific episode of distress. They also attempt to modify meaning making through consistent practice of CBT interventions, which widen clients' scope to consider all facts of a situation, rather than conclusions formed from emotional dominance (Månsson et al., 2016).

CBT's triadic focus on the interplay of thoughts, emotions, and behaviors can result in significant long-term therapeutic

gains. Three elements of this sequence that have particular application to animal companion loss are described subsequently.

Cognitive distortions

Cognitive distortions – negative biases and beliefs against the
self – may result when a person excludes, ignores, or minimizes
important contextual information or overemphasizes the negative aspects of a memory or situation (Spiegler & Guevremont,
2010; Beck & Fleming, 2021). For example, an animal companion
steward may erroneously believe that their failure to take timely
action heightened an animal's distress or pain. Or they may
engage in painful rumination about a decision to euthanize,
which retriggers negative core beliefs about competency, trust,
and abuse. The extent to which clients may believe and feel
emotional distress from distorted conclusions may be mitigated
through CBT's exacting analysis of all contributing facts. The
goal is not necessarily to reverse such conclusions, but to arrive
at a more objective realistic conclusion.

Distortions related to animal companion loss may include
assuming excessive responsibility for the death of the animal.
Other results may include feelings of worthlessness, incompe-
tence, or defectiveness; feeling intentionally abandoned by the
animal due to inadequacies as a steward; or anger toward the
animal for the perceived abandonment (Zilcha-Mano et al.,
2011b). Such beliefs may erase awareness of years of diligent
stewardship.

Emotional dysregulation

Stewards who did not expect to experience an intense degree of
despair over the loss of a companion animal, or who have histories of cumulative losses, may find that their previous coping
skills are insufficient to mediate the current crisis. Without
the introduction of new coping skills, such clients may spiral
into extreme emotional distress, which they are unable to

calm. Unmitigated emotional states can wreak havoc on one's relationships, life, health, and well-being, potentially leading to thoughts of self-harm or suicide, or intensifying a wish to join the departed animal (Clark, 2017).

Maladaptive behaviors

Stewards may attempt to manage extreme discomfort by engaging in destructive behaviors, including self-harm associated with shame. Despite initial relief, the unexplored emotions may continue, fueling more dysregulation and behavioral destruction. For example, the steward's continuance of activities shared with the animal may now only protract grief. This could lead to difficulties in letting go of the animal, delaying decisions about the disposition of its body, or feeling unable to release the physical representation of the animal. Steward with histories of substance abuse may reengage in these behaviors (Caparrós & Masferrer, 2021).

Case study: a better balance

Blaze was a stunning dapple-gray equine who lived on a rural Pennsylvania farm with Howard and his partner, James, both Philadelphia-based attorneys. Adopted as a colt to serve as a riding companion for Howard, and stablemate to an aging pony, Blaze lived among the farm's creatures, including chickens, geese, a border collie, two llamas, and four sheep.

Blaze and Howard enjoyed long rides on their 40-acre farm, which bordered miles of conservation trails. Even after a long workday and an hour's commute home, Howard, who had grown up with horses, looked forward to an outing. James was more interested in tending their gardens, where he cultivated herbs and vegetables.

When Blaze heard Howard's car coming up the long driveway, he would whinny loudly. If he was in the paddock, he galloped to the fence nearest the driveway and stomped his hoof in the grass. Their time together helped Howard unwind, and Blaze enjoyed exploring the many paths they roamed. They would stop by a brook or pause on the crest of an open field. Sometimes Howard would dismount on that hilltop, and they would watch the setting sun together. Blaze was a nuzzler, his large, looming body a protective presence. Howard frequently spoke to Blaze, whose ears would turn quickly to take in these confidences.

Their deeply bonded relationship was of great solace to Howard, especially when James passed away after a sudden illness. During the two years that followed, Blaze carried Howard and his heavy grief over the trails and paths, determined to release his steward's sadness. When Howard's grief was especially intense, Blaze would break into a thundering gallop, as if to ground his steward's sorrow.

The stream where James's ashes had been scattered was a favorite stop. Blaze seemed to know when Howard needed to visit and would find his way there with no directive. Such was the strength of their connection.

Faced with loneliness and disabilities, Howard decided to semi-retire and move to the city. Keeping the farm going felt isolating and impractical, given the cost of its upkeep. Over the next 18 months, most of the farm animals were placed at neighboring barns. The pony, now arthritic and blind, was gently let go.

Syd was rehomed with a neighbor whose young children and outdoor space would guarantee plenty of exercise. An out-of-state couple came to meet the formidable Blaze and quickly fell in love. With assurances of daily rides and visits to inspect his new accommodations, Howard agreed to the adoption.

But the day that Blaze left for his new home, Howard felt an anxious doubt. Blaze continued to whinny and pull against the reins as he was led into his new steward's trailer. Howard became distressed by his vocalizations but remained firm in his decision. Blaze left, the farm was sold, and Howard moved into his city condo.

A year later, he learned that the couple who adopted Blaze met with financial misfortune and were forced to rehome their animals. Howard learned that Blaze had been sold to a public riding facility in upstate New York.

Howard drove up to see Blaze but met a completely different animal from the proud equine he had known. Blaze was indifferent to Howard, showing no sign of recognition. His personality was subdued, his spirit resigned. Aware of the stress placed on equines in public stables, Howard attempted to purchase Blaze, thinking he would board him outside Philly, but the new owner refused to sell. Even doubling the price brought no results; docile Blaze was too much of a favorite.

Howard assured the stable owner that he would purchase Blaze upon his retirement and cover any veterinary costs, but his subsequent phone calls were ignored. After several months, Howard learned that the riding studio had been sold. The new owner informed Howard that Blaze had been euthanized for ligament injuries. He claimed he had not been informed of Howard's willingness to adopt him or cover his care.

Sobbing, Howard could barely drive the six hours home. Guilt-ridden and despairing, he began experiencing nightmares and panic attacks. He felt overwhelmed with regret for selling the farm.

But his primary torture was having let go of Blaze. He felt that he had been selfishly unable to consider Blaze's needs in the aftermath of James's death. If he had waited for his grief to resolve, perhaps he might have eventually found the farm to be a comfort, not a burden.

Unaccustomed to the acuity of negative feelings and associated emotions, Howard sought treatment from a local therapist who listed animal companion bereavement among his treatment specialties.

Assessment

The therapist began with a thorough psychosocial assessment and review of Howard's symptoms, which led to a diagnosis of prolonged grief disorder. It had been nearly four years since James's death and 18 months since Blaze's euthanasia.

CBT was deemed to be the best intervention, as negative thoughts – ruminations about himself and his decisions, coupled with guilt over the fate of Blaze and deep regret that he had sold his farm – plagued him day and night.

As he dropped off to sleep, Howard would recall the day James had seconded his decision to purchase Blaze or would imagine hearing Blaze's welcoming whinny. He thought of himself as a heartless steward who had abandoned a loving and loyal animal.

His thoughts were endless cycles of self-recrimination and feelings of failure: He should have been more forceful about reclaiming Blaze; his contract to sell Blaze should have specified that Blaze be returned if the new stewards could not keep him.

He felt hopelessly lost, his life without meaning. He felt his own death would not be unwelcome.

Howard's initial assessment was supplemented with the questionnaire, the responses to which indicated that Howard had not felt a connection of the depth he had shared with Blaze – not even with James. He felt guilty that he had shared more of his most intimate thoughts, conversations, and demonstrations of affection with Blaze than with James.

Howard had not attempted to create any kind of legacy for Blaze, feeling that he had lost that right by surrendering the animal. He felt unworthy of a peaceful life and thought his self-torture was justice for his neglect.

Treatment plan

Treatment goals prioritized addressing Howard's negative thoughts and pervasive feelings of guilt about Blaze, incomplete mourning of James, possible alcohol abuse, and disrupted sleep. Careful review of Howard's self-doubt and negative conclusions were warranted through CBT interventions designed to evaluate thoughts. Even if guilty ruminations were partially substantiated, some relief might be found by understanding and validating the context of choices that had led to his decisions.

Through Socratic questioning, a CBT intervention that inquires into all aspects of a difficult situation (Clark & Egan, 2015), client conclusions may be found to be faulty or excessively negative. The lens of depression can be a narrow one; when negative self-talk is amplified by grief, some aspects of the triggering situation may be amplified or overlooked.

This process of questioning, a skill widely used in the legal profession, was familiar and acceptable to Howard. Through these questions, it appeared that Howard's need to blame himself for letting go of Blaze and for the animal's subsequent death was not balanced by equally compelling facts about his exemplary care for Blaze and his other animals. Howard had released Blaze for adoption into what he thought would be a life of similar quality. Blaze had no legal status beyond that of property, making it difficult to trace his whereabouts once Howard's stewardship ended. With no power to intervene unless there was extreme cruelty, Howard was unable to ensure continuing optimal care.

After such review, Howard's belief that he was solely responsible for Blaze's death fell from a 10 to a 7 on the cognitive continuum, a scale that rates the intensity with which a belief is held (Beck & Fleming, 2021).

Howard's accompanying belief – that he would never again have such a close relationship with another human or animal – was also explored in the context of his guilt over confiding more of his feelings to Blaze than to James. In this process, he acknowledged that James was not particularly affectionate and was rather closed about his deepest feelings; Howard had often felt frustrated by his attempts to become closer to James. This recollection reduced his feelings of guilt, as he now saw Blaze as providing what his relationship with James lacked: deep feelings of connection, lack of judgment, and the sharing of confidences.

While it was accepted that Howard was unlikely to ever experience the kind of relationship he had with Blaze, the idea that he would never again have meaningful connections was found to be unproven. The possibility that Howard still had the capacity to form relationships with humans and animals reduced his depressive conclusions.

For example, a friend had approached Howard about adopting his sister's 9-year-old golden after she moved into assisted living. Howard had met the dog, named Merry, and instantly loved her. But regarding himself as a poor steward made him conclude that he did not deserve the companionship of another animal.

He completed the Beck Thought Record, which looks at facts, rates feelings and beliefs, and guides the client to more adaptive conclusions (Burger, 2021). This, in combination with his responses from the questionnaire, yielded indisputable evidence that he had been a trustworthy steward to the animals in his care, with this one exception. Howard decided that he would adopt the dog.

Other CBT techniques

♦ Journaling: Because expressing his feelings verbally was initially difficult for Howard in session, he used a process of daily writing to reflect or associate events of the day with the feelings that described his most distressing thoughts (Sohal et al., 2022). He was encouraged to write about times and activities he had shared with Blaze, including his repeated attempts to rescue the animal. Recording these meaningful interactions gave Howard a resource he could access when negative thoughts began to plague him, offering evidence of his careful stewardship.

♦ Relaxation exercises: To combat panic attacks, Howard was taught methods of relaxation to help reduce escalating anxiety. Paced breathing – a form of ratio breathing that begins with a normative intake of breath, which is followed by a longer exhale accompanied by a whistling sound as the air escapes – was introduced and found to be somewhat effective (Steffen et al., 2021). He completed an exercise, the Safe Place Exercise, in which he identified time spent in the barn grooming Blaze, who was clearly enjoying the exchange, as evoking feelings of relaxed safety. The smell of the hay, the creaking barn boards, their shared sweat, the feel of Blaze's fur as the brush moved across his giant back – all these brought an instant visceral feeling of connection and peace.

♦ Physical exercise: Howard's level of physical activity over the past two years had greatly decreased due to his more confined lifestyle. A significant weight gain was discussed as potentially contributing to feelings of lethargy and aversion to socialization (Alimoradi et al., 2020).

Howard initially stated that walking in nature brought feelings of sadness as he thought of Blaze. By changing those to joyful recollection, the more prominent emotion, Howard was able to go for walks, which helped reduce his anxious symptoms and allowed more peaceful sleep. Physical exertion helped Howard ground himself, by reducing his tendency to defensively intellectualize and to not be fully present in his body.

♦ Increasing social support: While insisting that he had no desire to socialize, Howard did acknowledge a loneliness that he accepted as part of aging. His retirement from a once-vital career felt like he had also retired from life. Howard was encouraged to consider using his legal expertise for animal advocacy, perhaps proposing ethical treatment guidelines for equines working in public trail riding. Howard was enthusiastic about this suggestion, which offered an opportunity to moderate the systemic failures that had doomed Blaze. He began seeking affiliation with other lawyers committed to animal advocacy, which helped him feel more connected and less depressed (Scott et al., 2020).

Outcome

Although Howard's negative thought patterns were quickly moderated, it took time for him to consistently accept the more adaptive conclusions. But he was now able to balance guilt with the equal truth that he had given Blaze the best care possible for most of their lives together, fostering a deep bond from which they both benefited.

Howard's expanded view about lifestyle options for senior life resulted in his adopting Merry. He joined an animal advocacy group as a legal consultant, with the goal of elevating animals' status to that of family members (Ascione & Shapiro, 2009).

He began a renewed regimen of self-care to relieve depressive symptoms and possibly attract other human companions.

Through the application of CBT interventions for the depressive symptoms associated with prolonged bereavement, along with the responses to the questionnaire, Howard was able to resolve feelings of guilt, find renewed hope in life's remaining options, and allow himself the company of a new animal companion. Through the adoption of Merry, Howard began his first emotional connection with animals since he had lost Blaze. Howard had once avoided thinking about his time with Blaze, but now he reflected on it with satisfaction, especially given that the majestic creature's legacy was embodied in his steward's pursuit of animal rights.

Dialectical behavior therapy, developed by Marsha Linehan in 1993, also has its foundational basis in cognitive behavior therapy, but adds a critically and previously underemphasized focus on management of emotion dysregulation. With its biosocial theory – that environment and biology are coconspirators in activating emotion dysregulation in vulnerable individuals – (Linehan, 1998) it reduces client shame while still assigning client responsibility for healing (i.e. "You may not have caused your problems, but you have to solve them anyway"). Through teaching skills to better identify triggers and creating strategies for emotional containment, clients are empowered to more effectively manage triggering situations. Lack of skills to manage difficult emotions can greatly reduce the effectiveness of interpersonal transactions and quality of life (Stone, 2006). While CBT also explores the association among thoughts, emotions, and resulting behaviors, less emphasis was placed on the skills to initially reduce emotional lability; instead, attention to thoughts was prioritized. DBT skills have been successfully applied to the symptoms of grief reactions (Barrett et al., 2017).

DBT was initially conceptualized as a yearlong treatment, consisting of a weekly 90-minute skills training group, an individual session, consultation team meetings, and coaching calls from DBT therapists to help clients generalize taught skills during difficult moments. Homework is an essential aspect of the therapy as DBT seeks to help clients apply newly learned skills to their biological, emotional, and social environments (Linehan, 1993, 2014).

As an essential goal of DBT is to help clients identify vulnerable emotional states and associated feelings and then employ "skillful means" to cope with those triggered emotions (Robins et al., 2004), DBT focuses on practicing skills from its five modules: Mindfulness, Emotion Regulation, Interpersonal Effectiveness, Distress Tolerance, and Walking the Middle Path (Rathus et al., 2015). Mindfulness is at the core of DBT skills, because it offers different methods to center the self by grounding fully in the present.

At initial assessment, DBT prioritizes client behaviors which threaten life, followed by behaviors which threaten behavior and then quality of life. While its first priority is obvious in terms of immediate containment of life-threatening behaviors, its second priority touches upon the therapist-client relationship in a realistic way.

While we repeatedly acknowledge the role of the sound therapeutic alliance as essential to treatment gains (Stubbe, 2018), protecting and enhancing this crucial relationship by remediating threats to its effectiveness received scant attention prior to DBT's introduction. When there are difficulties in managing emotions when triggering content is discussed, therapist-client attachment is greatly compromised, rendering even the most effective or evidenced approach impotent (Allen, 1997).

Therefore, much attention is given to therapy-interfering behaviors, which can include lateness, emotional explosiveness, overreliance on the therapist, not respecting boundaries, and refusal to engage in homework. Such behaviors can equally originate in either the client or the therapist; therefore, responsibility for a sound alliance is shared. The intrusion of such behaviors are not judged, but rather they are addressed, their impact explored, and then breaches repaired (Chapman & Rosenthal, 2016).

CBT, conversely while acknowledging emotional influences, does not specifically focus on teaching methods to change or contain them. For example, while the Beck Thought Record asks clients to rate the intensity of their beliefs and emotions, and questions how emotions might be moderated as a result of a new belief, its containment strategies rest more on cognitive restructuring than on skills to immediately reduce them. Without remediating clients' lack of skills for emotional management, therapy itself may become a triggering event, causing an abrupt end to even the most promising therapeutic encounter (Dimeff & Linehan, 2001).

DBT also offers therapists and clients critical support in the management of suicidal and self-harming behaviors. Its strategies help distinguish nonsuicidal self-injury from true suicidal intent, and the skills practiced to reduce emotional lability have led to reductions of inpatient hospitalizations for this issue (DeCou et al., 2019). In one such study of incarcerated women with a history of self-harm, the combination of DBT with animal-assisted therapy resulted in enhanced effect (Eaton-Stull et al., 2021).

DBT's acceptance – but insistence on change – of clients' previous strategies for reduction of difficult emotions (i.e. cutting, disordered eating behaviors, use of substances) helps reduce client shame (Stone, 2008). Given the emotional lability that animal companion grief may elicit, especially for those who have difficulty managing such emotions, DBT can be a pivotal form of treatment to help manage those reactions (Barrett et al., 2017). Even when a client does not suffer from significant deficits in the ability to self-regulate, DBT's skills and strategies are still incredibly useful in any affective disturbance that would benefit from restoration of emotional equilibrium.

For example, in the aftermath of animal death, a client's dependence on the animal to help self-soothe and manage difficult emotions may be revealed, as the steward has lost not only a cherished relationship but also an important resource for emotional grounding. In some ways, the animal may have been the first "therapist" in the steward's life, that essential transitional object and secure base.

Like CBT, some DBT interventions incorporate numeric scales to help clients better identify the intensity of emotional experiencing and associated beliefs. For example, the DBT Diary Card helps clients and clinicians track progress through daily assessment of emotions and urges (Probst et al., 2018). This intervention makes it possible to track the intensity of grief, as well as environmental influences that reduce or increase it. DBT also encourages more specific description of feeling states, for example, Are you experiencing fury or simply irritation? The former may bring a surge of more anger, while the latter might reduce its intensity.

Case study: the skills to manage life

Meredith was a college sophomore living in off-campus housing with four other young women. During her adolescence, Meredith – an only child – had struggled with emotional control manifested by labile moods, disordered eating, and intermittent self-harm. Her first romantic relationship failed due to her extreme responses to imagined slights. The resulting feelings of shame and worthlessness were long-lasting. Disordered eating ranged from binges to severe food restriction with excessive exercise.

Meredith's parents had also struggled with affective disturbances throughout her life. Her mother's severe depression resulted in a suicide attempt two months after her birth, and relatives cared for her during her mother's monthlong hospitalization. Meredith's father battled intermittent substance use disorders, resulting in two unsuccessful inpatient rehab hospitalizations, when she was an adolescent.

Her parents were loving during periods of mental stability, but the atmosphere in Meredith's home was often chaotic and emotionally charged. When one or both were struggling with mental illness, Meredith found herself isolated and lonely, reliant on other friends and their families to provide normalcy. Although Meredith loved her parents, she often felt shame, because her home life was so unpredictable.

She struggled with feelings that she was not important enough to motivate her parents to maintain their recovery. At these times, she found it difficult to manage destructive impulses, which resulted in further alienation of her limited social support. She would frequently disassociate, a defense mechanism to manage overwhelming emotion (Lynn & Rhue, 1994). But Meredith's strengths included high intelligence, as well as artistic and original creativity; her compelling writing won her entrance to a prestigious journalism program.

While Meredith had engaged in family and individual therapy throughout her teens, the focus was primarily on her parents' continuing difficulties; her individual issues with emotional management were never acknowledged or addressed.

Meredith had always found comfort in the family's dog and two cats. But as the animals passed away, no new animals were adopted. Therefore, one of Meredith's goals in moving to off-campus housing was to adopt a cat. After consulting with her roommates and gaining their enthusiastic support, Meredith visited a local animal shelter and adopted a seemingly healthy, well-socialized orange and cream-colored feline thought to be around 6 years old. They all decided to name the calm, laid-back cat Mellow.

For a while, Mellow's presence was uplifting. Meredith was her primary caretaker, but all the roommates enjoyed and interacted with Mellow, so she was not often alone. Mellow would sometimes wait by the door, hoping to escape into the yard with its interesting birds and squirrels. After a couple of quick escapes, it was determined that Mellow could no longer have free run of the house until all roommates were home for the night.

One evening, Meredith returned home with a date, seeking privacy in her own room. As Mellow's presence became a bit of a nuisance, Meredith placed her outside in the hallway.

A few hours later, Meredith awakened to pounding on her door. Apparently, as other roommates came home, wily Mellow saw an opportunity to escape and had run into the street, where she'd been struck by a car. Despite transport to a local veterinary hospital, Mellow succumbed to her injuries.

Meredith was inconsolable, blaming herself for Mellow's death. In the days that followed, she became increasingly distraught, isolating in her room and missing classes. She began restricting food, which is not unusual in young adults following trauma (Farber, 2002), especially in those who have suffered from abuse. She also began cutting her upper thighs in an attempt to relieve the unremitting guilt and pain of loss.

Without skills to cope with the traumatic loss, she began to experience suicidal thoughts. A visit to the college health center revealed scars in varying stages of healing. Meredith stated that she "could not go on" without Mellow. How could she live when she had caused Mellow's death?

It was determined that Meredith needed immediate treatment and was referred to an off-campus clinic.

Assessment

At intake, it seemed most appropriate to refer Meredith to the clinic's DBT program. She began meeting with her individual therapist, who conducted a thorough assessment and provided psychoeducation regarding the various components of the DBT program in which Meredith would be engaged.

Next was the identification of feelings and thoughts that prompted the self-harming behaviors and suicidal ideation. It was determined that Meredith's guilt over Mellow's death was the primary triggers of those symptoms. But her parents' ongoing mental health issues – during which hers remained unconsidered – were equally brought into focus.

Meredith's DBT therapist prioritized her behavioral and cognitive goals as reduction of self-harming behaviors and redirecting suicidal ideation respectively. She was also presented with a DBT contract that encouraged mutual acceptance of responsibility for outcomes, as well as an agreement to attend individual and skills training sessions for six months. These treatment goals align with DBT's priority of first addressing problems that threaten life, followed by problems that threaten therapy, as clients cannot improve if they are not involved in therapy (Perseius et al., 2003).

Meredith had never heard of DBT before and was initially hesitant to engage in the time commitment required, but she was unable to resume a full class schedule until her participation was confirmed. She ultimately signed the contract.

In responding to the questionnaire, Meredith shared the many names Mellow had been given, from terms of endearment like Mellow Yellow Fellow to playful monikers like Creamsicle.

Her responses indicated surprise that they had spent a great deal of time together. It had never occurred to Meredith that adopting Mellow satisfied a deep need for stable companionship that would help maintain affective stability. Meredith had felt safe in this exchange of unconditional love and physical affection. She now felt a sort of psychic death at Mellow's loss and was less able to manage her emotions.

These realizations brought Meredith comfort, altered her thoughts about her stewardship, and contributed to the development of treatment goals. Meredith had never been taught coping skills, nor did she believe it was even possible to self-moderate emotional states.

Treatment plan

It was determined that Meredith would attend the full DBT program, including the weekly skills training group and individual therapy for six months until the school year ended, at which point she would be referred to a supplemental program near her home.

The skills training group rotated through the five modules of DBT, including the following:

♦ Mindfulness Skills, which form the essential core of DBT skills, enhance the ability to stay in the moment to extract the fullness of a positive experience and to trust that a distressing moment will ultimately self-moderate if the person does not attempt to amplify or suppress its expression (Linehan, 2015b). Meredith was given guided meditations to help her practice returning to the present moment. She especially enjoyed the chart called Wise Mind, which helped determine when her emotions were less informed by logic.

♦ Interpersonal Effectiveness Skills are meant to help individuals manage interpersonal transactions more effectively by first clarifying what they want or need from an encounter and how much they are willing to negotiate to achieve their goal (Linehan, 2015b). Although it was important for Meredith to process her disappointment over her roommate's carelessness, she did not wish to alienate them. She was able to practice exactly what she would say about Mellow's death, acknowledging it as a series of errors, rather than blaming any one person, including herself.

♦ Emotion Regulation Skills better manage emotions (Linehan, 2015b). Meredith was encouraged to return to healthy eating and sleeping by planning meals and setting a regular bedtime. Thought stopping and redirection toward happier memories helped her manage thoughts of Mellow, which inevitably appeared during quiet times. She engaged in a Safe Place Exercise and Paced Breathing to calm bedtime tension.

♦ Distress Tolerance Skills are primarily intended for difficult circumstances that arise suddenly and focus on getting through the crisis as effectively as possible (Linehan, 2014). Such skills may include holding ice, utilizing all the senses, or grounding physical exercise. When Meredith overheard a friend observing that there should have been signage on both sides of the locked door, she became upset. Rather than participate in this triggering discussion, Meredith returned to her own room, washed her face with cold water, and turned on some loud music as emotional homeopathy mirroring her own amplifying emotions.

♦ Walking the Middle Path (Linehan, 2015a) was a strategy Meredith was encouraged to adopt, seeing Mellow's death as a series of events over which no one person had complete control. Part of that acceptance included acknowledging that Mellow herself knew she was not allowed to go outside yet continued to defy this mandate. That a car was passing at the moment she stepped onto the road was a fact that no one could have foreseen. Meredith's acceptance of responsibility for one aspect of the tragedy did not mean accepting total responsibility for Mellow's death.

Other interventions in Meredith's treatment plan included the following:

♦ Diary Card was a task that Meredith was encouraged to complete every day. The card noted the intensity of her most problematic emotions, which were listed as grief, anger, loneliness, and fear. The card helped Meredith recognize how multiple emotions can coexist and that they had specific environmental triggers.

◆ A chain analysis is a detailed behavioral assessment that reviews vulnerabilities in the client's environment that trigger maladaptive responses the client is trying to avoid (Linehan, 2015a). For example, when engaged in binge eating, Meredith was encouraged to make note of every thought and feeling that preceded the urge and then note what alternative actions or thoughts she could have utilized. Such triggers included missing Mellow, which inevitably led to feelings of guilt and pain over how she had died. Redirecting her thoughts or engaging in physical exercise were options that helped Meredith reduce the intensity of negative emotions.

◆ Radical acceptance is a term that does not imply agreement with a difficult circumstance or outcome, or that suggests that no remedial action will be taken. Rather, by fully accepting one's circumstance in the present moment, the energy of rumination about its unfairness or difficulty can instead be more constructively directed. By ceasing protest over what is, the person may move from negative rumination to the more constructive endeavors of problem-solving, rebuilding, and remediation (Linehan, 2014; Robins et al., 2004). Accepting the reality of Mellow's death – aside from transient feelings of culpability – released Meredith from the constant rumination of the "what ifs" and "should haves," which can protract action planning and prolong mourning.

◆ Noticing joy is a skill that suggests that there are moments that can offer respite, even among life's most aversive events. For example, friends' love and support during bereavement can foster a sense of gratitude. Meredith's roommates were mourning Mellow's loss with her, and her initial anger had eliminated access to this support. Noticing joy brought intentional focus to the fact that they were also grieving. It felt good to reconnect with them; often they would order pizza and recollect Mellow's most amusing antics. Such moments are important to capture and hold as comforting resources to be revisited in moments of distress.

Outcome
Eventually, after several months, Meredith's guilt began to subside as she practiced new skills for management of her grief and guilt. She was now able to view Mellow's death as a tragic accident, after which her regret was relegated to one behavior. Meredith particularly enjoyed mindfulness exercises to maintain emotional control. With practice, her ability to regulate her emotions included reduction of suicidal ideation and elimination of self-harming behaviors. She felt committed to staying alive and creating a "life worth living," as Linehan describes it. Finally, with the adoption of effective skills to manage emotions, she was able to accept that her capacity to derive joy and peace from an animal was a gift and not indicative of any deficit. She knew she would eventually welcome another animal into her home. Meredith continued treatment for her other childhood traumas for an additional two years. Perhaps Mellow's legacy to Meredith was bringing her to healing.

Chapter summary

This chapter focused on utilizing cognitive behavioral therapies to help stewards heal from animal companion loss. Two models were presented, cognitive behavior therapy and dialectical behavior therapy, both evidence-based options for the treatment of depression and anxiety, including that emanating from grief.

Basic CBT finds its curative power in the identification and moderation of cognitive distortions that lead to difficult emotions and maladaptive behaviors, while dialectical behavior therapy focuses on improvement of clients' abilities to regulate emotions through skillful use of coping strategies. With its biosocial theory that emotion dysregulation is a product of biology and environment, DBT relieves client shame, but not the responsibility for remediating skills deficits. Both models can be effectively applied to animal companion grief reactions, as guilt and trauma can create negative self-appraisals and emotional tsunamis for which stewards may lack management skills.

Two case studies were presented, one in which maladaptive cognitions thwarted mourning's progress and the other in which difficulties with emotion regulation were reactivated by guilt and grief. In each case study, specific strategies, tasks, and interventions were referenced. Both case studies recognized that an animal's loss can trigger significant grieving, and also that the deceased animal may have served as an important coping mechanism whose purpose must now be incorporated into healing. Finally, the knowledge, strategies, and coping skills gained from these models can have lasting benefits to clients well beyond healing from the loss of companion animals.

7

Trauma approaches to healing animal companion loss

I cannot walk to that field without imagining how lost Trixie felt. She did not know where to go. Sometimes I wake up sweating, gasping, thinking I feel her panic. I will never know her fate. – Janet, seven months after her miniature greyhound ran away

So spoke a young woman whose animal had bolted into nearby woods when an explosion frightened her. Trixie had never pulled on her leash or wandered far, but in an instant, she was gone. Months later, Janet was still experiencing flashbacks and nightmares of calling out repeatedly for a nonresponsive Trixie. While she gave immediate chase, and the ensuing search lasted three months, Trixie was never found.

Traumatic symptoms, which may follow animal companion death, can become their own treatment target when they complicate the grieving process. Such symptoms may occur after witnessing, perceiving, or experiencing an atrocity or threat to the health, life, or well-being of oneself or a loved one while feeling powerless to change or impact the outcome or circumstances (Herman, 1997). Without treatment that specifically addresses traumatic reactions like hyperarousal, flashbacks, or nightmares, this co-occurring disturbance may persist for years in vulnerable individuals (McFarlane, 2010; van der Kolk, 2000).

DOI: 10.4324/9781003145929-8

In this chapter, we will consider two evidence-based models that are effective for the treatment of trauma, secondary trauma, or PTSD, all of which may complicate grief following animal companion loss (Stamm, 1999). They are trauma-focused cognitive behavior therapy (TF-CBT), developed by Michael White (2007), and eye movement desensitization and reprocessing (EMDR), developed by Francine Shapiro, 2001; Shapiro & Forrest, 2016; van der Kolk, 2014; Hoogsteder et al., 2022).

Both TF-CBT and EMDR address symptoms of trauma expressed across multiple realms, including:

◆ biological (somatic manifestations; reactions to sounds, smells, and tastes; nightmares that disrupt sleep),
◆ cognitive (maladaptive ruminative thoughts, misattributions, cognitive errors),
◆ behavioral (risk-taking or potentially destructive behaviors),
◆ affective (hyperarousal, hypervigilance, or difficulty regulating emotions), and
◆ social or interpersonal states (withdrawal or difficulties in interpersonal transactions due to easily triggered emotions).

These two approaches have been successfully utilized for grief work and can be embedded within, or concurrently offered with, other ongoing forms of therapy (Solomon & Rando, 2014; Cohen et al., 2011).

The goals of both approaches, while differently achieved, are to reduce the biological/somatic severity of PTSD symptoms; mediate intrusive ruminative thoughts; correct cognitive errors; teach coping skills; and restore feelings of self-advocacy, control, and safety within one's environment while working to place the experience permanently in the past (Vanderschoot & Dessel, 2022; Jensen et al., 2022).

Persistent traumatic symptoms make it feel as if the threatening event is still occurring (van der Kolk, 2014). Without rapid intervention, emotional disequilibrium may result immediately after the event, several months following its occurrence, or even years later. Development of traumatic symptoms may be even more likely after experiencing traumas that created affective vulnerability, even though the current trauma may not seem as significant as the earlier experience (Breslau et al., 1999).

For example, veterans of war may successfully adapt to civilian life. But as they age, and distractions from family life or career diminish, environmental triggers may reawaken the buried trauma through dreams or renewed distress (Mota, 2016).

Traumatic aspects of animal companion death – including euthanasia, accidents, running away, kidnapping, the sudden discovery of an animal's terminal diagnosis, or awareness of animal mistreatment – are all too common. Such experiences can cause reactions of overwhelming guilt, grief, and powerlessness, which may retrigger symptoms of earlier traumas, complicating and delaying the initiation of normative grieving and a return to normative life (Domino et al., 2021).

For example, witnessing the process of euthanasia – during which disturbing vocalizations or unanticipated movements may occur – could lead to obsessive ruminations and flashbacks now associated with an event that was supposed to be peaceful. For this reason, as Donald Sawyer notes (Sawyer, 1988), it is important to consider "minimizing undesirable psychological effects on observers, and operative personnel and the animals involved."

Even when the process is smooth, the simple act of witnessing the death of a beloved companion animal, and feeling "responsible" for that choice, can prompt long-term reactions that can thwart normative grieving. During those critical moments, stewards may forget, revisit, or rage against the medical advice or regard themselves as the animal's murderer.

In addition, the person who brought the animal for treatment or made the decision to euthanize may be resented by others if there is disagreement or a lack of acceptance about how ill the animal was. They may then experience a complex form of traumatic grief, which could remain unresolved unless that person receives treatment.

In addition, if the death was that of an emotional-support or service animal, their loss may retrigger the symptoms of the previous trauma or disability acquisition, especially if that circumstance was the main reason for their adoption (Ferrell & Crowley, 2023).

In all probability, most animals – domestic or wild – could potentially be designated as emotional-support animals due to their ability to distract, comfort, or awe humans simply by their presence in the room, fields, seas, or skies! But in the case of domestic animals, the mutually satisfying exchanges of affection and companionship have definite health and mental health benefits (Jau & Hodgson, 2018). The allowed presence of emotional-support animals in areas from which they were previously excluded (planes, restaurants, hospitals, government agencies, stores) is based on multiple studies which repeatedly demonstrate their indisputable ability to reduce fear in anxious individuals, motivate healthy, constructive behaviors, and provide guidance and companionship to disabled individuals, be those disabilities mental or physical.

Like any significant loss, the death of an animal companion may represent a wide variety of additional losses. Successful therapy extends and explores the client's insight to include all aspects of the loss; thus understood, new perceptions and beliefs may emerge. For this reason, both TF-CBT and EMDR focus on all the thoughts, feelings, circumstances, and somatic experiences that may manifest in traumatic responses to loss.

Supplementing both approaches with the Animal Companion Bereavement Questionnaire may be especially helpful, as the trigger for traumatic symptoms may not be obvious; delving into the details of an animal's death or illness, and the steward's role in each, can help define the reaction and what is needed for the restoration of safety and functional homeostasis.

Trauma-focused cognitive behavior therapy (TF-CBT)

TF-CBT, developed by Anthony Mannarino, Judith Cohen, and Esther Deblinger (Paul, 2017; Cohen et al., 2017), was initially conceptualized as a short-term trauma-treatment model, primarily for children and adolescents. An important component of this treatment is the inclusion of parents – at least those who are not the source of the trauma and are regarded as safe and supportive helpers and attachment figures (Cohen & Mannarino, 2015; Pleines, 2019).

Although TF-CBT is highly effective at improving youth post-traumatic stress disorder symptoms, a PTSD diagnosis is not required to receive this treatment. It appears that this treatment's most facilitative component, like other forms of trauma therapy, is controlled exposure to the traumatic memory, followed by processing and interpreting its meaning (Lowe & Murray, 2014).

Many children and adolescents present with varying internal or external symptoms after a traumatic event. TF-CBT comprehensively assesses all symptoms across cognitive, emotional, and behavioral realms, while also attending to the distress that may be evidenced by their caregivers. Both caregivers and children are introduced to coping skills designed to reduce symptoms and increase supportive interactions (Cohen et al., 2012). It has been found to be more effective than EMDR in child/adolescent populations (Lewey et al., 2018). TF-CBT has also been successfully applied to adult and family populations (Mavranezouli et al., 2020) although its primary efficacy rests with children, adolescents, and their families.

TF-CBT utilizes the acronym PRACTICE to describe its focal points: psychoeducation; relaxation; affective modulation; cognitive coping; trauma narrative and emotional processing; in vivo desensitization, conjoint session, and enhancing safety (Cohen et al., 2017).

It is essential in any treatment for trauma, but especially for children, that the therapist provides a sense of a safe caregiver, as the client seeks to assimilate the traumatic experience through measured reexposure. TF-CBT focuses on restoring or enhancing cognitive coping with the trauma, that is, untangling the cognitive distortions about the self, other, and the world from the influence of the trauma. In addition, skills introduction enhances management of triggered affect, moderating reactions to the reexposure. The pairing of relaxation exercises amidst exposure helps contain triggered affect.

TF-CBT addresses clients' perception of the trauma – why it happened and what it means for the future – with an eye toward moderating cognitive distortions about how they interpret it. The process of desensitization is a safely controlled environment in which they can work toward a more objective recollection.

Case study: the struggle for breath

Eight-year-old Matthew had been treated for childhood leukemia for the past two years. His inpatient treatments sometimes caused severe nausea, which provoked breathing difficulties due to a sensation of choking. Still, Matthew had been doing well in school and sports, and evidenced a keen interest in chess. He was popular among his friends and extremely responsible.

The child, who was interested in biology and all forms of animal life, had been asking his parents to acquire a fish tank for the past year. After careful consideration, they bought and stocked a 20-gallon tank with discus, rasboras, and tetras.

Matthew cared for the tank's inhabitants diligently. He spent many hours watching the fish, as did his friends. He particularly admired one beautifully colored discus, whom he named Tiki.

One afternoon, during a visit from a group of classmates, one of them emptied a bottle of soda into the tank. Matthew was not present at the time, but after his friends left, he returned to find all the fish floating lifelessly on the water's surface, including his much-adored Tiki.

His parents attempted to comfort Matthew, eventually determining that the culprit was one of his friends, who had no idea about the consequences of his actions. But that did not console Matthew for the loss of his fish, especially Tiki. He kept imagining how they had been unable to breathe, and these thoughts triggered recollection of his own experiences with nausea and breathlessness.

At home, Matthew became tearful whenever he entered his room and saw the empty place where the tank had been. He experienced anxiety attacks at school when smells from the cafeteria permeated his class, prompting recollection of hospital odors during his illness. He became distracted, withdrawn, and estranged from the classmate who had caused the catastrophe.

After conferring with his concerned teachers, his parents brought Matthew to a social worker they'd met in the hospital.

Assessment

As a social worker assigned to the children's oncology unit, the therapist was already familiar with Matthew, his health history, and his supportive parents, and Matthew trusted her. She recalled Matthew as a brave, cooperative child who had rarely protested throughout his years of treatment. Together, they confirmed his symptoms of anxiety, weight loss, and ruminative guilt.

The therapist, who was trained in TF-CBT, frequently brought her Cavalier King Charles pup to the office, as she knew that Matthew and many of her other clients loved animals. While it does not yet appear that the addition of animal-assisted therapy to TF-CBT delivers consistently more effective impact (Allen et al., 2022), there are some reports of enhanced outcomes. More studies suggest that the presence of animals in the therapy room enhances communication and fosters a safe environment (Compitus, 2021; Sable, 2013).

Matthew reported feeling fine over the last year, rarely thinking about his treatment for leukemia. Instead, as his strength grew, he looked forward to adopting an animal, and starting with fish seemed like the easiest way.

After Matthew's primary assessment, his therapist introduced questions from the Animal Companion Bereavement Questionnaire to better understand his relationship with his fish, especially Tiki.

Matthew became very animated when talking about the fish, associating his full recovery from leukemia with his parents' allowing him to acquire them. The fish tank seemed to confirm that he was now well and cured of his illness.

Matthew saw aspects of himself in Tiki, the strongest fish in the tank, who had been given as a reward for his survival. He had expected that Tiki would live for many years. The child then shared that he had often wondered if there had been doubt that he himself would live, but he had never posed this question directly to his caregivers.

Observing how the boy associated the fish with his recovery, the therapist pointed out that there had been a large fish tank in the room where he had received chemotherapy treatments. Matthew appeared startled by this revelation – he did not remember it at all.

Treatment plan

The therapist then described the course of TF-CBT treatment, its inclusions, and goals to Matthew and his parents. The therapist then began the three phases of treatment associated with TF-CBT, stabilization, trauma narration, and integration (Peters et al., 2021).

Stabilization phase: The therapist met with Matthew individually to further explore his experience and understanding of his symptoms. Matthew's problems included a high degree of reactivity toward environmental triggers of memories associated with his cancer treatment such as smells that provoked symptoms of nausea, feelings of suffocation and breathlessness, negative projections about his health and future, and guilt that he had not been more watchful over his aquarium friends on that fateful day. He was also experiencing school avoidance, protesting the bus ride, which made him feel claustrophobic. Matthew's appetite fluctuated with his symptoms of nausea and anxiety, resulting in a significant weight loss.

The primary targets of the stabilization phase would be reducing Matthew's symptoms of anxiety and moderating his cognitive error in assuming total guilt for the deaths of Tiki and his other fish; reinforcing feelings of safety in his immediate environment; and exploring his experience and understanding of what he had endured while hospitalized. It was clear that the incident had indeed retriggered Matthew's distressing experience of those two years.

As Matthew's anxiety was a prominent, ongoing symptom, the therapist began treatment by introducing a method of relaxation. She presented the Safe Space exercise, in which Matthew could envision a place where he felt completely safe. At one time that had been his room, watching the hypnotic movements of his fish swimming. But now, as Matthew could not think of any current safe place, he constructed an imaginary one: a beautiful spring meadow at the top of a hill overlooking a valley. The meadow was full of animals of all kinds, many of them tame. They approached Matthew as he sat cross-legged, waiting to pet them. He was wearing a short-sleeved shirt, which signified that he was well and had no port in his arm or chest for medications associated with his illness.

As Matthew described this scene, his therapist watched him visibly relax. She encouraged him to think of this safe place on the ride to school to distract from any building anxiety.

Matthew's primary cognitive issue was believing that he was the cause of the fishes' death, because he had not been watchful enough. To help correct that distortion, Matthew was encouraged to recall in great detail all that he had done to care for them: his diligence with regard to the cleanliness of their tank, the quality of their food, and the appropriate levels of light and temperature.

Trauma narration and processing phase: Matthew's initial recollection narrative of his fishes' death centered on his failure to watch over their tank while his friends were with him. He repeatedly returned to the fact that he had left his bedroom to go to the kitchen to have a snack, instead of bringing the food back to his bedroom.

How could he possibly know, his therapist asked, that one of his friends would even think of pouring soda into the tank? He had not abandoned his fish, she further pointed out; he had been out of his bedroom for only half an hour. His friend's actions were not his fault.

Matthew struggled with letting go of self-recrimination until his therapist asked how he would feel if his parents had been home when this occurred. In that situation, he was able to understand; he would have blamed his friend, not his parents. Matthew was able to adopt a new cognition that gave his narrative a different perspective: Although he had done everything he could for his fish, he could not control or anticipate the behavior of others.

Once Matthew separated his feeling of responsibility from the facts of the tragedy, he was able to begin mourning a double loss – that of his fish, as well as the two years he had lost to cancer treatment.

Integration and consolidation phase: Matthew's reluctance to adopt another animal was addressed, as were the two aspects of his school avoidance: the bus ride to school, during which he felt claustrophobic, and the smells that sometimes led to nausea.

Matthew successfully used his Safe Place exercise during bus rides. It also helped that his father followed behind the bus in his car for a few weeks. After that experimental period, Matthew was able to ride the bus on his own.

The smells from the cafeteria and from industrial detergents proved more challenging. Matthew and his therapist constructed a one-to-ten scale to determine which odors were most triggering. He was then asked to recall appealing fragrances, like chocolate, newly cut grass, and fresh-baked cookies. The therapist would occasionally insert more problematic scents – garlic, cooking oil, cleaning agents – into the list.

The goal was to tolerate the smells or to ask his teacher's permission to leave the room. Matthew's seat was moved closer to a window, and he was assured that he could leave the room if he felt overwhelmed. It appeared that these options greatly reduced his reactivity.

The final challenge was to revisit his hospitalization. He had sensed that his predicament was serious, even though it was never addressed. His parents' lack of acknowledgment during his illness had only increased Matthew's fear.

Now he was able to directly ask his parents if his life had been in danger. He was reassured by their honest response: He indeed might have died, but medical interventions rapidly improved his prognosis, and his tolerance and endurance had brought him to full remission. This appeared to help Matthew restore trust in his parents.

Outcome

Matthew gradually became less anxious about going to school in the morning. After being prescribed medication to address his lack of appetite, he began to feel hungry again, the smells from the cafeteria now associated with food he liked rather than anxiety.

He was eventually able to speak with the boy who had poisoned the fish tank and accept his apology. This social remediation also helped Matthew feel safer at school and reduced his anxiety.

Matthew's parents acknowledged that they had only been trying to protect him by withholding the seriousness of his condition. They now understood that this very intelligent, intuitive, and cooperative child would have benefited from ongoing feedback about his condition. After several months without further symptoms, Matthew adopted a turtle, and the following year, a parakeet.

Eye movement desensitization and reprocessing (EMDR)

EMDR was developed by Francine Shapiro in 1987 as a treatment for PTSD or associated symptoms. It incorporates theory from several other evidence-based approaches, like psychodynamic, cognitive behavioral, attachment theory, communications theory, and trauma theory (Shapiro, 2001).

Named for its most novel and controversial component – bilateral stimulation through eye movements – this treatment was initially met with skepticism even while producing consistently excellent results among its recipients. Such results included rapid reduction in symptoms of PTSD (including the ability to recall the trauma without feeling it was in the present), reduction of overwhelming affect, restoration of emotional stability, reduction of hypervigilance, remediation of cognitive errors, reinstallation of trust in the self, and creating a meaning that does not blame the victim, restoring the client's self-worth and agency (Wilson et al., 2018).

One study applying EMDR to the treatment of grief after COVID showed how comparisons can be drawn to losses of animal companions, as stewards may face similar circumstances following their deaths. For example, during the pandemic, mourners were often not able to say goodbye, families had no access to social rituals and funeral services, and many of the deaths were sudden and unexpected (Solomon & Hensley, 2020).

One theory explaining the efficacy of EMDR is that it facilitates the processing of traumatic material thought to be "stuck" in the amygdala. Shapiro describes this as a "digestive process," in which such material then moves to the frontal lobes, which are our meaning-making systems, where it can finally be processed and released (Shapiro, 1998, 2002). Bessel van der Kolk et al. (2007) describes this facilitative component as helping to reposition the trauma, finally, in the past.

Recently, the utility of bilateral eye movements as part of treatment has been likened to the information processing that occurs during REM sleep (Farrell, 2018), which also prompts bilateral movement of the eyes. While many practitioners employ other methods to facilitate this effect, including alternate tapping of clients' hands, it appears that eye movements are more effective.

EMDR's protocol guides the client through eight stages: history taking, preparation, assessment, desensitization, installation, body scan, closure, and reevaluation, each of which is carefully introduced to avoid potentially retriggering or exacerbating the symptoms of PTSD (Menon & Jayan, 2010; Shapiro, 1998).

As EMDR can elicit unknown or forgotten aspects of the trauma, the client should have reliable soothing skills in order to reduce retriggered memories or associations. If the client does not have such skills or is experiencing one of the contraindicated factors, the possibility of reintroducing EMDR may be revisited once the client has achieved a degree of emotional stability through coping skills or medication. Careful assessment is advised when offering EMDR to clients who have verbalized suicidal ideation, due to the potential for escalated affect the intervention may trigger (Spector, 2009). In addition, when numbness, denial, or dissociative symptoms are being experienced, the delivery of EMDR may be premature or contraindicated (Solomon, 2018; Solomon & Hensley, 2020).

Case study: professional and personal devotion

Next to the flag-draped casket stood an easel featuring a portrait of a majestic German shepherd whose multihued fur shone and whose eyes radiated intelligence. A nearby table was heaped with plaques, trophies, and newspaper clippings, all evidence of a hero's life. Dozens of chairs in this suburban town hall were filled by those who had come to mourn Apollo, the highly trained K-9 killed in the line of duty, literally taking a bullet for his partner.

Sam, a DEA agent and Apollo's human partner for five years, stood by in full uniform. Apollo had been assigned to Sam upon his promotion from research to field work. Sam had never had a dog before and was not thrilled to be assigned a canine partner. But their intensive training and living together over eight months forged a collaboration that resulted in many seizures and apprehensions.

No human partner could have heard the faint creak of a floor-board, indicating the approach of the criminal they'd arrived to arrest. But Apollo heard it and turned to face the threat from the man, whose gun was already drawn.

By the time Sam also saw him, Apollo was in the air, intercepting the bullet. Sam returned fire and wounded the per-petrator, after which his colleagues emerged from their positions to assist.

Sam collapsed on the floor, watching the light leave Apollo's eyes. He let out a primal sound he had never made in his life.

Sam did not attend the arraignment of the suspect, fearful of what he might do when face-to-face with Apollo's killer. The loss of Apollo was an experience unlike any Sam had endured in his 52 years – and such losses included the deaths of family members, close friends, and other DEA officers. Sam had been unable to sleep or eat for the past four days. Now, in the arms of an agency friend, Sam was sobbing, repeating Apollo's name. Feeling broken and defeated at the sight of his partner's casket, he could not imagine how he would ever recover. His strong and constant faith failed him. His worried family could not comfort him.

Sam wanted to change places with Apollo – or to join him. His thoughts about doing so were dark and persistent. He felt a frantic grief, a disconnection from himself, a loss of spirit. He never imagined the death of a dog could cripple his soul, even though he had loved Apollo as he had loved no one else.

After three months of unremitting grief expressed through guilt, irritability, anger, and flashbacks of the moment Apollo was shot, Sam's boss insisted he get help. He had become short with colleagues and detached from a job that required total focus and rapid response.

Sam reluctantly engaged with a therapist in their employer-sponsored network but felt invalidated by the counselor's insistence that his extreme grief must also be the result of other cumulative losses in his life. Feeling invalidated and misunderstood, Sam stopped going to therapy. He felt alone in his alienated state; family and friends were perplexed by his unremitting grief, although they claimed to understand it.

The only time Sam felt at peace was when he took his boat out to fish in the lake. Apollo had often accompanied him there, with nothing but the rippling water and the boat's gentle rocking to disturb their peace. Occasionally, Apollo would sniff the air, delighting in new smells, or stare into Sam's eyes in a deep communion before lowering his magnificent head and closing his eyes. Sam would stroke the soft fur of Apollo's back, the sun emblazoning his coat with glistening colors. This time together was a restorative off-duty paradise.

Eventually, Sam's family physician prescribed hypnotic and antianxiety medication to help ease his persistent symptoms. These were helpful in restoring his sleep, but Sam's intense mourning continued. While he no longer felt suicidal, he had lost his robust attachment to life, his vibrant personality, and his passion for his work. Intimacy and activities with his children became sporadic.

He remained full of guilty regret that he could not shield or save Apollo, even though he had always known their work together might end this way. That Apollo had been lost in the line of duty – fulfilling his mission to bring criminals to justice and protect his partner – was of little solace to Sam.

Assessment

With his irritation and anger still easily provoked, Sam was directed to return to his EAP therapist, who now recommended that he seek EMDR treatment. Upon meeting with his certified EMDR therapist, Sam was deemed to be an appropriate candidate because he continued to experience symptoms of PTSD via flashbacks, nightmares, and mood dysregulation. Sam's suicidal ideation had ceased, so that potential contraindication was removed. It was also relevant that he had a loving, supportive family and was taking medication to restore his sleep.

EMDR has been found to be an effective intervention for first responders (Morris et al., 2022); more specifically, in one cited case study, EMDR was found to be effective for an adult male's grief over the loss of his dog (Dworkin, 2005, pp. 129–133).

Sam liked his therapist, who lived in the same community and who had brothers working as firefighters. Sam felt he was a down-to-earth, "no-bullshit" therapist who understood the challenges of public service. In addition, his therapist had a picture of his own two Labrador retrievers placed prominently on his desk, which felt validating.

Sam was given a thorough psychoeducation regarding EMDR, including the theory and research that made it an evidence-based treatment for trauma. He agreed to participate, hoping it would help calm intrusive memories and reduce emotional reactivity. To this history taking, his therapist added specific questions from the Animal Companion Bereavement Questionnaire; most relevant was how his relationship with Apollo had evolved from one of uncertain acceptance to the deepest emotional attachment of Sam's life. The therapist reviewed the activities and work ethic they shared; how Apollo had changed him through the uniqueness of their relationship and the strength of their bond; Sam's admiration for Apollo's intelligence and loyalty; and how Apollo had died, giving his own life to save Sam's.

Treatment plan

The therapist began applying the eight phases of EMDR to Sam's case according to its accepted protocols (Leeds, 2016):

History taking: Sam had grown up in a middle-class family, and while his parents were strict disciplinarians, Sam did not experience it as abuse. He felt loved and well regarded by his family. After earning a degree, he chose to enter the police force, like his father.

He had been married for 17 years, describing his marriage as warm and supportive. His three children were faring well. He had loved his work until this tragedy occurred. Other than normative life events, such as the death of his mother, Sam could not recall any other events which had so deeply affected his sense of well-being, will to live, and emotional stability.

> **Preparation:** During the next phase, the establishment of the therapeutic alliance was a prominent fe3ature. The client and therapist discussed the goals of the treatment, including how any triggered affect will be managed.

An effective form of relaxation is an important component of EMDR (and any treatment for trauma). Clients are encouraged to consistently practice methods of relaxation so they may be quickly introduced if the client becomes activated during the exposure phase.

Sam was introduced to progressive muscle relaxation, developed by Edmond Jacobson (Toussaint et al., 2021), in which groups of muscles are successively tensed and released. By listening to a guided meditation every evening, Sam found his body began to habituate and relax upon hearing even the beginning of the recording. In this way, the therapist had only to play the first few moments of the recording and Sam would begin to relax.

Finally, the clinician and Sam created a Subjective Units of Distress Scale, a system developed by Joseph Wolpe (Toussaint et al., 2021). To create a scale unique to Sam's reactions, he was asked to describe physical sensations of anxiety as they escalated and where he felt them in his body; he would then associate them with a number on the scale. In this way, the clinician can better understand the intensity of the triggered affect and deescalate the exposure if necessary.

For example, when discussing his love for Apollo, Sam felt an aching in his chest, which he rated a 4 or 5 level of distress. But when describing the moment that Apollo was shot, his hands would sweat, and he would feel a sense of dizziness, as if his throat were closing. Such reactions rated a 9 or 10. While it was considered unlikely that Sam would ever recall that moment with zero distress, the goal was for Sam to be able to think of it without feeling unbearable emotion, as if it were still continuing.

> **Assessment:** Now Sam was ready for the actual processing and desensitiszation. He was asked to recall an image that represented the most disturbing aspect of the trauma. For Sam, that moment was when he turned to see Apollo fall to the floor. He was then asked to associate that moment with a negative cognition, which for Sam was: "I failed to protect Apollo; I was a bad partner."

When prompted to extend this thought, Sam expressed the belief that Apollo died because he was incompetent and unfocused, that he did not deserve Apollo's loyalty and that he failed to accurately assess the degree of danger.

Sam was then asked to describe (Shapiro, 2001) how much, on a scale of 1 to 7, he actually believed this negative cognition. Initially, he stated his total belief in the negative cognition, rating it a 7. Next, Sam was asked to consider a more positive, substitute cognition. After much thought and hesitation, Sam softly said, "Apollo and I were just doing our jobs. We were both courageous. I was a trustworthy partner for five years."

> **Desensitization:** Sam was asked to recall and hold the image of Apollo falling while considering the negative cognition. From a predetermined, comfortable distance of about four feet, the therapist used his hand to direct Sam's eye movements back and forth. Sam was encouraged to articulate any new material that arose during this phase.

(Although there are other methods of bilateral stimulation for clients engaged in EMDR, following the therapist's hand may help continue the trusted connection during a period of great vulnerability. The therapist can also more easily control the speed of the movements, stopping to ground the client if there is evidence of substantial distress.)

The therapist carefully observed Sam for any somatic symptoms. The bilateral stimulation continued for several rounds until Sam's belief in the negative cognition began to decrease.

Installation: During this phase, Sam was again reminded to share any new material that arose. He was now asked to pair the same troubling image with the positive cognition – that he was a reliable, responsible partner and they were both just doing their jobs. Again, several rounds of bilateral stimulation occurred. At this point, Sam began to recall other details, including the fact that the gunman had emerged from an open window in the back room, which he had already checked. In fact, Sam realized that he had indeed completed all standard safety protocols.

In addition, Sam recalled and felt the experience of sitting in his boat with Apollo on the lake. He was able to feel the depth of the loving bond they shared for the first time since Apollo's death. While this memory brought instant tears, it also brought great relief that Sam's connection to Apollo remained. He was able to consider that their unique bond of five years far outweighed the ten seconds that took Apollo's life.

Body scan: Sam was asked to close his eyes and trace any remaining feelings of distress, and identify where they were located in his body. (Such feelings may linger after installation and are not necessarily associated with a negative outcome. Clients should be advised that this "processing" may continue for several hours or days, in dreams or daydreams. The numbing aspects of trauma may resolve through finally experiencing the grief.)

Sam felt more able to accept Apollo's death as a tragic event that occurred during the very dangerous work they performed together. He realized that they both constantly risked their lives and that Apollo's enthusiastic barks once in the van together evidenced his own enjoyment of their work. Sam described these feelings as being deep within his chest. While sad, they no longer evoked panic.

> **Closure:** Because the memories elicited through EMDR therapy may continue to emerge after the session, Sam was assured that if any uncomfortable memories or feelings arose, this was a normal occurrence, but he could reach out to his therapist if they became troubling. He was encouraged to use progressive muscle relaxation to calm residual anxiety and to note any additional thoughts that arose.

Sam did indeed have vivid dreams of Apollo in the days that followed. Not all of them were related to the tragedy – some were pleasant recollections of their off-duty time together in which Sam felt that Apollo was assuring him that he was okay.

> **Reevaluation:** During this final phase of treatment, the therapist and Sam reevaluated the sustained impact of the sessions to determine what level of resolution has been achieved, and if there are other aspects of the trauma that needed review or further processing. Sam felt he was now able to balance his distress at Apollo's death with his pride in their work and life together. He now appropriately attributed Apollos' death to the criminal who caused it. While he still felt extreme sadness at the loss of Apollo, his feelings of guilt were extinguished.

Outcome

After eight sessions of EMDR, Sam's belief about his role in Apollo's death had changed from assuming complete guilt to the acknowledgment that Apollo's death in the line of duty was similar to that of any other DEA agent. Apollo was an eager partner, whose mastery of all aspects of his job made him a stellar officer. These gifts and loyal dedication ultimately allowed Apollo to save his partner's life.

Sam's evolving belief about his role in Apollo's life and death had an almost immediate impact on his symptoms of PTSD. After four months, he was able to go off his medication. Questions from the ACB Questionnaire helped Sam to imagine himself beyond his immediate grief as a steward and partner, able to eventually accept, incorporate, internalize, and honor Apollo's life. He was able to begin creating a legacy for Apollo without the persistent guilt he had experienced.

While Sam could not yet tolerate the idea of working with another dog, he decided to pursue the training of K-9 teams. Taking such an active role helped Sam overcome his feelings of helplessness and allowed him to describe his life with Apollo to each new class of recruits. His legacy to Apollo was the honoring of their work through his renewed involvement in team development.

Chapter summary

As elements of trauma are frequent components of animal companion loss, two approaches to helping stewards heal from traumatic symptoms of loss were introduced: trauma focused cognitive behavior therapy (TF-CBT) and eye movement desensitization and reprocessing (EMDR). Both expedient, highly effective forms of treatment may be used when severe symptoms of trauma or PTSD emerge after animal companion death or if an animal's death becomes a retriggering event for previously unexplored and unhealed traumas. Both protocols may be effective as stand-alone treatment or adjuvant therapy. While TF-CBT is primarily evidence-based for children, it has found efficacy among adult populations as well. EMDR has been studied primarily in adult populations as an effective and expeditiously relieving treatment for trauma.

Including questions from the Animal Companion Bereavement Questionnaire may be especially important, as the symptoms and causes of PTSD from the loss of the relationship may not be immediately evident to the steward or the therapist.

8

Anticipatory mourning in animal companion loss

I know I don't have much longer with Lucy, but when we are together, she still seems so alive that it is hard to believe I will lose her. – Candace, whose senior feline was receiving cancer treatments

Previous chapters have focused on the experiences of human stewards following their companion animals' deaths. But anticipatory mourning, the subject of this chapter, has different challenges. This sometimes fulfilling, mostly distressing limbo – the time period between the steward's awareness of their animal's impending death and their actual death – may last for weeks, months, or sometimes years (Rando, 2000).

Caregiving stewards must hold two truths while administering interventions necessary for palliative comfort and maintenance of very ill animals: The animal is still alive and will benefit from my care, yet despite that care, the animal will die.

It takes bravery, awareness, and commitment to provide an animal with intensive, home-based treatments that could extend its life. Although it might be assumed that any extra time spent with a beloved animal will bring a more peaceful resolution to grief when the end finally does arrive, that is not always the case.

DOI: 10.4324/9781003145929-9

Jocelyn D'Antoni was writing about human caregivers mourning other humans when she wrote (2014), "The grief of caregivers is complex and often greater in intensity than the grief experience following death" (p. 104). But her conclusion is no less applicable to a steward anticipating the death of an animal family member.

A staff member at the clinic where Candace's cat was being treated wondered if she would benefit from attending the practice's animal companion bereavement group. Yet the idea could be problematic, as she would be confronted with the futile result of her caregiving, which could cause a premature detachment (Rando, 2000). Again, these findings reference human experiences of anticipatory mourning, but they may be applied to animal companion loss once the views of the majority of human stewards – that animals are family members – are taken into account.

In addition, exposing caregivers to the intensity of emotions following animal death could have further negative impact on an already-stressful situation. For example, witnessing the acute grief expressed by group members in mourning could cause the steward to withdraw from their own animal. In that case, caregiving could be resented, or it might cease entirely, potentially denying both animal and steward the opportunity for reciprocal comfort as death approaches.

Animal hospice programs

In the past, formal hospice and palliative care programs for chronically or terminally ill animals were few, and the decision to euthanize an animal or provide pain medication at home was more likely. Thus, animal stewards usually experienced a rather brief period between a terminal diagnosis and the animal's death or euthanasia, a time that could be referred to as "silent grief" or "anticipatory grief" (Rando, 2000).

The common attitude of wanting to sustain human life at all costs did not necessarily translate to animals with terminal illnesses. The lack of animal health insurance we've previously discussed usually precluded costly, life-prolonging interventions.

But advanced technology and pharmacological interventions have now made it possible for animal illnesses to be detected months or years before they become lethal, providing new treatment options and medications that effectively reduce pain or curb disease progression (Aparicio et al., 2022).

Nonetheless, the end result will not be a cure or the resumption of activities that defined the relationship. Instead, the caregiver will likely witness the animal's continuing decline and sometimes its discomfort. As with terminally ill humans, the frustration of providing constant care with no evidence of improvement may evoke feelings of helplessness (Hebert et al., 2007). The absence of emotional support during this time has been linked with protracted and complicated mourning, as caregivers – for humans and animals alike – must face the results of their "failed" caregiving (Reisbig et al., 2017).

The tasks of anticipatory mourning

Challenges and tasks noted in the following paragraphs subsume some of the "generic operations" Rando (2000) associates with anticipatory mourning, including grief and mourning, coping, interaction, psychosocial reorganization, planning, balancing conflicting demands, and facilitating an appropriate death.

Biological: Tasks for caregiving stewards may include maintenance of their own biological needs (like sleeping and eating), balancing self-care with care of the animal, and acknowledging and accepting their limits. Home-based animal care may involve invasive procedures like giving shots and providing medications and special foods, even when the animal is aversive to them. It may include more intimate procedures such as expressing anal glands or cleaning up after incontinent animals. Stewards may need enough strength to carry animals outside or to the litter box.

Psychological: If an animal companion steward is already in treatment for a psychological issue or has a history of affective disturbance, contact with their mental health provider may be prudent, as the stresses of caregiving may increase psychological vulnerabilities. Learning coping skills to manage difficult emotions, facilitate relaxation, or improve interpersonal communication can be helpful. Addressing troubling thoughts, negative self-concepts, or unfounded assumptions about the animal's response to care are best addressed prior to its death. Beginning to articulate a narrative or capture important memories before the animal dies can be a worthy exercise that may lead to a solid foundation for legacy creation. In addition, this period may subject caregivers to renewed or unresolved grief from past losses or put them in touch with their concept of spirituality and the creation of new meaning within the relationship (Doka, 2000).

Social: Challenges for the animal steward may include role restructuring (i.e. "Who am I without my animal?"), imagining the future without the animal, disruption of previous routines, reduced socialization, less opportunity to engage in favorite activities or hobbies, planning for increased caretaking time, and managing the loss of the animal's companionship. Maintaining positive, supportive contact with the animal's medical care providers is essential, along with the need to establish or alter social support networks that may offer respite care or support once the animal passes.

Economic: Financial challenges must be addressed objectively, and stewards should set a potential limit for related expenditures, balancing the costs of animal medical care with their own financial obligations. Loan providers sometimes work with medical practices to offer clients financing at reduced interest rates. Regardless, stewards may experience feelings of guilt arising from setting a limit on the value of their animal companion.

Stewards have been known to accumulate great debt, remortgage homes, max out credit cards, and accept the burden of new loans to obtain treatment for their animals. According to a 2020 Lending Tree survey, nearly half (47 percent) of pet owners have gone into debt for their pet's benefit, up from 36 percent in 2019. Such loans may take years to pay back, long after the animal dies.

Veterinary practices are often generous with discounts for lifesaving care, yet they too have limits. It has been suggested that through the offering of a spectrum of care (Quain et al., 2021), some of the economic disparities might be moderated. In addition, there are national programs that offer grants to supplement veterinary care (Pet Helpers, 2023). There may also be local programs: For example, in New Jersey, CLAWS provides a multitude of services to help stewards manage economic challenges to medical care and access to food. In human hospice programs, economic issues do not as heavily influence treatment decisions due to the presence of public and private insurance. When economic limits do arise, an immediate application for charity care, Medicaid, or community or sponsored programs can help cover such costs.

Mental health support: Many hospice programs for humans help loved ones process the many difficult questions that arise regarding end-of-life care. Families of those in hospice care frequently write letters stating they could not have completed the journey without such support (Aparicio et al., 2022). Many hospice programs also offer emotional care in the form of bereavement groups or staff social workers.

But such support is rarely embedded in animal hospice programs, despite the need. While veterinary staff members may exhibit great compassion, they are not trained to provide mental health services. Human caregivers must usually traverse these challenges by themselves.

As a consequence, stewards may abandon palliative options as their emotional stress increases – potentially clouding the final period of the relationship with stress, regrets, and resentment (Schulz & Sherwood, 2008).

Respite care: Taking time off from intense caregiving is encouraged in human hospice programs, and its value has been well researched (Utz, 2022). Family leave programs can ease the economic difficulties of reduced income while providing home care. Stipends from federal programs for caregivers or private insurance may cover home visits from nurses or other aides.

Such programs and stipends are not available to those caring for dying animals. While animal hospice programs have compassionate staff ready to assist with home visits, these are less likely to be covered services, depending on the limits of the animal's health insurance plan.

Ethical guidance: In dealing with ethical dilemmas affecting human treatment decisions, if the family cannot agree on a course of action and the patient is too incapacitated to make such choices, there is guidance from physicians, social workers, and even bioethics committees. Beyond a beleaguered veterinarian who has no legal recourse when steward disagreement results in a questionable choice, there is often no additional guidance. While a few months or a year of medical interventions does not seem an unreasonable period of time to save or extend the life of a human with an 80-year life span, it represents a significant loss for older or more fragile creatures with much shorter life expectancies. The diminished quality of life for an animal resulting from invasive treatments or chemotherapy may not bring commensurate benefits. Humans can still have quality of life despite many disabilities. For animals, restricted movements are far more life-diminishing.

An animal's awareness of its increasing limitations (avoiding stairs or no longer attempting to jump on the bed) does not mean awareness of its own impending death. The steward, who understands the inevitability of loss, must therefore carry that awareness alone.

The desperation stewards sometimes feel can influence treatment decisions. It is understandable, but ethically challenging, when the steward's anticipatory grief results in choices in which the animal's best interests are no longer the priority, potentially prolonging its suffering (Goldberg, 2019). There are no advanced directives, no conversations that lay out the animal's preference for or against life-extending or invasive treatments.

Disagreements between the steward and the animal's medical team can place veterinary caregivers in a position in which their advice is sought but not taken. Because of animals' legal status as property, veterinarians have little standing to challenge a treatment choice with which they disagree. In one study, up to 57 percent of veterinary respondents indicated they faced one to two ethical dilemmas a week; indeed, "veterinarians are the only healthcare professionals trained to both preserve and end life" (Goldberg, 2019). Animals may endure deaths of great suffering, because human stewards cannot let them go.

The challenging circumstances and tasks associated with anticipatory mourning within the human-animal dyad could greatly benefit from the same mental health, economic, ethical, and practical supports available in human hospice programs. But such resources seem even more scant than the paucity of services for bereavement support.

Case study: a deepening bond

Candace, a 48-year-old woman with a highly stressful job, came into the veterinary hospital with her 16-year-old feline. Lucy had recently lost weight despite a healthy appetite, was shedding fur, drank water voraciously, and used the litter box constantly. It was determined that Lucy was experiencing an acute case of feline diabetes, which had already resulted in organ compromise. She would need insulin, a special diet, and frequent monitoring of vitals and glucose levels.

Candace was uncertain if she would be able to undertake this regimen by herself. She dreaded the thought of having to give shots to her cat. Making more office visits and purchasing insulin and special food would greatly tax her budget. She worried that she would be unsuccessful in caregiving efforts, further compromising Lucy's health.

But Candace received a great deal of support from the devoted staff. Once the vet tech expertly demonstrated how to give Lucy a subcutaneous shot, Candace became more comfortable with the idea.

Lucy appeared to stabilize on the new regimen of insulin, special food, and toys purchased to entice physical play. Candace became more confident in her ability to care for Lucy.

Previously, the pair had been rather independent of each other: Candace worked long hours, while Lucy was content to wander from her window perch to the bed to hunting for rodents or insects.

Previously, most of their time together had occurred in the evenings. Candace and Lucy now began and ended their days together. Although Lucy initially fled as Candace prepared the syringe, she came to understand that it had to be tolerated. As Candace began to feel more competent with these new tasks, she found ways to make the experience less upsetting. She would hold out one of Lucy's favorite treats, which was given only with or immediately following the shot. Their new routines developed a rhythm of their own. Their relationship reached a new level of closeness. For seven months, all went well.

Unfortunately, Lucy's improved health did not last. She lost more weight and became listless. She would not eat. Candace brought her back to the vet, convinced that a simple modification of her diet or medication would restore her to good health. But this time, the diagnosis was sad and shocking: Lucy now had lymphoma, a terminal illness. Since her diabetes precluded several treatment options, Lucy's prognosis was poor. The veterinarian compassionately informed Candace that if she wanted to consider euthanasia, the practice would support this choice.

But Candace was not ready to let Lucy go. Instead, she agreed to introduce medications that might modestly extend her life.

The animal hospital had recently added a hospice program, and Candace and Lucy were invited to enroll. A vet tech would come to her home to monitor Lucy's vitals and glucose levels and ensure that the introduction of the new medications was not compromising her health. Candace herself would receive more consistent support from a dedicated 24-7 hotline, through which she received empathic feedback.

For two more months, Lucy was stable, with most of her symptoms in remission. Their growing closeness no longer made expenditures of time or money feel like a sacrifice, but a worthy investment in a relationship that nurtured them both.

But as spring arrived, the lymphoma returned. When confronted with the reality of Lucy's looming death, Candace was distraught, but Lucy's spirit was still strong, and she sometimes still played like a kitten.

A support group for those in the hospice program was initiated to address the stressors of caregiving, including the anxiety of living within uncertain time frames, recollection of shared pre-diagnosis activities, identifying new gifts emerging from the caregiving relationship, and discussing quality-of-life issues related to euthanasia decisions. Stewards could decide, for instance, where the euthanasia would take place, if they wanted to be present, and rituals could be prearranged, leading to fewer decisions and regrets once the animal passed away.

Candace agreed to attend the group. Appreciating its many benefits, she also contacted one of the therapists referred by the veterinary practice for individual work.

Assessment

Candace began weekly meetings with her new therapist, who herself lived with two canines and one feline. The usual psychodynamic assessment was completed, noting Candace's history of an anxiety disorder and her past experiences with loss, including family members and friends. The goal of therapy was not only to support Candace while moving through the final stages of anticipatory mourning but to assess any associated symptoms that her caretaking of Lucy might trigger as the inevitability of death approached. Candace's therapist supplemented her assessment with questions from the ACB Questionnaire in order to gain more specific information on the history and current status of Candace's evolving relationship with Lucy.

How did Lucy come into your life?

Lucy was an impulsive purchase at an adoption event. When she spotted Lucy, Candace was drawn to her cool, seemingly wise demeanor, her multicolored beauty, and the arresting gaze of her vivid green eyes. The sponsoring agency convinced Candace that Lucy was the perfect animal for her, as she was independent, well-behaved, and quite healthy.

While Candace never regretted adopting Lucy, she had given no thought to what might occur if Lucy became ill. She assumed, as many new animal stewards do, that when the time came to let her go, she would "put her to sleep" under the care of a dedicated veterinarian. She had never considered how a protracted decline in Lucy's health might impact her life, let alone the need for personal involvement in her caregiving.

Candace expressed gratitude that the caregiving experience had added new dimensions to their relationship, including greater closeness and a new self-view as a capable steward, able to demonstrate great compassion. Verbally acknowledging and writing these thoughts could help dispel any associated doubt about her caretaking once Lucy passed.

What names do you have for Lucy?

It is not unusual for stewards to have many names for their domestic or feral animals, reflecting different feelings or stages of life. Candace called Lucy by several names: Lucille Ball when she would scramble after a light-up ball, sometimes crashing into an end table; Lucifer, when she would proudly parade a squirming cockroach in her mouth; Lucky Lucy when receiving her favorite treats during her shots; and Linda Lucy ("linda" being the Spanish word for beautiful) during moments of affection.

As she recalled the instances that triggered each name, Candace's face softened considerably. She noted that she had never before felt so much tenderness toward an animal. Recollection and journaling of these names would provide reminders of the experiences associated with each name following Lucy's death.

Where does Lucy sleep?

While this circumstance may change as an animal becomes increasingly disabled, tracing its evolution can elicit humorous discussion, as stewards may have gone from "No animals on the bed" to welcoming them.

Lucy had always slept on Candace's bed, but now Candace sometimes had to lift her there in response to her short meow. Through this conscious decision to keep Lucy next to her throughout the night, Candace was made aware of the comfort she had felt from Lucy's presence, an acknowledgment that only reinforced her willingness to care for Lucy.

How is this relationship different from past stewardship of animals or other species of animals?

As Candace had never stewarded an animal previous to Lucy, she had no way of comparing this experience, but had not expected to feel the degree of attachment to Lucy that developed during their final months together. Candace had previously found the degree of devotion and sentimentality expressed by her friends toward their animals to be extreme and even strange. She now had an understanding of the strength of such connections.

How much time did you spend with Lucy? All day, evenings, weekends? Did the animal travel on vacations with you?

In the past, Candace and Lucy had spent time together primarily in the early evenings. But now Candace interacted with Lucy intensively at least twice a day.

While they had never vacationed together, some holidays resulted in celebration with nearby family. At these times Candace would purchase and wrap gifts for Lucy, who would play with the ribbon until the box's contents were revealed. Then they would play until the feline raised her tail and walked away, indicating she was now bored with the new toy!

When Candace recalled these memories with Lucy, the cat would gaze deeply into Candace's face as if to say that she too remembered those times.

The intensity of caregiver involvement can be affected by proximity, so those who do not live with the dying person or animal can better balance the idea of their death, even while life continues (Empeño et al., 2013). Candace's intense, live-in involvement with a dying being made mental health support all the more valuable. While such support will not necessarily extinguish the intensity of mourning following death, it may leave the caretaker better prepared to confront the tasks of rebuilding.

Candace concluded that spending more time together had enhanced her life, giving it a purpose beyond any previous relationship. Despite the inconvenience and considerable expense, Candace expressed gratitude for Lucy's presence in her life. Through articulating the gifts inherent in her bond with Lucy, Candace was creating a resource of positive remembrance that could be an important reference after Lucy's death. This can be a lonely time for caregivers as they confront the inevitability of grief and their own limits of endurance.

What activities did you do with Lucy? Did you socialize with the animal?

Candace did not really socialize with Lucy beyond their personal interactions. Animals who are primarily housebound usually socialize only when the steward's friends visit. Candace did not entertain much, but as Lucy's illness continued, friends would sometimes come to the apartment to visit them both.

What special qualities does this animal have?

Candace was impressed that despite Lucy's growing disability and discomfort, she still sometimes managed to act silly and kittenish. In addition, Lucy often stared into Candace's eyes with a knowingness that made Candace feel deeply connected to her. This silent communication brought an otherworldly peace to Candace. She was fascinated by the unwavering stare and dimensional depth in Lucy's eyes.

What qualities does the animal bring out in you?

Candace felt herself to be a more loving and compassionate person, capable of making and keeping a commitment. No other situation in her life had required such constancy, emotional investment, and daily commitment. Because Candace had altered her life and her budget to care for Lucy, she now viewed herself as a compassionate and devoted steward who had done everything in her power to make Lucy's final days as pain-free and peaceful as possible.

Did you talk to this animal?

Candace spoke to Lucy frequently, especially prior to administering her twice-daily shot. She would murmur words of support and encouragement, calling her "Baby" and "Lovey." She would speak to her upon arriving home and while preparing meals for them both. She would share stories about her day at the office, people who had annoyed her, or project challenges she faced. Lucy would listen with ears forward, occasionally swishing her tail if she noticed a tone of annoyance.

Candace began expressing her love to Lucy, telling her how much their life together had enriched her. This included "listening" to the animal, allowing a rich but silent exchange, even if such wordless exchanges were facilitated solely through the eyes. It is possible to hold this communion with any sentient being, allowing a nonverbal exchange that nonetheless communicates a clear response.

Was Lucy healthy or ill most of her life?

Candace realized that Lucy was quite healthy for most of their time together. When caretaking becomes intense at the end of life, it may obscure the reality of sharing times of health. Candace acknowledged that most of their time together was what she had expected: Lucy was a life-enhancing presence, an affectionate feline who accommodated her existence around Candace's schedule. These recollections reminded Candace that Lucy had previously required very little beyond basic caretaking.

How did caretaking impact your life?

Candace was surprised by her response to this question. At first she had considered surrendering Lucy, as she doubted she could provide the needed care. But as she accepted the burden of caretaking through the education provided by the veterinary practice, confidence in her abilities grew. Eventually, Candace felt herself to be a more humane being, one who had been transformed by the love of an animal. Previously, Candace had thought of herself as selfish and unlikely to disrupt her life for another – let alone for a feline! Now their exchanges had become more tactile, more physically intimate and affectionate. Such displays of affection were now part of a treasured aspect of their daily ritual.

Another aspect of this discussion was how Candace's identity would change once Lucy died. Who will she be without Lucy, and how will she rebuild her social life? The expression of expected relief at the freedom which will follow the end of caregiving is not unusual and can benefit from the validating acknowledgment of a clinician.

Do you have regrets about your time with this animal? Do you feel you gave the animal a good life?

Lucy was at peace in feeling that she was giving everything she could to Lucy without jeopardizing her own livelihood. She felt that Lucy got the "best of me" during the months that preceded her death.

This is an important acknowledgment for stewards passing through anticipatory mourning, one that will greatly diminish residual guilt once the animal dies. Of all the tasks of anticipatory mourning associated with mitigating grief, steward participation in facilitating an appropriate or "good" death appears to carry great weight. It appears that the steward's in arranging a good death helps caregivers transition to post-death challenges (Rando, 2000). Constant evaluation of the effectiveness of pain management is an important aspect of helping stewards feel they are providing maximum comfort as death approaches.

Consulting with veterinary staff regarding euthanasia is also important to discuss. Some associated decisions might include the following: Do you want to be present for euthanasia? Where will it be held? Who will perform it? Are there other individuals you would like to be present? Do you want to stay with the animal's body or have it removed? What are your thoughts on the disposition of the animal's body via cremation or burial? What might your needs be following euthanasia? Would you find comfort in a religious ritual with friends, family, clergy? Do you believe in an afterlife for animals? Has your sense of life's continuance or finality been affected by this animal's life and death?

These decisions were Candace's alone. She wanted to invite her best friend and sister to accompany her. Candace also decided she would take time off from work, if the euthanasia could be planned at least a few days in advance.

What do you feel is the legacy of this animal's presence in your life? Have you thought about what the animal would want you to say or feel in its absence?

Candace was readily able to think about Lucy's legacy, as she had now already considered her responses to the questionnaire. Ultimately, her legacy involved donating money to further the study and treatment of feline lymphoma and diabetes. In addition, Candace began volunteering as a community outreach coordinator for the hospice program, from which she had derived so much support during Lucy's decline. Her assignment involved fielding calls from prospective clients and sharing her positive experiences of the program with those hesitant to enroll.

Do you think attending an animal companion bereavement support group would be helpful to you? What is your experience of other forms of social or mental health support during difficult times?

After Lucy's death, Candace did attend the animal companion bereavement support group. Her focused work during the anticipatory mourning phase of Lucy's life made her more comfortable continuing with a group process. She was a valuable member of the bereavement group, sharing thoughts and experiences that had helped her accept Lucy's death. She was also able to share the coping skills she had learned, and was still using, to help her through the early stages of mourning.

Outcome

Mental health support during the phase of anticipatory mourning offered Candace many benefits as she considered the life and impending death of her animal companion. She felt better prepared for Lucy's death and more aware of the tasks she would encounter during healing. She was able to articulate what had been gained through time with Lucy, not just what she had lost. Having gathered memories while the animal still lived gave her direction in creating a legacy for Lucy. She found that she missed the presence of an animal in her life and adopted a kitten the following year.

Chapter summary

Anticipatory mourning describes the period of time between the steward's realization of chronic or terminal illness and the animal's actual death. Hospice programs for animals are increasing and may comfortably extend an unwell animal's life from weeks to months or even years. The caregiver may then need to assume interventive, life-prolonging tasks they did not anticipate. The costs associated with such programs may be beyond the steward's economic means, which may introduce feelings of guilt. Decisions about animal quality of life may lead to suspension of treatment and further caregiver stress. Without support for the many decisions they will confront, caregivers may feel overwhelming stress or guilt, which could cause prema- ture abandonment of the caregiving needed to keep the animal alive. This may complicate the grief that follows with guilt, self-blame, and regret.

Mental health services frequently embedded in human hospice programs which help manage associated stressors are not yet consistently available in hospice programs for animals. Including them or having ready referrals available could be highly beneficial, not only for the stewards facing new caregiving tasks but for the veterinary practice, so they do not become overwhelmed with their stewards' emotional needs during this time. With mental health support, the experience of anticipatory mourning could enrich the final stage of the human-animal bond, helping stewards more closely align with their animal's needs and discover their own capacities for empathy and commitment. The ACB Questionnaire can help clinicians elicit information to incorporate into treatment planning and capture recollection of life with the animal while it still lives, increasing the likelihood that an eventual legacy of their unique bond will include more objective assessment. The case study of Lucy and Candace highlighted both the use of this instrument and the benefits of receiving mental health support during this period and after the animal's death. Other discussions could include exploring or revisiting spirituality, as well as assessment of their bond with the animal and its meaning in their lives.

9

Legacy creation following animal companion loss

How will I move on? It's been months, and I see that empty cage and feel part of me has died. There seems to be no end to my grief. – Owen, proprietor of an exotic avian store, after the sudden death of his 27-year-old cockatoo, Billy

Among those grieving companion animals, many will not quickly find peaceful resolution. Legacy creation – or "finding meaning" in the lost relationship – is described by David Kessler (2019) as the "sixth stage of grief."

There is little information available related to the benefits of legacy creation for animal companions. For humans, life review may bring peace to a dying person (Huang et al., 2020); help satisfy the need to be remembered through "symbolic immortality" (Waggoner et al., 2023); and help resolve the "psychosocial crisis" (Erikson, 1984) of generativity vs. stagnation (Newton, 2020).

But acute grief felt after the death of an animal companion (Weissman et al., 2017, p. 45) cannot be qualified or quantified only by that which is being mourned but by the significance of the loss, its qualities, depth, and expressed behaviors. Therefore, those mourning companion animals may benefit from creating a legacy in which the deceased is not forgotten simply because grief resolves, but rather is internalized.

DOI: 10.4324/9781003145929-10

In my experience with those mourning companion animals, encouragement for legacy creation, or this internalization process, is often lacking.

We will explore how the process of legacy creation for a companion animal may differ from that of a human loved one, but the goal is the same: internalization of the relationship to provide a reference point of support, guidance, and continuance while the mourner returns to full functionality in their life. The process can include expressed values, activities, and beliefs shared by the human-animal dyad, and will therefore vary depending on its qualities, level of engagement, reciprocity, and summary of what was experienced. It restructures "what was" into "what is" – the essence of the bonding that the steward will carry forward as an internalized comforting reference point.

As discussed in the previous chapter, legacy creation may begin during anticipatory mourning. This may be an optimal time to begin recording the feelings which animal companions elicit as well as their reactions to us, in writing or audio or video exchanges. Though their responses may be limited to a soft meow, a quick lick of the face, or a tender gaze, such reactions can foster and reinforce the relationship that existed before health challenges fade those memories. But for most animal companion stewards, the process will not initiate until after the animal has died, sometimes not until months later.

The purpose of legacy creation following animal companion loss

The establishment of a meaningful legacy can offer great comfort after animal companion death, supporting the steward's ability to move on and redirect their grief into constructive activities that help express and rebuild the practical, emotional, and social aspects of what was lost.

It offers stewards the opportunity to articulate a narrative about their unique experience with an animal and to end feelings of alienated emptiness through the incorporation of the lost relationship, the benefits of which they can then carry forward. The mourner's ability to recollect this association will no longer rely solely on the animal's physical presence in order to maintain the cherished connection. Without this stage of mourning, stewards may find it hard to relinquish their only remaining association with the animal: that of their grief. They may, therefore, hold onto grief as the last connection to their departed animal (Parkes, 1998).

Despite the clear benefits of legacy creation to the human mourner (Lewis & Hoy, 2011), this intentional activity may be perceived as an unnecessary or indulgent process when applied to animal companion loss, an exercise that encourages continuing attachment to a deceased animal rather than releasing grief. Legacy creation for the 30-year stewardship of a parrot may seem odd. Or it may be wondered why relief is found in a retrospective valuing of a 20-year-old dapple-gray pony after its death. There may even be a bit of species racism in assuming which creatures "deserve" to have the meaning of their lives honored within this process (Cordeiro-Rodrigues, 2022). The erection of a town statue depicting a canine who repeatedly located missing people may be understood. But what of a child's insistent request to create a plaque remembering their goldfish, perhaps the first animal with whom they experienced an interspecies connection?

As in all other therapeutic encounters for grief, it is essential to "start where the client is" (Vakharia & Little, 2017), acknowledging and accepting that all living creatures are capable of having significant impact on the humans with whom they coexisted. To begin this transformative process, stewards must first acknowledge and accept the loss. Instead of counting the days since the animal died, mourners benefit from redirecting their energy toward the creation of a new, internalized connection with the deceased companion. Even beginning to speak about the animal in the past tense during an animal companion bereavement group helps stewards integrate the loss and create an urge to capture and internalize what remains, rather than lose it all to grief.

But with only physical objects and clay paw prints remaining, it takes dedicated introspection to transform the remains of a primarily visceral relationship into one that still has life through its internalization. Associations with animals – beyond the activities shared – may also be imbued with qualities outside, beyond, and experientially different from relationships with humans. Capturing this otherworldly essence is an integral part of legacy creation, best guided by those whose intention is to help the steward explore all of the relationship's richness, not subdue its importance in an attempt to reduce grief.

Creating a legacy for a specific animal – or group of animals or species with whom have shared aspects of our lives – takes time, painstaking recall, and scrutiny of the steward's life, not just the animal's, before, during and after the animal's death. It includes the valuing of profound changes that may have occurred within us, and which further define who we are.

Such conclusions not only help clarify the relationship's most positive characteristics but moderate steward appraisal after the death. For example, while steward guilt is often an undeserved conclusion, reflection finds it appropriate in certain circumstances. This allows for reparative actions that can foster ethical or moral growth.

Challenges and tasks of legacy creation

Creating a legacy for an animal companion may be perceived by some as indulgent, unnecessary, excessively encouraging of continuing attachment, and denying the reality of death. The ability of a steward to form a close relationship with an animal may feel minimized by such dismissal of healing rituals, especially if the species being mourned is deemed unworthy of remembrance at all.

To those obstacles, let us identify other potential challenges that mourners themselves may encounter:

Denial of death
In early grieving, it may be too challenging to balance the concept of physical loss with the spiritual continuance offered through legacy creation. A mourner may feel that it is impossible

to imagine how such a visceral connection could be transformed into a meaningful but invisible one. They simply want that animal back. They would give anything for one more walk, one more peaceful evening together. Therefore, in order to fully participate in legacy creation, a steward must reach a beginning acceptance that the animal is gone and will not return.

Determining cause of death

Animals often die suddenly, and their stewards may remain unsure of what actually caused their deaths. Sometimes, multiple health issues, some present for years, emerge in a single storm of life-threatening symptoms. Circumstance may cloud the determination of a death's exact cause beyond an obvious failure of heart or lungs. As with the deaths of all loved ones, there is a need to understand what took them from us (Burns, 2022).

Any confusion can retrospectively challenge the decision to euthanize or cause hindsight doubt about treatment choices. It is helpful to determine, to the best of the medical provider or steward's ability, death's specific cause, as doing so will offer more concrete closure, confirming that treatment choices, including choice of the "good death" were appropriate.

Cause of death questions are not as frequent in human loss as illness progression is generally well-documented. Many human obituaries briefly include reference to the cause of death. Knowing why a person died seems to give survivors reassurance that death is not some random act, but has causative factors that may be treated or avoided. The absence of a clear reason following animal companion death can prolong anxiety about the future of other seemingly healthy animals, and even of the steward himself.

Disposition of body

Stewards may feel rushed into decisions about the disposition of the animal's body. Decisions to euthanize are often made during periods of emotional crisis, without consideration of the choices that will follow (Goldberg & Brackenridge, 2019). Under such circumstances, exploration of burial or cremation options may be lacking. For example, stewards may not be aware of the difference in both outcome and cost for group cremations and individual cremations.

There are (albeit very few) animal cemeteries that will collect an animal's body from the veterinary hospital and transport it to an animal funeral home. Those that do will then offer stewards options for a memorial service along with burial plots or cremation urns.

Being able to bury an animal's remains and subsequently visit its grave may comfort the mourner and help facilitate the transition from denial to acceptance. These benefits are similar in human loss (Schuurman & Redmalm, 2019), but not yet widely available for animal companion stewards.

Animal's belongings

To some, quickly discarding these reminders feels relieving. To others, even the thought of this process is initially too painful.

What might best honor the animal's life? Donating a dog bed or a cat tower to a shelter? Transporting bales of hay to nearby farms to feed neighboring equines? Or would it feel better to gather the animal's remaining belongings to create a kind of memorial? Many people initially opt for this option, lighting candles, playing music, and substituting this process for a formal funeral. Animals do not leave specific bequests, they have no wills; it is up to the surviving steward to make such determinations.

Solo process

The legacy being created is formed by the surviving steward or family, without the direct participation of the animal itself. The steward alone recounts its life, remembering achievements realized, life milestones, and transformations that occurred during their time together. Unlike legacy creation for humans, the animal itself has no direct awareness of, investment in, or interest in how it is remembered. Only its stewards have the need to attach and internalize the value and impact of its life.

There is also a lack of other mourners participating in the grieving process. Family and friends, who might journey from many miles away to bear witness to human loss, are less inclined to be there in the aftermath of animal companion death. Shared grief will likely include a very small circle of friends, animal caretakers, and immediate family.

What may follow animal companion death is a shocking, lonely walk to an empty car after an emergency vet visit. The creature who may have ridden in the passenger seat only an hour earlier, stoically hiding the extent of its pain, is now absent, its body left behind.

Mourners may feel isolated in their grief, yearning to reach out but afraid that drawing others into their loss will feel somehow burdensome or inappropriate.

Paucity of community resources

The majority of those mourning companion animals do not have the benefit of recognized social rituals to transform grief into acceptance. The intentional rapidity with which human burials and funerals occur helps human mourners move out of denial (Rando, 1984). Watching a casket lowered into the ground, amidst others who shared life with the deceased, helps ease the mourner toward acceptance. Even if the body of the deceased is never found, memorial services are held, legal declarations of death are made, and social and religious observances help confirm the reality of death. No such closure for animals who have run away or been kidnapped will be offered. The bereaved steward is left to find such solace alone, a process that could linger for many years.

Absence of documentation

Writing timely obituaries for deceased humans requires imme-diate review of the lost life. Mourners can draw on well-documented experiences: achievements, activities, perspectives, education, politics, affiliations, and relationships. Certificates verify birth, graduation, marriage, becoming parents. Scrapbooks, pictures, school transcripts, and letters give confirmation of professions pursued and charities supported. Each person with whom the deceased had a relationship can contribute to the narrative through remembered conversations, whether their experience was positive or conflicted.

But there is seldom such documentation of animals' lives. They are sold or given to us without much more than a page defining their lineage – often unverifiable. Their entire existence may be focused on one person or family, their alliance and love singularly invested. They did not run for office, converse about politics, discuss religious or philosophical beliefs, challenge our choice of companions, demand behavioral consistency for the receipt of affection, or chastise our choices. Their world is small. If animal companions have careers of helping, assisting, emotionally supporting, or protecting humans, such work does not necessarily reflect their choice, but their ability to be trained and to maintain behavioral standards for such work.

There may be pictures of the animal when first adopted, photos at holidays or vacations. But there are seldom any written accounts, and our verbal exchanges are one-sided. We may feel we cannot truly discern what these creatures felt, what they considered to be the pivotal points of their lives, what brought them the most contentment or frustration, joy, or anxiety. What they might have thought of us remains unknown.

We are, instead, left with toys, leashes, saddles, huts, perches, empty stalls, bags of food, water bowls, cat towers, animal beds. These external manifestations do little to capture the depth of our association.

Collecting memorabilia

During the early stages of grief, it may feel unbearable to review photographs, videos, or other memorabilia. Sometimes those mourning companion animals may assume that they have many such items, only to scrutinize phones and computer drives in order to find more at a later point. Most activities done with animals happen spontaneously, and the need to capture those moments may be at odds with the goal of being fully present, immersing oneself in the experience.

Talking with others

Discussing the animal's life with other human or animal family members may yield new information or recollections. Noting the behavior and watching the expressions of others in mourning can reveal a fuller impact of their deaths. An animal's own grieving for the lost housemate may be obvious or may be absent, especially if the death allows another animal to assume a leadership position within the pack of those remaining. Where did the deceased animal fall within the hierarchy of the pack? Who will be the new leader? If discussing farm animals, is the horse mourning the pony? Are the llamas mourning the burro?

Identifying routines

Take note of routines that will now change. For example, during early-morning walks, was there a specific place where you both would pause to watch the sunrise? What were those exchanges like? Did the animal have a favorite place they liked to lie? How did you arrange yourselves to sit together or play ball? If a cage needed cleaning, a stall needed mucking, or a seed container needed refilling, how will the absence of those daily chores feel? Try to capture such reflections in as much detail as possible.

Exploring recollections can help define aspects of the lost relationship, which may help stewards move toward life without the animal. This is especially true if the animal was the source of exchanges or activities that existed only in that relationship. Creating a legacy may involve three types of review: the qualities of the human steward, the qualities of the animal, and the qualities of the dyad they created together. This process may be challenging and helpful in equal measures, as it considers the unique alchemy that went into the human-animal bond.

Responses to the ACB Questionnaire

What special qualities did this particular animal have? What qualities did this animal bring out in you?

The mourner is asked to describe the animal's personality, perhaps eliciting how those characteristics were reflected within the dyad. Often the mourner may have possessed similar attributes yet anthropomorphically projects them onto the animal. For example, the mourner might describe the animal as non-judgmental, responsive, and comforting.

This question can bring awareness that each being contributed equally to the experience of emotional reciprocity. Or if there was frustration or mismatched attunement, such disconnects can be more specifically described and discussed.

> *Did you talk to the animal? Share experiences of your day? Do you think the animal knew what you were feeling and thinking? Do you think you knew what the animal was feeling and thinking?*

Such recollections may reveal a degree of distance or closeness or a conclusion that the animal was the steward's primary confidant. Too frequently, others may assume that a steward's emotional reliance on an animal indicates a paucity of human relationships. But even among those with many friends and family members, an animal companion may still have been the preferred connection for such exchanges.

Responding to these questions helps mourners realize the extent to which they felt a connection or shared communication. These are no small gifts.

> *Do you have regrets about your time with this animal? Do you feel you gave the animal a good life? A good death? What are you imagining the animal felt throughout this process?*

The responses to this question will help the clinician identify challenges to satisfactory legacy creation. If there is guilt, it must be addressed and accepted, remediated, or challenged. Projections regarding the animal's potential anger at the steward around caretaking decisions are also important to explore or dispel and can be difficult for mourners to discern on their own.

Mourning stewards may wonder if they will be judged in some future incarnation based on perceived omissions in their care for this animal.

Has your view of [cats, dogs, horses, small mammals, birds, feral or wild animals] changed as a result of your experience with this animal?

Responses to this question may help lead to suggestions of activities that would further legacy creation. For example, if the steward now feels a deeper responsibility and connection to animals, they may find solace through volunteering or animal advocacy. It may also prompt a philosophical shift challenging the hierarchical position of humans as superior to other sentient beings.

Has your perception of the afterlife or spirituality evolved since the animal died? Have you had any experiences in which you thought you felt the animal's presence, saw it, or heard it?

Many stewards continue to feel a connection reflected in dreams or even experiences in which they think they have felt, heard, or seen the animal or imagined that its spirit is guiding their thoughts. Feelings that the departed animal is close by, while at the same time acknowledging its death, are not infrequent.

We readily accept the idea that humans may be organically bound to one another; we have studied the chemistry of human melding, the hormonal influences that imprint human or animal infants to caregivers (Panksepp, 2017), support intimacy between lovers, and cement friendships through aligned purpose.

Similarly, animals – domesticated or feral – are constantly engaging their instinctive senses, achieving closeness through sight, sound, smell, and touch. Through these exchanges, visceral and even spiritual connections deepen – one reason stewards may have trouble disposing of leashes, toys, and blankets. The smell of the saddle, the fur remaining on the bed, ears still attuned to their call – these memories may be held within our own sensory networks.

When humans articulate a visceral recollection of a loved one, the sound of their voice, their scent, their eyes, these feelings are often accepted as benign manifestations of grief (Kamp et al.,

2020). Discussing how an animal felt – its softness, its scent, its beauty, the touch of its inner ear, the strength of the powerful body beneath the saddle – are also organic memories not easily released.

I have had many encounters in my work with individuals who did not believe in an afterlife but, when faced with the unimaginable loss of a companion animal, began to consider aspects of spirituality. Likewise, many stewards who firmly believe in an afterlife seek to somehow confirm that their animal will be awaiting them there after death.

The creation of a legacy can help revisit or refine spiritual beliefs. Such discussions, while not always resulting in conclusive determinations, can trigger growth and spirituality for the surviving steward, another gift of the animal's legacy.

> *Did you memorialize the animal? Are you interested in any rituals to mark its life and death? How did you grieve or memorialize other significant losses in your life?*

This discussion can evoke creative responses, reflecting the unique qualities of the dyad. Perhaps a memorial service can still be held, even if participants are few or one. Some clergy members are willing to facilitate such services, reading favorite passages of comfort and including the animal in prayers.

Reviewing responses to previous losses may help stewards clarify what was most helpful. Was something missing which can now be incorporated into a new ritual?

One advantage of the lack of templates for mourning companion animals is that stewards may create their own. Perhaps over time they might develop a series of rituals to speak to their experience of life together.

> *What do you feel is the legacy of the animal's presence in your life? Have you thought about what the animal would want you to feel in its absence? Do you feel connected to the animal now?*

This question helps mourners review what has been most transformative as a result of this relationship. What do they consider to be the most precious aspects of the lost relationship, the qualities they most wish to maintain through activities or behaviors?

Activities helpful to legacy creation

Once mourning stewards have responded to the earlier questions, activities that might be most helpful to healing become more evident and help further the process of legacy creation. These suggestions are not exhaustive, but solid options that may be considered during various stages of healing and legacy creation.

Joining a bereavement group

In the immediate aftermath of death, such groups can help guide recollection of special qualities within the human-animal dyad (Park & Royal, 2020). Hearing other stewards' stories may trigger forgotten memories, which may now be joyfully recalled. In addition to receiving validation and support, mourners have a chance to begin compiling their own stories, greatly contributing to legacy foundation. Individual counseling may also help mourners process their animal companions' deaths and find meaning in them (Leonhardt-Parr & Rumble, 2022).

Journaling

Making a daily habit of writing can help derive meaning from the early stages of grief, when the intensity of loss may feel unending (Lichenthal & Neimyer, 2012). In comparing their feelings to those of the previous week or month, mourners may find their grief has slightly remitted, sleep has improved, appetite increased, and recollections have become less distressing. It is also helpful to chart how a few hours of relief are again followed by renewed intensity, indicating that recovery from mourning is not a linear process. Journaling can reinforce that healing continues even when it feels stalled during a difficult day. It may lead to a willingness to finally accept the loss.

Creation of an in-home memorial

Assembling an altar of sorts within the home, where the animal's cremains, possessions, pictures, or comforting religious icons can be displayed, may offer the mourner a location to meditate, visit, commune with, or recollect the departed animal. How long such a memorial remains in place is not limited; a year or longer is not unusual for those who enjoyed deep closeness with a departed companion animal.

Creation of an exterior memorial

When access to an animal cemetery is not possible or preferred, some stewards bury an animal's remains on their own property, depending on local regulations. If there is space, mourners can also create a garden, plant a tree in a location the animal favored, or place a seat nearby where they may privately reflect on their memories. Perennials like forget-me-nots reinforce life's continuity and give evidence of the eternal existence of deep love. Some veterinary practices send packets of forget-me-nots to their mourning clients.

Absent a physical location for the animal's remains, posting virtual memorials can create an alternate location for stewards to connect with their lost companions. Statistics kept on *www. petlosshelp*.org indicate that newly bereaved stewards visit their memorial postings on the site an average of five times a week during early bereavement.

Creation of a narrative

As described in Chapter 5, the often comforting process of telling the story of an animal's life may be facilitated within a form of treatment (like narrative therapy), within an animal companion bereavement support group, among family and friends, or posting the story on a website. If typing feels too burdensome, mourners may record voice memos on smartphones, which can be easily accessed when needed for comfort. New recollections may be added as they arise.

Creative expression

For those who find solace in the arts, creating videos, dance routines, or paintings to capture the essence of the relationship may offer relief and resolution of grief as a final step in legacy creation. Writers, poets, and musicians may find that channeling their grief into these individual expressions uniquely reflects the love that continues for their lost animal.

Donating to animal-related causes

Grieving stewards may find meaning in donations made to animal-related causes, and some veterinary practices may make donations in the names of their departed clients, to acknowledge their steward's loss as well as their own sadness after having cared for an animal for years. There are many animal welfare or breed-specific organizations in need of such support to continue their missions.

Volunteer work

For mourning stewards who are not ready to consider adopting another animal, the need to be near animals may still be prominent. This urge to interact with animals may be temporarily fulfilled by working at animal shelters, at adoption events, or even by caring for other animals in their stewards' absences. Fostering animals who have not yet found permanent homes is another way to connect with animals.

Such volunteer work may include working with organizations devoted to the protection of animal habitats. Examples include patrolling the shoreline to protect nesting turtles, cleaning debris or chemicals from habitats, and remaining alert within your community about pesticides that threaten birds and bees. Writing or speaking about the importance of animal life for local news, sponsoring animal-related events, advocating for the designation of animal spaces in town, volunteering to be on the board of animal organizations, and fundraising for associated events are all worthy endeavors that can turn lasting love into future hope.

Adopting another animal

While some mourners cannot imagine adopting another animal – feeling that doing so would be disloyal to their deceased companion or that they could not endure experiencing loss again – others stewards need to maintain their connection to the animal world by adopting soon after a loss. They may feel the best way to honor their deceased companion is through offering a good life to another. In addition, the comfort and distraction offered through readoption helps healing.

Sometimes stewards wonder if their work schedules or tiny apartments are insufficient to give an animal a good life. To this one might respond: What is the better choice for an existing animal's well-being, the concrete floor of a shelter pen or eight hours on your living room couch awaiting your loving return?

Legal advocacy

For stewards with professional skills or affiliations, legal advocacy to elevate the status of animals is a worthy pursuit. For example, the right of aging stewards and their animal companions to remain housed together is an important issue.

Advocacy is yet another way to demonstrate continuing care for the plight of animals (Peek et al., 1996). Whether protecting habitats or elevating animals' legal status (Tarlton, 2018), funneling the energy of grief into such pursuits can bring great satisfaction. Those wishing to advocate can review their state's ranking in terms of animal welfare and work with associated agencies to improve or maintain a good ranking (Animal Legal Defense Fund, 2023).

Legacy opportunities for mental health professionals

If the grieving steward is an experienced mental health professional, they might consider animal companion bereavement as an additional clinical focus. Offering secondary trauma debriefings to veterinary employees, shelter workers, zookeepers, and others who care for animals can help process difficult emotions. Counseling despairing environmentalists, naturalists, or animal researchers can help heal grief related to animal loss. They can also become a resource for veterinary practices by conducting animal companion bereavement groups or individual counseling.

Another option which may follow readoption is eventual pursuit of AAI certification in order to work with your animal within your practice, being careful, of course, to query your clients about the potential effects of its presence. Mental health professionals may also help advance animal status by engaging in clinical research that explores and further substantiates their positive impact on human health, then publishing or presenting their findings in professional journals or books.

For stewards who undertake the thoughtful creation of animal companion legacy, its most fulfilling and healing aspect is giving life to that legacy. By refusing to accept that the death of a beloved animal permanently ends a cherished experience, its gifts may benefit many others.

Legacy creation for wilder creatures

How do we create a legacy for animals whose lives are mostly hidden from ours, but who deeply affect us?

I'm referring to animals whose existence enhances our lives but whose absence evokes great sadness: the missing annual migrations that used to mark our seasons, the millions of animals lost to forest fires, floods, and other natural disasters. Despite their distance, they are nonetheless our neighbors, a bridge to the natural world.

We may feel such losses acutely, whether our sense of wonder and connectedness to the natural world is stimulated by regenerating numbers of bats or despairing by diminished sightings of bees in spring orchards. All are unique beings who reflect important aspects of ourselves and cause us to ponder our responsibilities to our living world.

Most animals live beyond our view. We may notice only evidence of their presence – fleeting shadows, footprints in the snow, morning and evening calls – but still we are captivated by the dignity and magnificence of their lives.

We innately sense that any threat to their existence is a threat to our own. Our alliance is indisputable; we are linked by our mutual reliance on Earth's health to sustain us.

Whether calling to us from the couch, perch, forest floor, tree canopy, roiling seas, or soaring skies, their welcome presence comes with an awareness that their time is brief and all life is fragile. Great love is worth mourning, regardless of source. Such it is with a dog named Dickens, source of ceaseless inspiration.

Chapter summary

In this chapter, the purpose and importance of creating an animal companion legacy is explored, along with the process itself. Obstacles to that process are defined in terms of the absence of many societal rituals associated with human loss and other challenging aftermaths unique to animal companion death. The process of legacy creation is explained, including suggested tasks and activities. Items from the ACB Questionnaire are proposed to facilitate a thoughtful introspection to further define the unique qualities of each dyad. Finally, the application of legacy creation to those mourning threats to the natural world is validated.

Bibliography

Abbate, C. (2022). Animal ethics. In A. Knight, C. J. C. Phillips & P. Sparks (Eds.), *Routledge handbook of animal welfare* (pp. 353–365). Routledge.

Adrian, J. A. L., & Stitt, A. (2017). Pet loss, complicated grief, and post-traumatic stress disorder in Hawaii. *Anthrozoös, 30*(1), 123–133.

Ainsworth, M. D. S. (1992). A consideration of social referencing in the context of attachment theory and research. In S. Feinman (Ed.), *Social referencing and the social construction of reality in infancy* (pp. 349–367). Springer US.

Ainsworth, M. D. S. (1993). Attachments and other affectional bonds across the life cycle. In C. M. Parkes, J. Stevenson-Hinde & P. Marris (Eds.), *Attachment across the life cycle* (pp. 33–51). Routledge.

Alcaro, A., Carta, S., & Panksepp, J. (2017). The affective core of the self: A neuro-archetypical perspective on the foundations of human (and animal) subjectivity. *Frontiers in Psychology, 8*, 1424. https://doi.org/10.3389/fpsyg.2017.01424

Alimoradi, Z., Golboni, F., Griffiths, M. D., Broström, A., Lin, C. Y., & Pakpou, A. H. (2020). Weight-related stigma and psychological distress: A systematic review and meta-analysis. *Clinical Nutrition (Edinburgh, Scotland), 39*(7), 2001–2013.

Allan, B. A., Campos, I. D., & Wimberley, T. E. (2016). Interpersonal psychotherapy: A review and multicultural critique. *Counselling Psychology Quarterly, 29*(3), 253–273.

Allen, B., Shenk, C. E., Dreschel, N. E., Wang, M., Bucher, A. M., Desir, M. P., Chen, M. J., & Grabowski, S. R. (2022). Integrating animal-assisted therapy into TF-CBT for abused youth with PTSD: A randomized controlled feasibility trial. *Child Maltreatment, 27*(3), 466–477.

Allen, D. M. (1997). Techniques for reducing therapy-interfering behavior in patients with borderline personality disorder. Similarities in four diverse treatment paradigms. *Journal of Psychotherapy Practice and Research, 6*(1), 25–35.

American Pet Products Association. (2021). *2021–2022 APPA national pet owners survey: Business/finance fact sheet.* American Pet Products Association. https://americanpetproducts.org/Uploads/NPOS/21-22_BusinessandFinance.pdf

American Psychiatric Association. (2022). *Diagnostic and statistical manual of mental disorders* (5th ed., text rev.; DSM-5-TR). American Psychiatric Association Publishing.

American Psychiatric Association. (2023, March 1). *Americans note overwhelming positive mental health impact of their pets in new poll; Dogs and cats equally beneficial* [News release]. www.psychiatry.org/news-room/news-releases/positive-mental-health-impact-of-pets#:~:text=Among%20pet%20owners%2C%20a%20strong,a%20part%20of%20their%20family

American Veterinary Medical Association. (2022). *AVMA pet ownership and demographics sourcebook: 2021–2022 edition.* AVMA, Veterinary Economics Division. https://ebusiness.avma.org/files/ProductDownloads/eco-pet-demographic-report-22-low-res.pdf

Animal Legal Defense Fund. (2023, February). *2022 U.S. state animal protection laws rankings.* https://aldf.org/project/us-state-rankings/

Aparicio, M., Centeno, C., Robinson, C. A., Palliative, A. M. (2022). Professionals' experiences of receiving gratitude: A transformative and protective resource. *Qualitative Health Research*, *32*(7), 1126–1138.

Archer, J., & Ireland, J. L. (2011). The development and factor structure of a questionnaire measure of the strength of attachment to pet dogs. *Anthrozoös*, *24*(3), 249–261.

Arkow, P. (2019). The "dark side" of the human-animal bond. In L. Kogan & C. Blazina (Eds.), *Clinician's guide to treating companion animal issues* (pp. 319–346). Academic Press.

Arkow, P. (2020). Human–animal relationships and social work: Opportunities beyond the veterinary environment. *Child and Adolescent Social Work Journal*, *37*(6), 573–588.

Ascione, F. R. (2001, September). Animal abuse and youth violence. In *Juvenile Justice Bulletin*. [NCJ 188677]. Office of Juvenile Justice and Delinquency Prevention.

Ascione, F. R., & Shapiro, K. (2009). People and animals, kindness and cruelty: Research directions and policy implications. *Journal of Social Issues*, *65*(3), 569–587.

Attig, T. (2000). Anticipatory mourning and the transition to loving in absence. In T. A. Rando (Ed.), *Clinical dimensions of anticipatory mourning: Theory and practice in working with the dying, their loved ones, and their caregivers* (pp. 115–133). Research Press.

Bandura, A. (1975). The ethical and social purposes of behavior modification. In C. M. Franks & G. T. Wilson (Eds.), *Annual review of behavior therapy: Theory & practice: 1976* (pp. 13–20). Brunner/Mazel. https://repository.library.georgetown.edu/handle/10822/770156

Barbisan, G. K., Moura, D. H., Lobato, M. I. R., & da Rocha, N. S. (2020). Interpersonal psychotherapy for gender dysphoria in a transgender. *Archives of Sexual Behavior, 49*(2), 787–791.

Barrett, J. J., Tolle, K. A., & Salsman, N. L. (2017). Dialectical behavior therapy skills training for persistent complex bereavement disorder. *Clinical Case Studies, 16*(5), 388–400.

Bartholomew, T. T., Kang, E., Joy, E. E., Robbins, K. A., & Maldonado-Aguiñiga, S. (2022). Clients' perceptions of the working alliance as a predictor of increases in positive affect. *Journal of Psychotherapy Integration, 32*(3), 310–325.

Beck, A. T., Freeman, A., & Davis, D. D. (2006). *Cognitive therapy of personality disorders* (2nd ed.). Guilford Press.

Beck, J. S. (1995). *Cognitive therapy: Basics and beyond*. Guilford Press.

Beck, J. S. (2020). *Cognitive behavior therapy: Basics and beyond* (3rd ed.). Guilford Press.

Beck, J. S., & Fleming, S. (2021). A brief history of Aaron T. Beck, MD, and cognitive behavior therapy. *Clinical Psychology in Europe, 3*(2), 1–7.

Bekoff, M. (2007). *The emotional lives of animals* (p. 15). New World Library.

Bekoff, M., & Gould, S. J. (2000). *The smile of a dolphin: Remarkable accounts of animal emotions*. Discovery Books.

Boelen, P. A., & Smid, G. E. (2017). Disturbed grief: Prolonged grief disorder and persistent complex bereavement disorder. *British Medical Journal, 357*, j2016.

Bouma, E. M. C., Reijgwart, M. L., & Dijkstra, A. (2021). Family member, best friend, child or 'just' a pet, Owners' relationship perceptions and consequences for their cats. *International Journal of Environmental Research and Public Health, 19*(1), 193.

Bowlby, J. (1982). Attachment and loss: Retrospect and prospect. *American Journal of Orthopsychiatry, 52*(4), 664–678.

Bowlby, J. (1988). *A secure base* (Reprint ed.). Basic Books.

Breslau, N., Chilcoat, H. D., Kessler, R. C., & Davis, G. C. (1999). Previous exposure to trauma and PTSD effects of subsequent trauma: Results from the Detroit area survey of trauma. *American Journal of Psychiatry, 156*(6), 902–907. https://doi.org/10.1176/ajp.156.6.902

Bretherton, I. (1992). The origins of attachment theory: John Bowlby and Mary Ainsworth. *Developmental Psychology, 28*(5), 759–775. https://doi.org/10.1037/0012-1649.28.5.759

Brewer, D. (2020). *Quotes of Mahatma Gandhi, A words of wisdom collection book.* Lulu.com

Bridges, M. R. (2006). Activating the corrective emotional experience. *Journal of Clinical Psychology, 62*(5), 551–568.

Broadfield, K. (2020). *Can animal-assisted therapy aid recovery from alcohol and drug addiction? A brief review of the literature.* James Cook University.

Brockington, I. (2008). *Maternal attachment and bonding disorders in perinatal and postpartum mood disorders: Perspectives and treatment guide for the health care practitioner* (Stone & Menken, edits). Springer Publishing Company.

Brown, A. (2023). *About half of U.S. pet owners say their pets are as much a part of their family as a human member.* Pew Research Center.

Brown, O. K., & Symons, D. K. (2016). "My pet has passed": Relations of adult attachment styles and current feelings of grief and trauma after the event. *Death Studies, 40*(4), 247–255.

Brunke, D. B. (2008). *Shapeshifting with our animal companions: Connecting with the spiritual awareness of all life.* Bear & Company.

Burger, F., Neerincx, M. A., & Brinkman, W.-P. (2021). Natural language processing for cognitive therapy: Extracting schemas from thought records. *PLoS One, 16*(10), e0257832.

Burns, K. (2022). When death comes suddenly to a pet. *Journal of the American Veterinary Medical Association, 260*(6), 585–597.

Butler, S., & Northcut, T. (2013). Enhancing psychodynamic therapy with cognitive-behavioral therapy in the treatment of grief. *Clinical Social Work Journal, 41*(4), 309–315.

Cable, A. B., Willcox, E. V., & Leppanen, C. (2022). Contaminant exposure as an additional stressor to bats affected by white-nose syndrome: Current evidence and knowledge gaps. *Ecotoxicology, 31*(1), 12–23.

Caparrós, B., & Masferrer, L. (2021). Coping strategies and complicated grief in a substance use disorder sample. *Frontiers in Psychology, 11*, 624065. https://doi.org/10.3389/fpsyg.2020.624065

Carucci, R. (2019, December 9). Getting to the bottom of destructive behaviors. *Harvard Business Review.* https://hbr.org/2019/12/getting-to-the-bottom-of-destructive-behaviors

Chapman, A. L., & Rosenthal, M. Z. (2016). *Managing therapy-interfering behavior: Strategies from dialectical behavior therapy.* American Psychological Association. www.apa.org/pubs/books/4317388

Cherniack, E. P., & Cherniack, A. R. (2014). The benefit of pets and animal-assisted therapy to the health of older individuals. *Current Gerontology and Geriatrics Research, 2014*, e623203.

Chur-Hansen, A., McArthur, M., Winefield, H., Hanieh, E., & Hazel, S. (2014). Animal-assisted interventions in children's hospitals: A critical review of the literature. *Anthrozoös, 27*(1), 5–18.

Clark, A. (2017, April 5). What if the pain of pet loss becomes too much to bear? *Psychology Today.* www.psychologytoday.com/us/blog/animal-attachment/201704/what-if-the-pain-pet-loss-becomes-too-much-bear

Clark, G. I., & Egan, S. J. (2015). The Socratic method in cognitive behavioural therapy: A narrative review. *Cognitive Therapy and Research, 39*(6), 863–879.

Cohen, J. A., & Mannarino, A. P. (2015). Trauma-focused cognitive behavior therapy for children and families. *Child and Adolescent Psychiatric Clinics of North America, 24*(3), 557–570. https://doi.org/10.1016/j.chc.2015.02.005

Cohen, J. A., Mannarino, A. P., & Deblinger, E. (2017). *Treating trauma and traumatic grief in children and adolescents* (2nd ed.). Guilford Press.

Cohen, J. A., Mannarino, A. P., & Iyengar S. (2011). Community treatment of posttraumatic stress disorder for children exposed to intimate partner violence: A randomized controlled trial. *Archives of Pediatrics and Adolescent Medicine, 165*(1), 16–21. https://doi.org/10.1001/archpediatrics.2010.247

Cohen, J. A., Mannarino, A. P., Kliethermes, M., & Murray, L. A. (2012). Trauma-focused CBT for youth with complex trauma. *Child Abuse & Neglect, 36*(6), 528–541.

Compitus, K. (2019). Traumatic pet loss and the integration of attachment-based animal assisted therapy. *Journal of Psychotherapy Integration, 29*, 119–131.

Compitus, K. (2021). *The human-animal bond in clinical social work practice*. Springer International Publishing.

Constantino, M. J., Morrison, N. R., Coyne, A. E., & Howard, T. (2017). Exploring therapeutic alliance training in clinical and counseling psychology graduate programs. *Training and Education in Professional Psychology, 11*(4), 219–226.

Corcoran, J., Stuart, S., & Schultz, J. (2019). Teaching interpersonal psychotherapy (IPT) in an MSW clinical course. *Journal of Teaching in Social Work, 39*(3), 226–236.

Cordeiro-Rodrigues, L. (2022). Connecting racial and species justice: Towards an Afrocentric animal advocacy. *Philosophy and Social Criticism, 48*(8), 1075–1098.

Curtis, P. (1988). Euthanasia of a pet: A personal experience. In W. J. Kay, S. P. Cohen, C. E. Fudin, A. H. Kutscher, H. A. Nieburg, R. E. Grey & M. M. Osman (Eds.), *Euthanasia of the companion animal: The impact on pet owners, veterinarians, and society* (pp. 70–74). Charles Press.

Cusack, O. (2014). *Pets and mental health*. Routledge.

D'Antonio, J. (2014). Caregiver grief and anticipatory mourning. *Journal of Hospice & Palliative Nursing, 16*(2), 99–104.

Daniel, T. (2021). Adding a new dimension to grief counseling: Creative personal ritual as a therapeutic tool for loss, Trauma and transition. *OMEGA – Journal of Death and Dying, 87*(2), 363–376.

Davies, B. (2000). Anticipatory mourning and the transition of fading away. In T. A. Rando (Ed.), *Clinical dimensions of anticipatory mourning: Theory and practice in working with the dying, their loved ones, and their caregivers* (pp. 135–153). Research Press.

Davis, C. G., Lehman, D. R., Silver, R. C., Wortman, C. B., & Ellard, J. H. (1996). Self-blame following a traumatic event: The role of perceived avoidability. *Personality and Social Psychology Bulletin, 22*(6), 557–567.

Davis, K. L., & Montag, C. (2019). Selected principles of Pankseppian affective neuroscience. *Frontiers in Neuroscience, 12*, 1025.

DeCou, C. R., Comtois, K. A., & Landes, S. J. (2019). Dialectical behavior therapy is effective for the treatment of suicidal behavior: A meta-analysis. *Behavior Therapy*, *50*(1), 60–72. https://doi.org/10. 1016/j.beth.2018.03.009

Dimeff, L., & Linehan, M. M. (2001). DBT in a nutshell: A step-by-step on how to merge "radical acceptance" with a "technology of change. *California Psychologist*, *34*(3), 10–13.

Doka, K. J. (2000). Re-creating meaning in the face of illness. In T. A. Rando (Ed.), *Clinical dimensions of anticipatory mourning: Theory and practice in working with the dying, their loved ones, and their caregivers* (pp. 103–113). Research Press.

Domino, J. L., Whiteman, S. E., Davis, M. T., Witte, T. K., & Weathers, F. W. (2021). Sudden unexpected death as a traumatic stressor: The impact of the DSM–5 revision of criterion A for posttraumatic stress disorder. *Traumatology*, *27*(2), 168–176.

Doyon-Martin, J., & Gonzalez, A. (2022). 'It brought life back to prison': Content analysis of prison-based dog training programs in four midwestern prisons. *Contemporary Justice Review*, *25*(1), 82–99.

Dugas, M. B., Wamelink, C. N., Killius, A. M., & Richards-Zawacki, C. L. (2016). Parental care is beneficial for offspring, costly for mothers, and limited by family size in an egg-feeding frog. *Behavioral Ecology*, *27*(2), 476–483. https://doi.org/10.1093/beheco/arv173

Dworkin, M. (2005). *EMDR and the relational imperative: The therapeutic relationship in EMDR treatment*. Routledge.

Eaton-Stull, Y., Wright, C., DeAngelis, C., & Zambroski, A. (2021). Comparison of DBT skills groups with and without animal-assistance for incarcerated women with self-harm histories. *Corrections*, *6*(3), 217–228.

Eckstein, M., Mamaev, I., Ditzen, B., & Sailer, U. (2020). Calming effects of touch in human, animal, and robotic interaction-scientific state-of-the-art and technical advances. *Frontiers in Psychiatry*. Published online November 4, 2020. https://doi.org/10.3389/fpsyt.2020.555058

Einstein, A. (2015). *Bite-size Einstein: Quotations on just about everything from the greatest mind of the twentieth century* (p. 15). St. Martin's Press.

Empeño, J., Raming, N. T. J., Irwin, S. A., Nelesen, R. A., & Lloyd, L. S. (2013). The impact of additional support services on caregivers of hospice patients and hospice social workers. *Omega*, *67*(1–2), 53–61.

Erikson, E. H. (1984). Reflections on the last stage – and the first. *Psychoanalytic Study of the Child, 39*, 155–165.

Esquivel, G. B., Oades-Sese, G. V., & Jarvis, M. L. (2010). *Culturally sensitive narrative interventions for immigrant children and adolescents.* University Press of America.

Falabella, G. S., Johnides, B. D., Hershkovich, A., Arett, J., & Rosmarin, D. H. (2022). CBT/DBT-informed intensive outpatient treatment for anxiety and depression: A naturalistic treatment outcomes study. *Cognitive & Behavioral Practice, 29*(3), 614–624.

Farber, S. K. (2002). *When the body is the target: Self-harm, pain, and traumatic attachments* (Rev. ed., p. 25). Jason Aronson, Inc.

Farrell, D. (2018). The neurobiology of eye movement desensitization reprocessing therapy. In A. R. Beech, A. J. Carter, R. E. Mann & P. Rothstein (Eds.), *The Wiley Blackwell handbook of forensic neuroscience* (Vol. 2, pp. 755–782). Wiley Blackwell.

Ferrell, J., & Crowley, S. L. (2023). Emotional support animal partnerships: Behavior, welfare, and clinical Involvement. *Anthrozoös, 36*(3), 471–487.

Figley, C. R. (1999). Police compassion fatigue (PCF): Theory, research, assessment, treatment, and prevention. In J. M. Violanti & D. Paton (Eds.), *Police trauma: Psychological aftermath of civilian combat* (pp. 37–53). Charles C Thomas Publisher, Ltd.

Fine, A. (2019). The human animal bond over the lifespan: A primer for the mental health professional. In C. Blazina & L. R. Cogin (Eds.), *Clinicians guide to treating animal companion issues* (pp. 1–19). Academic Press.

Fine, A. H. (2010). *Handbook on animal-assisted therapy: Theoretical foundations and guidelines for practice* (3rd ed.). Academic Press.

Forbes Advisor (2023). *Pet Ownership Statistics 2023.* www.forbes.com/advisor/pet-insurance/pet-ownership-statistics/

Frank, E., Ritchey, F. C., & Levenson, J. C. (2014). Is interpersonal psychotherapy infinitely adaptable? A compendium of the multiple modifications of IPT. *The American Journal of Psychotherapy, 68*(4), 385–416.

Frei, D. (2011). *Angel on a leash: Therapy dogs and the lives they touch.* Companion House Books.

Fujisawa, H., Kumasaka, T., Masu, H., & Kataoka, M. (2016). Changes in mood among 4th year elementary school students when interacting with dogs and considerations: The need for animals in elementary education. *International Medical Journal*, *23*(6), 633–635.

Goldberg, K. (2019). Considerations in counseling veterinarians: Addressing suffering in those who care for animals. In L. Kogan & C. Blazina (Eds.), *Clinician's guide to treating companion animal issues* (pp. 421–434). Academic Press.

Goldberg, K., & Brackenridge, S. (2019). Following the loss of a companion animal: Aftercare and pet loss support. In L. Kogan & C. Blazina (Eds.), *Clinician's guide to treating companion animal issues* (pp. 435–456). Academic Press.

Grams, N. (2019). Homeopathy – Where is the science? *EMBO Reports*, *20*(3), e47761. https://doi.org/10.15252/embr.201947761

Guillen Guzmán, E., Sastre Rodríguez, L., Santamarina-Perez, P., Hermida Barros, L., García Giralt, M., Domenec Elizalde, E., Ristol Ubach, F., Romero Gonzalez, M., Pastor Yuste, Y., Diaz Téllez, C., Romero Cela, S., Real Gisbert, L., Salmeron Medina, M., Ballesteros-Urpi, A., & Morer Liñan, A. (2022). The benefits of dog-assisted therapy as complementary treatment in a children's mental health day hospital. *Animals*, *12*(20), 2841.

Hamilton, N. (2019). *Coping with stress and burnout as a veterinarian: An evidence-based solution to increase wellbeing*. Australian Academic Press.

Hammer, T. R. (2011). Social learning theory. In S. Goldstein & J. A. Naglieri (Eds.), *Encyclopedia of child behavior and development* (pp. 1396–1397). Springer US.

Hebert, R. S., Arnold, R. M., & Schulz, R. (2007). Improving well-being in caregivers of terminally ill patients. Making the case for patient suffering as a focus for intervention research. *Journal of Pain and Symptom Management*, *34*(5), 539–546.

Hediger, K., Marti, R., Urfer, V., Schenk, A., Gutwein, V., & Dörr, C. (2022). Effects of a dog-assisted social- and emotional-competence training for prisoners: A controlled study. *International Journal of Environmental Research and Public Health*, *19*(17), 10553.

Heerink, M., Kröse, B., Evers, V., & Wielinga, B. (2010). Assessing acceptance of assistive social agent technology by older adults: The Almere Model. *International Journal of Social Robotics*, *2*(4), 361–375. https://doi.org/10.1007/s12369-010-0068-5

Henderson Metzger, L., Meyer, L., & Nadkarni, L. (2022). Laws governing animal maltreatment: Past, present, and future. In L. Henderson Metzger, L. Meyer & L. Nadkarni (Eds.), *Animal maltreatment evaluation basics for mental health practitioners, students, and educators* (pp. 5–15). Springer.

Herman, J. (1997). *Trauma and recovery: The aftermath of violence–From domestic abuse to political terror*. Basic Books.

Hermann, E. (2022). Anthropomorphized artificial intelligence, attachment, and consumer behavior. *Marketing Letters, Springer, 33*, 157–162. https://doi.org/10.1007/s11002-021-09587-3

Heywood, L., Conti, J., & Hay, P. (2022). Paper 1: A systematic synthesis of narrative therapy treatment components for the treatment of eating disorders. *Journal of Eating Disorders, 10*(1), 137.

Hoogsteder, L, Lott, T., Schippers, E., & Stams, G. (2002). A meta analysis of the effectiveness of EMDR and TF-CBT in reducing trauma symptoms and externalizing behavior problems in adolescents. *International Journal of Offender Therapy & Comparative Criminology, 66*(6–7), 735–757.

Horowitz, A. (2019). *Our dogs, ourselves: The story of a singular bond*. Simon and Schuster.

Horton, L., Griffen, M., Chang, L., & Newcomb, A. B. (2023). Efficacy of animal-assisted therapy in treatment of patients With traumatic brain injury: A randomized trial. *Journal of Trauma Nursing, 30*(2), 68–74.

Howie, A. R. (2021). *Assessing handlers for competence in animal-assisted interventions*. Purdue University Press.

Huang, M. H., Wang, R. H., & Wang, H. H. (2020). Effect of life review on quality of life in terminal patients: A systematic review and meta-analysis. *Journal of Nursing Research, 28*(2), e83. DOI: 10.1097/JNR.0000000000000335

Hunt, M., Al-Awadi, H., & Johnson, M. (2008). Psychological sequelae of pet loss following Hurricane Katrina. *Anthrozoös, 21*, 109–121.

Hunter, E. G. (2007). Beyond death: Inheriting the past and giving to the future, transmitting the legacy of one's self. *Omega, 56*(4), 313–329.

Iglewicz, A., Shear, M. K., Reynolds III, C. F., Simon, N., Lebowitz, B., & Zisook, S. (2020). Complicated grief therapy for clinicians: An evidence-based protocol for mental health practice. *Depression and Anxiety, 37*(1), 90–98.

Jau, J., & Hodgson, D. (2018). How interaction with animals can benefit mental health: A phenomenological study. *Social Work in Mental Health*, *16*, 20–33.

Jensen, T. K., Braathu, N., Birkeland, M. S., Ormhaug, S. M., & Skar, A.-M. S. (2022). Complex PTSD and treatment outcomes in TF-CBT for youth: A naturalistic study. *European Journal of Psychotraumatology*, *13*(2), 2114630.

Kamp, K. S., Steffen, E. M., Alderson-Day, B., Allen, P., Austad, A., Hayes, J., Larøi, F., Ratcliffe, M., & Sabucedo, P. (2020). Sensory and quasi-sensory experiences of the deceased in bereavement: An inter-disciplinary and integrative review. *Schizophrenia Bulletin*, *46*(6), 1367–1381.

Karkdijk, E. M., Duindam, H. M., Deković, M., Creemers, H. E., & Asscher, J. J. (2022). A friend in prison: Human-animal bond, stress and self-esteem of detained juveniles in Dutch cell dogs. *Animals*, *12*(5), 646.

Katcher, A. H., & Beck, A. M. (2010). Newer and older perspectives on the therapeutic effects of animals and nature. In A. Fine (Ed.), *Handbook on animal-assisted therapy: Theoretical foundations and guidelines for practice* (pp. 49–58). Academic Press.

Kaufmann, M. E., Beetz, A., Kinoshita, M., & Ross, J. S. (2015). Chapter 15 – Enhancing special education environments with animal-assisted interventions at green chimneys: Opportunities and practical considerations. *Handbook On Animal-Assisted Therapy*, 211–224.

Kessler, D. (2019). *Finding meaning: The sixth stage of grief.* Simon and Schuster.

Kiesler, D. J. (1996). From communications to interpersonal theory: A personal odyssey. *Journal of Personality Assessment*, *66*(2), 267–282.

Kim, S., Fonagy, P., Allen, J., Martinez, S., Iyengar, U., & Strathearn, L. (2014). Mothers who are securely attached in pregnancy show more attuned infant mirroring 7 months postpartum. *Infant Behavior and Development*, *37*(4), 491–504.

King, B. J. (2013). *How animals grieve.* University of Chicago Press.

Kipperman, B. (2010, August). *Economic euthanasia: A disease in need of prevention.* Human Society Veterinary Medical Association. www.hsvma.org/economic_euthanasia_disease_in_need_of_prevention

Klass, D. (Ed.). (1996). *Chapter 17: Continuing bonds: New understandings of Grief* (pp. 297–309). CRC Press LLC.

Klerman, G. L., & Weissman, M. M. (Eds.). (1993). *New applications of interpersonal psychotherapy*. American Psychiatric Association.

Krumwiede, A. (2014). *Attachment theory according to John Bowlby and Mary Ainsworth: Seminar paper*. GRIN Verlag GmbH. www.grin.com/document/270555

Kübler-Ross, E. (1970). *On death and dying*. Collier Macmillan.

Kübler-Ross, E. (2014). *On death and dying: What the dying have to teach doctors, nurses, clergy and their own families*. Scribner.

Kucharski, A. M. D. (1984). History of frontal lobotomy in the United States, 1935–1955. *Neurosurgery, 14*(6), 765–772.

Lahn, B. T. (2020). Social dominance hierarchy: Toward a genetic and evolutionary understanding. *Cell Research, 30*(7), 560–561.

Langston, S. (2019). Pets and the therapeutic process. In L. Kogan & C. Blazina (Eds.), *Clinician's guide to treating companion animal issues* (pp. 115–127). Academic Press.

Larkin, P. J., Jr. (2017). Death row dogs, hard time prisoners, and creative rehabilitation strategies: Prisoner-dog training programs. *Catholic University Law Review, 66*(3), 543–576.

Laube, J. J. (1998). Therapist role in narrative group psychotherapy. *Group, 22*(4), 227–243.

Leeds, A. M. (2016). *A guide to the standard EMDR therapy protocols for clinicians, supervisors, and consultants* (2nd ed.). Springer Publishing Company.

Leonhardt-Parr, E., & Rumble, B. (2022). Coping with animal companion loss: A thematic analysis of pet bereavement counselling. *OMEGA – Journal of Death and Dying*, 302228211073217. Advance online publication. https://doi.org/10.1177/00302228211073217

Lewey, J. H., Smith, C. L., Burcham, B., Saunders, N. L., Elfallal, D., & O'Toole, S. K. (2018). Comparing the effectiveness of EMDR and TF-CBT for children and adolescents: A meta-analysis. *Journal of Child & Adolescent Trauma, 11*(4), 457–472.

Lewis, L., & Hoy, W. G. (2011). Bereavement rituals and the creation of legacy. In *Grief and bereavement in contemporary society: Bridging research and practice* (pp. 315–323). Routledge/Taylor & Francis Group.

Lichenthal, W., & Neimyer, R. (2012). Directed Journaling to Facilitate Meaning-Making. In R. Neimyer (Ed.), *Techniques of grief therapy*. Routledge.

Lin, J. (2020). Palliative care and legacy creation: A medical student's journey in understanding death. *British Columbia Medical Journal, 62*(8), 292–293.

Lin, J. S., O'Connor, E., Whitlock, E. P., Beil, T. L. (2010). Behavioral counseling to promote physical activity and a healthful diet to prevent cardiovascular disease in adults: A systematic review for the U.S. Preventive Services Task Force. *Annals of Internal Medicine, 153*(11), 736–750.

Linehan, M. M. (1993). *Cognitive-behavioral treatment of borderline personality disorder*. Guilford Press.

Linehan, M. M. (1998). An illustration of dialectical behavior therapy. *Session: Psychotherapy in Practice, 4*, 21–44.

Linehan, M. M. (2014). *DBT skills training manual* (2nd ed.). Guilford Press.

Linehan, M. M. (2015a). *DBT Skills training handouts and worksheets* (2nd ed.). Guilford Publications.

Linehan, M. M. (2015b). *DBT skills training manual* (2nd ed.). Guilford Press.

Lorenz, K. (1952). *King Solomon's ring: New light on animal ways*. Thomas Y. Crowell Co.

Lorenz, K. (1970–1971). *Studies in animal and human behaviour* (Vols. 1 & 2). Harvard University Press.

Low, P. (2012). *The Cambridge declaration of consciousness* (J. Panksepp, D. Reiss, D. Edelman, B. Van Swinderen, P. Low, & C. Koch, Eds.). http://fcmconference.org/img/CambridgeDeclarationOnConsciousness.pdf

Lowe, C., & Murray, C. (2014). *Adult service-users' experiences of trauma-focused cognitive* behavioural therapy. *Journal of Contemporary Psychotherapy, 44*(4), 223–231. https://doi.org/10.1007/s10879-014-9272-1

Lynn, S. J. E., & Rhue, J. W. (Eds.). (1994). *Dissociation: Clinical and theoretical perspectives* (pp. 24–27). Guilford Press.

Malkinson, R. (2006). Grief and bereavement. In A. Freeman & T. R. Ronen (Eds.), *Cognitive behavior therapy in clinical social work practice* (pp. 521–550). Springer Publishing Co.

Månsson, K. N., Salami, A., Frick, A., Carlbring, P., Andersson, G., Furmark, T., & Boraxbekk, C.-J. (2016). Neuroplasticity in response to cognitive behavior therapy for social anxiety disorder. *Translational Psychiatry*, *6*(2), e727.

Markowitz, J. C., & Weissman, M. M. (2012). Interpersonal psychotherapy: Past, present and future. *Clinical Psychology & Psychotherapy*, *19*(2), 99–105.

Mathew, L. E. (2021). Braiding western and eastern cultural rituals in bereavement: An autoethnography of healing the pain of prolonged grief. *British Journal of Guidance & Counselling*, *49*(6), 791–803.

Mavranezouli, I., Megnin-Viggars, O., Daly, C., Dias, S., Welton, N. J., Stockton, S., Bhutani, G., Grey, N., Leach, J., Greenberg, N., Katona, C., El-Leithy, S., & Pilling, S. (2020). Psychological treatments for post-traumatic stress disorder in adults: A network meta-analysis. *Psychological Medicine*, *50*(4), 542–555. https://doi.org/10.1017/S0033291720000070

McConnell, A. R., Paige Lloyd, E., & Humphrey, B. T. (2019). We are family: Viewing pets as family members improves wellbeing. *Anthrozoös*, *32*(4), 459–470.

McFarlane, A. C. (2010). The long-term costs of traumatic stress: Intertwined physical and psychological consequences. *World Psychiatry*, *9*(1), 3–10.

Meehan, M., Massavelli, B., & Pachana, N. (2017). Using attachment theory and social support theory to examine and measure pets as sources of social support and attachment figures. *Anthrozoös*, *30*(2), 273–289.

Menon, S. B., & Jayan, C. (2010). Eye movement desensitization and reprocessing: A conceptual framework. *Indian Journal of Psychological Medicine*, *32*(2), 136–140.

Milot, M. (2023). The therapeutic alliance as an indicator of well-implemented and impactful employee counseling services: Deployment of the brief therapeutic alliance scale in an employee assistance program. *Journal of Workplace Behavioral Health*, *38*(1), 10–35.

Milot-Lapointe, F., Le Corff, Y., & Arifoulline, N. (2021). A meta-analytic investigation of the association between working alliance and outcomes of individual career counseling. *Journal of Career Assessment, 29*(3), 486–501. https://doi.org/10.1177/1069 072720985037

Mobbs, D., Hagan, C. C., Dalgleish, T., Silston, B., & Prévost, C. (2015). The ecology of human fear: Survival optimization and the nervous system. *Frontiers in Neuroscience, 9*, 55.

Morgan, A. (2000). *What is narrative therapy?: An easy-to-read introduction.* Dulwich Centre Publications.

Morris, C. C. (2006). *Narrative theory: A culturally sensitive counseling and research framework.* http://www.counselingoutfitters.com/ Morris.htm

Morris, H., Hatzikiriakidis, K., Savaglio, M., Dwyer, J., Lewis, C., Miller, R., & Skouteris, H. (2022). Eye movement desensitization and reprocessing for the treatment and early intervention of trauma among first responders: A systematic review. *Journal of Traumatic Stress, 35*(3), 778–790.

Morris, K., Flynn, E., Jenkens, M., Senecal, J., Gandenberger, J., Hawes, S., & Tedeschi, P. (2019). *Documentation of nature-based programs at Green Chimneys.* University of Denver, Institute for Human-Animal Connection.

Mota, N., Tsai, J., Kirwin, P. D., et al. (2016). Late-life exacerbation of PTSD symptoms in US Veterans: Results from the national health and resilience in veterans study. *Journal of Clinical Psychiatry, 77*(3), 348–353.

Mufson, L., Yanes-Lukin, P., Gunlicks-Stoessel, M., & Wickramaratne, P. (2014). Cultural competency and its effect on treatment outcome of IPT-A in school-based health clinics. *American Journal of Psychotherapy, 68*(4), 417–442.

Murray, A., Westervelt, A., & Gunlicks-Stoessel, M. (2017). Interpersonal psychotherapy. In A. Wenzel (Ed.), *The SAGE encyclopedia of abnormal and clinical psychotherapy* (pp. 1883–1887). SAGE Publications.

Muzik, M., Bocknek, E. L., Broderick, A., Richardson, P., Rosenblum, K. L., Thelen, K., & Seng, J. S. (2013). Mother-infant bonding impairment across the first six months postpartum: The primacy of psychopathology in women with childhood abuse and neglect histories. *Archives of Women's Mental Health, 16*(1), 29–38.

Nakajima, S., Masaya, I., Akemi, S., & Takako, K. (2012). Complicated grief in those bereaved by violent death: The effects of post-traumatic stress disorder on complicated grief. *Dialogues in Clinical Neuroscience, 14*(2), 210–214.

Napia.org (2023). *NAPHIA State of the industry report, 2023 – May 3, 2023 North America Statistics.* North American Pet Health Insurance Association. https://naphia.org/wp-content/uploads/2023/05/NAPHIA-SOI2023-Report-Highlights_Public-May9.pdf

National Institute of Mental Health (NIMH). (2021). *Mental health information, statistics, mental illness.* U.S. Department of Health and Human Services. https://www.nimh.nih.gov/health/statistics/mental-illness

National Philanthropic Trust (2021). *The 2020 annual report.* www.nptrust.org/annual-reports/the-2020-annual-report/

Neacsiu, A. D., Rompogren, J., Eberle, J. W., & McMahon, K. (2018). Changes in problematic anger, shame, and disgust in anxious and depressed adults undergoing treatment for emotion dysregulation. *Behavior Therapy, 49*(3), 344–359.

Neimeyer, R. A., & Feixas, G. (1990). The role of homework and skill acquisition in the outcome of group cognitive therapy for depression. *Behavior Therapy, 21*(3), 281–292.

New York State Department of Environmental Conservation (2018). *White-nose syndrome.* www.dec.ny.gov/animals/45088.html

Newmyer, S. T. (2006). *Animals, rights and reason in Plutarch and modern ethics.* Routledge. https://doi.org/10.4324/9780203350157

Newmyer, S. T. (2020). *Plutarch's three treatises on animals: A translation with introductions and commentary* (1st ed., p. 127). Routledge.

Newton, N. J., Chauhan, P. K., Pates, J. L. (2020). Facing the future: Generativity, stagnation, intended legacies, and well-being in later life. *Journal of Adult Development, 27*(1), 70–80.

NP Source (2023). *The ultimate list of charitable giving statistics for 2023: Charitable giving statistics.* https://nonprofitssource.com/online-giving-statistics/

O'Brien, F., Bible, J., Liu, D., & Simons-Morton, B. G. (2017). Do young drivers become safer after being involved in a collision? *Psychological Science, 28*(4), 407–413.

Ohio State University (2009, October 14). Microchips result in higher rate of return of shelter animals to owners. *ScienceDaily.* www.sciencedaily.com/releases/2009/10/091013185154.htm

Otani, K., Suzuki, A., Matsumoto, Y., & Shirata, T. (2018). Marked differences in core beliefs about self and others, between sociotropy and autonomy: Personality vulnerabilities in the cognitive model of depression. *Neuropsychiatric Disease and Treatment, 14*, 863–866.

Panksepp, J. (1998). *Chapter 13: Affective neuroscience: The foundations of human and animal emotions*. Oxford University Press.

Panksepp, J. (2000). The chemistry of caring. In M. Bekoff (Ed.), *The smile of a dolphin: Remarkable accounts of animal emotions*. Discovery Books.

Panksepp, J. (2005). Affective consciousness: Core emotional feelings in animals and humans. *Consciousness and Cognition, 14*, 30–80. https://doi.org/10.1016/j.concog.2004.10.004

Panksepp, J. (2011a). Cross-species affective neuroscience decoding of the primal affective experiences of humans and related animals. *PLoS One, 6*(9).

Panksepp, J. (2011b). Toward a cross-species neuroscientific understanding of the affective mind: Do animals have emotional feelings? *American Journal of Primatology, 73*, 545–561. https://doi.org/10.1002/ajp.20929

Panksepp, J. (2017). Affective consciousness. In S. Schneider & M. Velmans (Eds.), *The Blackwell companion to consciousness* (pp. 141–156). John Wiley and Sons.

Parish-Plass, N. (2008). Animal-assisted therapy with children suffering from insecure attachment due to abuse and neglect: A method to lower the risk of intergenerational transmission of abuse? *Clinical Child Psychology and Psychiatry, 13*(1), 7–30.

Park, R., & Royal, K. (2020). A national survey of companion animal owners' self-reported methods of coping following euthanasia. *Veterinary Sciences, 7*(3), 89.

Parkes, C. M. (1998). Bereavement in adult life. *BMJ, 316*(7134), 856–859.

Parthasarathy, V., & Crowell-Davis, S. L. (2006). Relationship between attachment to owners and separation anxiety in pet dogs (Canis lupus familiaris). *Journal of Veterinary Behavior, 1*(3), 109–120.

Paul, H. A. (2017). Review of the book [*Treating Trauma and Traumatic Grief in Children and Adolescents* (2nd ed.) by J. A. Cohen, A. P. Mannarino, & E. Deblinger]. *Child & Family Behavior Therapy, 39*(4), 318–324.

Pearlman, L. A., Wortman, C. B., Feuer, C. A., Farber, C. H., & Rando, T. A. (2014). *Treating traumatic bereavement: A practitioner's guide*. Guilford Press.

Peek, C. W., Bell, N. J., & Dunham, C. C. (1996). Gender, gender ideology, and animal rights advocacy. *Gender & Society*, *10*(4), 464–478.

Perseius, K.-I., Ojehagen, A., Ekdahl, S., Asberg, M., & Samuelsson, M. (2003). Treatment of suicidal and deliberate self-harming patients with borderline personality disorder using dialectical behavioral therapy: The patients' and the therapists' perceptions. *Archives of Psychiatric Nursing*, *17*(5), 218–227.

Pet Helpers. (2023, December). *Pet Helpers – Clinic: SNAP – Pet assistance program*. https://pethelpers.org/snap-pet-assistance-program/

Pet Ownership for the Elderly and Persons with Disabilities, 24 C.F.R. § 5.300 (2008). www.govinfo.gov/app/details/FR-2008-10-27/E8-25474

Peters, W., Rice, S., Cohen, J., et al. (2021). Trauma-focused cognitive–behavioral therapy (TF-CBT) for interpersonal trauma in transitional-aged youth. *Psychological Trauma: Theory, Research, Practice, and Policy*, *13*(3), 313–321.

Pierce, J. (2013). The dying animal. *Journal of Bioethical Inquiry*, *10*(4), 469–478. https://doi.org/10.1007/s11673-013-9480-5

Pierce, J. (2013). It hurts. www.psychologytoday.com/us/blog/all-dogs-go-heaven/201303/it-hurts

Pleines, K. E. (2019). An attachment-informed approach to trauma-focused cognitive behavioral therapy. *Clinical Social Work Journal*, *47*(4), 343–352. ttps://doi.org/10.1007/s10615-019-00701-7

Probst, T., Decker, V., Kießling, E., Meyer, S., Bofinger, C., Niklewski, G., Mühlberger, A., & Pieh, C. (2018). Suicidal ideation and skill use during in-patient dialectical behavior therapy for borderline personality disorder. A diary card study. *Frontiers in Psychiatry*, *9*, 152.

Pryor, K. (2002). *Don't shoot the dog!: The new art of teaching and training* (3rd ed.). Ringpress Books.

Quackenbush, J., & Graveline, D. (1985). *When your pet dies: How to cope with your feelings*. Simon and Schuster.

Quain, A., Ward, M. P., & Mullan, S. (2021). Ethical challenges posed by advanced veterinary care in companion animal veterinary practice. *Animals (Basel)*, *11*(11), 3010.

Quinn, L. (2017, July 20). Search and rescue dogs do their jobs despite travel stress. *ScienceDaily*. www.sciencedaily.com/releases/2017/07/170720113659.htm

Rajhans, P., Hans, G., Kumar, V., & Chadda, R. K. (2020). Interpersonal psychotherapy for patients with mental disorders. *The Indian Journal of Psychiatry*, *62*(Suppl. 2), S201–S212.

Rando, T. A. (1984). *Chapter 7: Grief, dying and death*. Research Press.

Rando, T. A. (1993). *Treatment of complicated mourning*. Research Press.

Rando, T. A. (Ed.). (2000). *Clinical dimensions of anticipatory mourning: Theory and practice in working with the dying, their loved ones, and their caregivers*. Research Press.

Rappaport, J. (1999). Maternal love and its manifestations in the therapeutic process. In C. Tosone & T. Aiello (Eds.), *Love and attachment: Contemporary issues and treatment considerations* (pp. 189–204). Jason Aronson.

Rathus, J., Campbell, B., Miller, A., & Smith, H. (2015). Treatment acceptability study of walking the middle path, A new DBT skills module for adolescents and their families. *American Journal of Psychotherapy*, *69*(2), 163–178.

Rehn, A. K., Caruso, V. R., & Kumar, S. (2023). The effectiveness of animal-assisted therapy for children and adolescents with autism spectrum disorder: A systematic review. *Complementary Therapies in Clinical Practice*, *50*, 101719.

Reisbig, A. M. J., Hafen, M., Siqueira Drake, A. A., Girard, D., & Breunig, Z. B. (2017). Companion animal death. *Omega*, *75*(2), 124–150.

Robins, C. J., Schmidt, H., Linehan, M. M. (2004). Dialectical behavior therapy: Synthesizing radical acceptance with skillful means. In S. C. Hayes, V. M. Follette & M. M. Linehan (Eds.), *Mindfulness and acceptance: Expanding the cognitive-behavioral tradition* (pp. 30–44). The Guilford Press.

Rogers, C. R. (1965). The therapeutic relationship: Recent theory and research. *Australian Journal of Psychology*, *17*, 95–108.

Rollin, B. (2008). Animal ethics and the law. *Michigan Law Review*, *106*, 143.

Rollin, B. E. (2011). Euthanasia, moral stress, and chronic illness in veterinary medicine. *Veterinary Clinics: Small Animal Practice*, *41*(3), 651–659.

Ross, S. B. (2011). *The extraordinary spirit of green chimneys: Connecting children and animals to create hope*. Purdue University Press.

Rowell, M. K., Pillay, N., & Rymer, T. L. (2021). Problem solving in animals: Proposal for an ontogenetic perspective. *Animals*, *11*(3), 866.

Russell, V. (2015). *Complicated grief therapy in pet loss: A clinical case study* (Publication No. 10001960) [Doctoral dissertation, Mississippi College, ProQuest Dissertations Publishing].

Sable, P. (2013). The pet connection: An attachment perspective. *Clinical Social Work Journal*, *41*(1), 93–99.

Savishinsky, J. (1988). Common fate, difficult decision: A comparison of euthanasia in people and in animals. In W. J. Kay, S. P. Cohen, C. E. Fudin, A. H. Kutscher, H. A. Nieburg, R. E. Grey & M. M. Osman (Eds.), *Euthanasia of the companion animal: The impact on pet owners, veterinarians, and society* (pp. 3–8). Charles Press.

Sawyer, D. C. (1988). Euthanasia in veterinary practice and laboratory animal medicine: Euthanasia agents and methods. In W. J. Kay (Ed.), *Euthanasia of the companion animal: The impact on pet owners, veterinarians, and society* (pp. 219–223). Charles Press.

Schmidt, C., & Garroway, C. J. (2022). Systemic racism alters wildlife genetic diversity. *Proceedings of the National Academy of Sciences*, *119*(43), e2102860119. https://doi.org/10.1073/pnas.2102860119

Schoenfeld-Tacher, R. M., & Kogan, L. R. (2019). The human-animal bond and hispanic clients in the United States. In Kogan, L. & Blazina, C. (Eds.) *Clinician's guide to treating companion animal issues, addressing human-animal interaction* (pp. 457–475). Academic Press. https://doi.org/10.1016/B978-0-12-812962-3.00024-1

Schore, A. N. (2015). *Affect regulation and the origin of the self: The neurobiology of emotional development*. Routledge.

Schroeder, K., & Clark, S. (2019, December). Traumatic pet loss. *Society for the Advancement of Psychotherapy*. https://societyforpsychotherapy.org/traumatic-pet-loss/

Schulz, R., & Sherwood, P. R. (2008). Physical and mental health effects of family caregiving. *American Journal of Nursing*, *108*(Suppl. 9), 23–27.

Schuurman, N., & Redmalm, D. (2019). Transgressing boundaries of grievability: Ambiguous emotions at pet cemeteries. *Emotion, Space and Society*, *31*, 32–40.

Scott, H. R., Pitman, A., Kozhuharova, P., & Lloyd-Evans, B. (2020). A systematic review of studies describing the influence of informal social support on psychological wellbeing in people bereaved by sudden or violent causes of death. *BMC Psychiatry*, *20*, 1–20.

Seponski, D. M., Bermudez, J. M., & Lewis, D. C. (2013). Creating culturally responsive family therapy models and research: Introducing the use of responsive evaluation as a method. *Journal of Marital and Family Therapy*, *39*(1), 28–42.

Shapiro, F. (1998). *EMDR: A closer look*. [Video-CDs]. EMDR Institute, Inc. www.emdr.com/product/emdr-a-closer-look/

Shapiro, F. (2001). *Eye movement desensitization and reprocessing (EMDR): Basic principles, protocols, and procedures* (2nd ed.). Guilford Press.

Shapiro, F. (2002). EMDR and the role of the clinician in psychotherapy evaluation: Towards a more comprehensive integration of science and practice. *Journal of Clinical Psychology*, *58*(12), 1453–1463.

Shapiro, F., & Forrest, M. S. (2016). *EMDR: The breakthrough therapy for overcoming anxiety, stress, and trauma*. Basic Books.

Shapiro, K., Randour, M. L., Krinsk, S., & Wolf, J. L. (2014). *The assessment and treatment of children who abuse animals: The AniCare child approach*. Springer International Publishing.

Sohal, M., Singh, P., Dhillon, B. S., & Gill, H. S. (2022). Efficacy of journaling in the management of mental illness: A systematic review and meta-analysis. *Family Medicine and Community Health*, *10*(1), e001154.

Solomon, R. M. (2018). EMDR treatment of grief and mourning. *Clinical Neuropsychiatry: Journal of Treatment Evaluation*, *15*(3), 173–186.

Solomon, R. M., & Hensley, B. J. (2020). EMDR therapy treatment of grief and mourning in times of COVID-19 (Coronavirus). *Journal of EMDR Practice and Research*, *14*(4), 162–174.

Solomon, R. M., & Rando, T. A. (2014). Utilisation of eye movement desensitisation and reprocessing in the treatment of grief and mourning. *Bereavement Care*, *33*(3), 3.

Spain, B., O'Dwyer, L., & Moston, S. (2019). Pet loss: Understanding disenfranchised grief, memorial use, and posttraumatic growth. *Anthrozoös*, *32*(4), 555–568.

Spector, J. (2009). Can I use EMDR with clients who report suicidal ideation? *Journal of EMDR Practice and Research*, *3*(2), 107 (© 2009 EMDR International Association).

Spiegler, M. D., & Guevremont, D. C. (2010). *Contemporary behavior therapy* (5th ed.). Cengage Learning.

Stamm, B. H. (1999). *Secondary traumatic stress: Self-care issues for clinicians, researchers, and educators*. Sidran Press.

Steffen, P. R., Bartlett, D., Channell, R. M., Jackman, K., Cressman, M., Bills, J., & Pescatello, M. (2021). Integrating breathing techniques into psychotherapy to improve HRV: Which approach is best? *Frontiers in Psychology, 12,* 624254.

Stone, S. D. (2006). Remembering our beloved companions during the holidays. *The Animal Companion, 3*(12).

Stone, S. D. (2007). Using dialectical behavior therapy in clinical practice. In T. Ronen & A. Freeman (Eds.), *Cognitive behavior therapy in clinical social work practice.* Springer.

Stone, S. D. (2008). Comorbid presentations in perinatal mental health: Dialectical behavior therapy as a treatment model. In S. D. Stone & A. Menken (Eds.), *Perinatal and postpartum mood disorders: Perspectives and treatment guide for the health care practitioner.* Springer Publishing Company.

Stone, S. D. (2022). *Veterinary social work: Opportunities and challenges.* Silver School of Social Work, New York University. https://socialwork. nyu.edu/a-silver-education/continuing-education/online-and-self-study/veterinary-social-work.html

Stuart, S., & Robertson, M. (2012). *Interpersonal psychotherapy: A clinician's guide* (2nd ed.). CRC Press.

Stubbe, D. E. (2018). The therapeutic alliance: The fundamental element of psychotherapy. *Focus, 16*(4), 402–403. https://doi.org/10.1176/appi.focus.20180022

Tarlton, M. (2018, February 8). Family or property: Pets and their changing protections under the law. *Campbell Law Observer.* http://campbelllawobserver.com/family-or-property-pets-and-their-changing-protections-under-the-law/

Teo, J. T., & Thomas, S. J. (2019). Psychological mechanisms predicting Wellbeing in pet owners: Rogers' core conditions versus Bowlby's attachment. *Anthrozoös, 32*(3), 399–417.

Topál, J., Gácsi, M., Miklósi, Á., Virányi, Z., Kubinyi, E., & Csányi, V. (2005). Attachment to humans: A comparative study on hand-reared wolves and differently socialized dog puppies. *Animal Behaviour, 70*(6), 1367–1375.

Tosone, C., & Aiello, T. (1999). *Love and attachment: Contemporary issues and treatment considerations.* Jason Aronson.

Toussaint, L., Nguyen, Q. A., Roettger, C., Dixon, K., Offenbächer, M., Kohls, N., Hirsch, J., & Sirois, F. (2021). Effectiveness of progressive muscle relaxation, deep breathing, and guided imagery in promoting psychological and physiological states of relaxation. *Evidence-Based Complementary and Alternative Medicine, 2021,* 5924040.

Trigg, R. (2021). Intersectionality – An alternative to redrawing the line in the pursuit of animal rights. *Ethics & the Environment, 26*(2), 73–119.

Uccheddu, S., De Cataldo, L., Albertini, M., Coren, S., Da Graça Pereira, G., Haverbeke, A., Mills, D. S., Pierantoni, L., Riemer, S., Ronconi, L., Testoni, I., & Pirrone, F. (2019). Pet humanisation and related grief: Development and validation of a structured questionnaire instrument to evaluate grief in people who have lost a companion dog. *Animals, 9*(11), 933.

Uccheddu, S., Ronconi, L., Albertini, M., Coren, S., Da Graça Pereira, G., De Cataldo, L., Haverbeke, A., Mills, D. S., Pierantoni, L., Riemer, S., Testoni, I., & Pirrone, F. (2022). Domestic dogs (Canis familiaris) grieve over the loss of a conspecific. *Scientific Reports, 12*(1), 1920.

Utz, R. L. (2022). Caregiver respite: An essential component of home – and community-based long-term care. *Journal of the American Medical Directors Association, 23*(2), 320–321.

Vakharia, S., & Little, J. (2017). Starting where the client is: Harm reduction guidelines for clinical social work practice. *Clinical Social Work Journal, 45*(1), 65–76.

van der Kolk, B. (2000). Posttraumatic stress disorder and the nature of trauma. *Dialogues in Clinical Neuroscience, 2*(1), 7–22.

van der Kolk, B. (2014). Letting go of the past: EMDR. In *The body keeps the score: Brain, mind, and body in the healing of trauma* (Reprint ed., pp. 250–264). Penguin Publishing Group.

van der Kolk, B. A., McFarlane, A. C., & Weisaeth, L. (Eds.). (1996). *Traumatic stress: The effects of overwhelming experience on mind, body, and society* (p. 190). Guilford Press.

van der Kolk, B. A., Spinazzola, J., Blaustein, M., Hopper, J., Hopper, E., Korn, D., & Simpson, W. (2007). A randomized clinical trial of eye movement desensitization and reprocessing (EMDR), Fluoxetine, and Pill Placebo in the treatment of posttraumatic stress disorder. *Journal of Clinical Psychiatry, 68,* 37–46.

Vanderschoot, T., & Van Dessel, P. (2022). EMDR therapy and PTSD: A goal-directed predictive processing perspective. *Journal of EMDR Practice and Research, 16*(3), 108–122.

Vanegas-Farfano, M., & González-Ramírez, M. T. (2016). Behaviors indicative of attachment with pets scale: An adaptation of the attachment during stress scale for companion animals. *Journal of Veterinary Behavior, 15*, 12–19.

Waggoner, B., Bering, J. M., & Halberstadt, J. (2023). The desire to be remembered: A review and analysis of legacy motivations and behaviors. *New Ideas in Psychology, 69*.

Wanser, S. H., Vitale, K. R., Thielke, L. E., Brubaker, L., & Udell, M. A. (2019). Spotlight on the psychological basis of childhood pet attachment and its implications. *Psychology Research and Behavior Management, 12*, 469–479. https://doi.org/10.2147/PRBM.S158998

Weiss, E., Slater, M., & Lord, L. (2012). Frequency of lost dogs and cats in the United States and the methods used to locate them. *Animals, 2*(2), 301–315.

Weissman, M. M., Markowitz, J. C., & Klerman, G. L. (2007). *Clinician's quick guide to interpersonal psychotherapy.* Oxford University Press.

Weissman, M. M., Markowitz, J. C., & Klerman, G. L. (2017). *Chapter 5: The guide to interpersonal psychotherapy* (expanded, updated ed.). Oxford University Press. https://doi.org/10.1093/med-psych/9780 190662592.001.0001

Weitz, E., Hollon, S. D., Kerkhof, A., & Cuijpers, P. (2014). Do depression treatments reduce suicidal ideation? The effects of CBT, IPT, pharmacotherapy, and placebo on suicidality. *Journal of Affective Disorders, 167*, 98–103.

White, J., & Morris, J. (2019). Re-thinking ethics and politics in suicide prevention: Bringing narrative ideas into dialogue with critical suicide studies. *International Journal of Environmental Research and Public Health, 16*(18), 3236.

White, M. (2007). *Maps of narrative practice.* W. W. Norton & Company.

White, N., Mills, D., & Hall, S. (2017). Attachment style is related to quality of life for assistance dog owners. *International Journal of Environmental Research and Public Health, 14*(6), 658.

White-Lewis, S. (2019). Equine-assisted therapies using horses as healers: A concept analysis. *Nursing Open, 7*(1), 58–67.

Wilson, D. M., Underwood, L., Carr, E., Gross, D. P., Kane, M., Miciak, M., Wallace, J. E., & Brown, C. A. (2021). Older women's experiences of companion animal death: Impacts on well-being and aging-in-place. *BMC Geriatrics, 21*(1), 470.

Wilson, G., Farrell, D., Barron, I., Hutchins, J., Whybrow, D., & Kiernan, M. D. (2018). The use of eye-movement desensitization reprocessing (EMDR) therapy in treating post-traumatic stress disorder-A systematic narrative review. *Frontiers in Psychology, 9,* 923.

Wisocki, P. (2018). Systematic desensitization. In E. Braaten (Ed.), *The SAGE encyclopedia of intellectual and developmental disorders* (pp. 1622–1624). SAGE Publications.

Wulfert, E. (2015). Social learning according to Albert Bandura. In *Encyclopedia of health* (vol. 5, pp. 1782–1786). Hackensack, NJ: Salem Press.

The Zebra (2023a, January 3). *Pet adoption statistics in 2023.* www.thezebra.com/resources/research/pet-adoption-statistics/#euthanized-pet-adoption

The Zebra (2023b, January 30). *Animal therapy statistics in 2023.* www.thezebra.com/resources/research/animal-therapy-statistics/

Zenithson, N. G. (2019). Advocacy and rethinking our relationships with animals: Ethical responsibilities and competencies in animal assisted interventions. In P. Tedeschi & M. A. Jenkins (Eds.), *Transforming trauma: Resilience and healing through our connections with animals.* Purdue University.

Zilcha-Mano, S., Mikulincer, M., & Shaver, P. R. (2011a). An attachment perspective on human–pet relationships: Conceptualization and assessment of pet attachment orientations. *Journal of Research in Personality, 45*(4), 345–357.

Zilcha-Mano, S., Mikulincer, M., & Shaver, P. R. (2011b). Pet in the therapy room: An attachment perspective on animal-assisted therapy. *Attachment & Human Development, 13*(6), 541–561.

Zilcha-Mano, S., Mikulincer, M., & Shaver, P. R. (2012). Pets as safe havens and secure bases: The moderating role of pet attachment orientations. *Journal of Research in Personality, 46*(5), 571–580.

Zisook, S., & Shear, K. (2009). Grief and bereavement: What psychiatrists need to know. *World Psychiatry, 8*(2), 67–74.

Index

abandonment 34–35

abuse 32–34

ACB Questionnaire *see* Animal Companion Bereavement (ACB) Questionnaire

acceptance stage of mourning 18

accidents 32

Adjustment Disorders F43.20 (unspecified) 86–87

adopted animals 8, 15

adopting animals 52–54, 188–189

Adrian, J. A. L. 28

Aiello, T. 50

Ainsworth, M. 48, 67

American Veterinary Medical Association 7–8

anger stage of mourning 17–18

animal adoption 188–189; attachment and 52–54

animal-assisted therapy (AAT) 7

animal belongings 179

animal companion bereavement group, facilitating 24–25

Animal Companion Bereavement (ACB) Questionnaire 3–4, 21, 58, 62, 73–85, 140, 143, 151; described 73–74; legacy creation and 182–186; psychodynamic therapy combined with 93–94; questions 74–85

animal companion loss 5–25; animal companion stewardship and 7–9; anticipatory mourning to 4, 157–173; aspects of 12–16; behavioral responses to 13; benefits to practice of including 23–25; clinician perspectives on, assessing 21–23; DSM diagnoses associated with 86–88; emotional responses to 12–13; experience of

5–7; four common presentations following 70–72; grief responses to 12–13, 52; healing (*see* psychodynamic therapy); legacy creation and 4, 174–191; psychological responses to 13–14; roles of animals in human lives 9–11; societal responses to 16–21; spiritual responses to 14; trauma approaches to healing (*see* trauma approaches to healing animal companion loss); *see also* attachment theory; cognitive behavior therapy; trauma

animal companion loss, assessment strategies for 68–89; ACB Questionnaire 73–85; contexts for mental health guidance 70–72; DSM diagnoses associated with 86–88; elements complicating grief resolution 72–73; overview of 68–70

animal companion mourners, societal responses to 17–21

animal companion stewardship 1–2, 7–9, 18; euthanasia and 29–30

animal deaths, causes of 27

animal hospice programs 158–159

animal law 3

animal roles in human lives 9–11

animals: adoption of, and attachment to 52–54; healing value and contributions of 10–11; loss of, coping with 2, 3–4; physical and emotional powers of 10; as primary attachment figures 48–49, 51; as property 37–38; roles of 2, 9–11; status of 2–3; as symbols of motivation and hope 11

anticipatory grief 158

anticipatory mourning 71, 157–173; animal hospice programs 158–159; biological tasks of 159; deepening bond case study 163–172; economic tasks of 160–161; ethical guidance tasks of 162–163; mental health support tasks of 161; overview of 157–158; psychological tasks of 159–160; respite care tasks of 161; social tasks of 160

anxious attachment 47

Arkow, P. 66

Ascione, F. R. 66

assessment strategies for animal companion loss 3, 68–89; ACB Questionnaire for 73–85; contexts for mental health guidance 70–72; DSM diagnoses associated with 86–88; elements complicating grief resolution 72–73; overview of 68–70

attachment figures, elements of 48

attachments, forming: biochemical impetus to 50; language role in 50

attachment styles, similarities in animal/human 49–51

attachment theory 3, 7, 45–67, 94; animal adoption and 52–54; animal companion grief and 52; animal/human attachment styles, similarities in 49–51; animals as primary attachment figures 48–49; basics of 46–47; dominant attachment styles 46; language role 50; mismatched partners case study 62–64; mutual saviors case study 59–62; overview of 45–46; quiet communion case study 54–59; therapists and 47; tragic spiral case study 64–66

avoidant attachment 47

Bandura, A. 94, 116

bargaining stage of mourning 18

Beck, A. 116; see also cognitive behavior therapy (CBT)

Beck Depression and Anxiety Inventories 117

Beck Hopelessness Scale 117

Beck Thought Record 124, 127

behavioral responses to animal companion loss 13

behavior therapy 115–116

Bekoff, M. 7

bereavement groups 186

better balance case study 119–126; assessment 121–122; CBT techniques 124–125; outcome 125–126; overview of 119–121; treatment plan 122–124

bilateral stimulation through eye movements 147, 148

biological tasks of anticipatory mourning 159

biosocial theory 126, 135

body, disposition of 178–179

Bowlby, J. 46–47, 50, 94; see also attachment theory

Brown, O. K. 52

Cambridge Declaration of Consciousness 7

case studies: better balance 119–126; clinic conflict 42–43; deepening bond 163–172; family of witnesses 106–111; harmonious connection 97–103; life management skills 129–135; mismatched partners 62–64; mutual saviors 59–62; nesting drive 40–42; professional and personal devotion 148–156; quiet communion 54–59; struggle for breath 142–147; tragic spiral 64–66

cause of death, determining 178

CBT see cognitive behavior therapy (CBT)

chain analysis 134

"Chemistry of Caring, The" (Panksepp) 50

chickens as companion animals 8

CLAWS 161

client stewardship, acknowledging 24

clinic conflict case study 42–43
clinician: benefits of including
    animal companion loss to practice
    23–25; perspectives on animal
    companion loss, assessing 21–23;
    see also animal companion loss,
    assessment strategies for
cognitive behavior therapy (CBT)
    114–126; better balance case study
    119–126; cognitive distortions 118;
    curative power of 135; described
    115–118; emotional dysregulation
    118–119; maladaptive behaviors
    119; overview of 114–115
cognitive distortions 118
Cohen, J. 140; *see also* trauma focused
    cognitive behavior therapy
    (TF-CBT)
communication analysis 102
community bonds, developing
    closer 24
community resources for legacy
    creation 180
companion animals: as equal family
    members 18; stewards attachment
    hierarchy
    and 48
consistency of response, secure
    attachment and 67
corrective emotional experience 47
creative expression 187–188
cultural competency 91–92

D'Antoni, J. 158
DBT Diary Card 128, 133–134
death, denial of 177–178
Deblinger, E. 140; *see also* trauma
    focused cognitive behavior therapy
    (TF-CBT)
deepening bond case study 163–172;
    assessment 165–172; outcome 172;
    overview of 163–165
denial stage of mourning 17, 177–178
depression stage of mourning 18
dialectical behavior therapy (DBT)
    126–135; biosocial theory and
    126, 135; described 126–129; five

modules of 127, 132–133; life
    management skills case study
    129–135; overview of 114–115
disenfranchised grief 95
disposition of body 178–179
Distress Tolerance Skills 133
documentation, legacy creation and
    180–181
donations to animal-related causes 188
Don't Shoot the Dog (Pryor) 115
DSM diagnoses associated with
    animal companion loss 86–88;
    adjustment disorders F43.20
    (unspecified) 86–87; prolonged grief
    disorder F43.8 87–88; PTSD 309.81
    88; uncomplicated bereavement
    Z63.4 86

economic euthanasia 31
economic tasks of anticipatory
    mourning 160–161
emotional dysregulation 118–119
emotional homeopathy 58
emotional responses to animal
    companion loss 12–13
Emotion Regulation Skills 133
endangerment of habitats 9
equine-based mental health
    programs 11
ethical guidance tasks of anticipatory
    mourning 162–163
euthanasia 29–30, 139, 158
evidence-based strategies to loss 4,
    91; *see also* psychodynamic therapy
exotic pets 7
extinction of animals 9, 10, 92, 95,
    112–113
eye movement desensitization and
    reprocessing (EMDR) 42, 147–156;
    assessment phase 153; body scan
    phase 154–155; closure phase 155;
    desensitization phase 153–154;
    elements of 147; goals of 138;
    history taking phase 151–152;
    installation phase 154; overview
    of 147–148; phases of 151–155;
    preparation phase 152–153;

professional and personal devotion case study 148–156; reevaluation phase 155; trauma symptoms addressed by 138

family of witnesses case study 106–111; assessment 109–110; outcome 111; overview of 106–109; treatment plan 110–111
Faunalytics 9
finding meaning stage of mourning 18, 174; *see also* legacy creation
first responder option 5–6
Forbes Advisor Pet Ownership Statistics and Facts 37
forced surrender 34–35
funding organizations, animal shelters and 10

generativity *vs.* stagnation 174
Green Chimneys 11
grief: assessment 3; attachment style influences on 52; elements complicating resolution of 72–73; expressions of 12; finding meaning stage of 4; levels of 2; responses to animal companion loss 12–16; sharing 2; stages of 69; trauma and 12, 28; treatment for, following animal companion loss 70–71; *see also* animal companion loss, assessment strategies for

habitats, endangerment of 9
harmonious connection case study 97–103; assessment 97–101; outcome 103; overview of 97; treatment plan 101–103
human-animal bond 3, 4, 47; transformative power of 7; *see also* Animal Companion Bereavement Questionnaire; attachment theory
human mourners, societal responses to 16–17
human stewards: introduction to 1–4; mental health support for 4
Hurricane Katrina, animal companion loss during 34

incarcerated individuals 11
incorporating animals 136
in-home memorial creation 187
insurance, lack of, and treatment choices 36–37
intentional destruction 36
interpersonal deficits 97
interpersonal disputes 96–97
Interpersonal Effectiveness Skills 132
interpersonal incident 102–103
interpersonal inventory 101–102
interpersonal psychotherapy (IPT) 91, 94–103; adaptability of 92; cultural competency and 91–92; grief and loss 95–96; harmonious connection case study 97–103; interpersonal deficits and 97; interpersonal disputes and 96–97; overview of 94–95; role transitions and 96; therapist's role in 93
interpersonal relationships theory 94

Jacobson, E. 152
journaling 124, 186

Kessler, D. 4, 18, 174
kidnapping 35–36
Kübler-Ross, E. 18, 69

language role in forming attachments 50
law enforcement, dogs working in 11
legacy creation 4, 174–191; ACB Questionnaire responses 182–186; activities helpful to 186–189; animal adoption and 188–189; animal's belongings and 179; bereavement groups and 186; cause of death and 178; challenges/tasks of 177–182; community resources for 180; creative expression and 187–188; denial of death and 177–178; disposition of body and 178–179; documentation and 180–181; donations to animal-related causes and 188; exterior

memorial creation 187; in-home memorial creation 187; journaling and 186; legal advocacy 189; memorabilia collecting and 181; mental health professionals and 189–190; narrative creation 187; overview of 174–175; purpose of 175–177; routines, identifying 182; as solo process 179–180; talking with others and 181–182; volunteer work and 188; for wilder creatures 190–191
legal advocacy 189
legal status of animals 37–38
Leonhardt-Parr, E. 92
life management skills case study 129–135; assessment 131–132; outcome 135; overview of 129–131; treatment plan 132–135
Linehan, M. 126; see also dialectical behavior therapy (DBT)
Lorenz, K. 50, 53
Love and Attachment (Tosone and Aiello) 50

maladaptive behaviors 119
Mannarino, A. 140; see also trauma focused cognitive behavior therapy (TF-CBT)
meaning making systems 116, 147–148
media stories and animal rescue 9–10
memorabilia, collecting 181
mental health practice 21–23; benefits to 23–25; equine-based 11; legacy opportunities for 189–190; need for 3, 4
mental health professionals, legacy creation and 189–190
mental health support tasks of anticipatory mourning 161
mindfulness 127
Mindfulness Skills 132
mirroring, secure attachment and 67
mismatched partners case study 62–64
mutual saviors case study 59–62
My Octopus Teacher (documentary film) 10

narrative creation 187
narrative therapy (NT) 91, 103–111; adaptability of 92; cultural competency and 91–92; family of witnesses case study 106–111; therapist's role in 93
Nature, animal adoption and 53
neglect 32–34
nesting drive case study 40–42
noticing joy 134–135

Panksepp, J. 7, 50
"Pet Attachment Questionnaire" (Zilcha-Mano) 48, 52
pet livestock and poultry 7
Pet Loss Help (www.petlosshelp.org) 5, 8, 18, 187
pet ownership by species 7–8
pet therapy programs 10–11
physical exercises 124–125
post-traumatic stress disorder (PTSD) 26–27, 28, 34, 44; treatment of 138
PRACTICE 141
professional and personal devotion case study 148–156; assessment 150–151; outcome 155–156; overview of 148–150; treatment plan 151–155
prolonged grief disorder F43.8 87–88
property, animals as 37–38
proximity seeking, attachment and 48, 67
psychodynamic therapy 90–113; ACB Questionnaire combined with 93–94; adaptability and 92; cultural competency and 91–92; family of witnesses case study 106–111; harmonious connection case study 97–103; interpersonal psychotherapy 94–97; narrative therapy 103–106; overview of 90–91; therapist's role in 93; see also interpersonal psychotherapy (IPT); narrative therapy (NT)
psychological responses to animal companion loss 13–14
psychological stability, animal contributions to 10

psychological tasks of anticipatory mourning 159–160
PTSD *see* post-traumatic stress disorder (PTSD)
PTSD 309.81 DSM diagnosis 88

quiet communion case study 54–59

radical acceptance 134
Rando, T. A. 159
reciprocity, secure attachment and 67
relaxation exercises 124
respite care tasks of anticipatory mourning 161
Rhode Island Red therapy rooster 8
role-play 102
roles of animals in human lives 9–11
role transitions 96
roosters as companion animals 8
routines, identifying 182
Rumble, B. 92
running away 35–36

Sable, P. 52
safe haven, attachment and 48, 67
Sawyer, D. 139
search-and-rescue animals 11
secondary trauma 38–40; treatment of 138
secure attachment 47
secure base, attachment and 48, 67
self-esteem, animal contributions to 10, 11
self-schemas 116
separation distress, attachment and 48, 67
service animals 11
severe illness, sudden realization of 28
Shapiro, F. 138, 147; *see also* eye movement desensitization and reprocessing (EMDR)
Shapiro, K. 66
shelter workers 23; euthanasia impact on 31; legacy opportunities for 189
silent grief 158
social learning theory 94, 116
social support, increasing 125

social tasks of anticipatory mourning 160
societal responses to animal/human mourning 16–21
Solomon's Ring (Lorenz) 53
spiritual responses to animal companion loss 14
Stitt, A. 28
struggle for breath case study 142–147; assessment 143–144; integration/consolidation phase of treatment 145–146; outcome 146–147; overview of 142–143; stabilization phase of treatment 144–145; trauma narration/processing phase of treatment 145; treatment plan 144–146
Subjective Units of Distress Scale 152
symbolic immortality 174
Symons, D. K. 52

talk therapy *see* psychodynamic therapy
therapeutic alliance, fostering 23–24
Topál, J. 51
Tosone, C. 50
tragic spiral case study 64–66
trauma 26–44; clinic conflict case study 42–43; grief and 12, 28; negative impacts of unaddressed 28; nesting drive case study 40–42; overview of 26–27; response triggers 28–38; secondary 38–40; treatment of 138
trauma approaches to healing animal companion loss 137–156; eye movement desensitization and reprocessing 147–156; overview of 137–140; trauma-focused cognitive behavior therapy 140–147; *see also* individual trauma approaches
trauma focused cognitive behavior therapy (TF-CBT) 3, 140–147; described 140–142; effectiveness of 141; goals of 138; PRACTICE acronym 141; struggle for breath case study 142–147; trauma symptoms addressed by 138

traumatic response triggers 28–38; abuse/neglect 32–34; accidents 32; economic euthanasia 31; euthanasia 29–30; forced surrender/abandonment 34–35; insurance, lack of, and treatment choices 36–37; intentional destruction 36; kidnapping/running away 35–36; legal status of animals 37–38; overview of 28; sudden realization of severe illness 28; verbal communication, lack of 31–32

unaddressed trauma, negative impacts of 28
Uncomplicated Bereavement Z63.4 86
underserved needs, addressing 24

van der Kolk, B. 148
verbal communication, lack of 31–32
veterinarians 43, 162; animal abuse/neglect and 32–33; secondary trauma and 38–40
volunteer work 188

Walking the Middle Path 133
Wanser, S. 48–49
Weissman, M. 92
White, M. 138; *see also* trauma focused cognitive behavior therapy (TF-CBT)
Wolpe, J. 152

Zilcha-Mano, S. 48

For Product Safety Concerns and Information please contact our EU
representative GPSR@taylorandfrancis.com
Taylor & Francis Verlag GmbH, Kaufingerstraße 24, 80331 München, Germany

www.ingramcontent.com/pod-product-compliance
Lightning Source LLC
Chambersburg PA
CBHW050642280326
41932CB00015B/2750

* 9 7 8 0 3 6 7 6 9 4 2 3 4 *